D1548923

Adapted Physical Education National Standards

SECOND EDITION

*National Consortium for
Physical Education and Recreation
for Individuals with Disabilities*

Adapted Physical Education National Standards

• SECOND EDITION •

National Consortium for
Physical Education and Recreation
for Individuals with Disabilities

Luke E. Kelly

Editor

Human Kinetics

Library of Congress Cataloging-in-Publication Data

National Consortium for Physical Education and Recreation for Individuals with Disabilities (U.S.)
  Adapted physical education national standards / National Consortium for Physical Education and Recreation for Individuals with Disabilities ; Luke Kelly, editor.--2nd ed.
      p. cm.
    Includes bibliographical references.
    ISBN-13: 978-0-7360-4603-9 (soft cover)
    ISBN-10: 0-7360-4603-8 (soft cover)
  1. Physical education for children with disabilities--Standards--United States. 2. Physical education teachers--Certification--United States.   I. Kelly, Luke. II. Title.
    GV445.N38 2006
    371.9'04486--dc22

                                     2005037754

ISBN-10: 0-7360-4603-8
ISBN-13: 978-0-7360-4603-9

Copyright © 2006 by National Consortium for Physical Education and Recreation for Individuals with Disabilities

All rights reserved. Except for use in a review, the reproduction or utilization of this work in any form or by any electronic, mechanical, or other means, now known or hereafter invented, including xerography, photocopying, and recording, and in any information storage and retrieval system, is forbidden without the written permission of the publisher.

The Web addresses cited in this text were current as of April 5, 2006, unless otherwise noted.

Acquisitions Editor: Bonnie Pettifor; **Managing Editor:** Jacqueline Eaton Blakley; **Assistant Editor:** Bethany J. Bentley; **Copyeditor:** Patsy Fortney; **Permission Manager:** Dalene Reeder; **Graphic Designer:** Robert Reuther; **Graphic Artist:** Dawn Sills; **Photo Manager:** Sarah Ritz; **Cover Designer:** Fred Starbird; **Photographs (interior):** © Les Woodrum, unless otherwise noted; photo on lower right-hand side of pages 1, 9, 21, 41, 55, 63, 89, 95, 105, 119, 133, 139, 145, 151, and 155 by Kim Thorne. **Printer:** United Graphics

Printed in the United States of America   10 9 8 7 6 5 4 3 2 1

Human Kinetics
Web site: www.HumanKinetics.com

United States: Human Kinetics
P.O. Box 5076
Champaign, IL 61825-5076
800-747-4457
e-mail: humank@hkusa.com

Canada: Human Kinetics
475 Devonshire Road Unit 100
Windsor, ON N8Y 2L5
800-465-7301 (in Canada only)
e-mail: orders@hkcanada.com

Europe: Human Kinetics
107 Bradford Road
Stanningley
Leeds LS28 6AT, United Kingdom
+44 (0) 113 255 5665
e-mail: hk@hkeurope.com

Australia: Human Kinetics
57A Price Avenue
Lower Mitcham, South Australia 5062
08 8277 1555
e-mail: liaw@hkaustralia.com

New Zealand: Human Kinetics
Division of Sports Distributors NZ Ltd.
P.O. Box 300 226 Albany
North Shore City
Auckland
0064 9 448 1207
e-mail: info@humankinetics.co.nz

CONTENTS

INTRODUCTION

Standards provide a guiding light—in terms of basic knowledge, skills, and attitudes—for people within a professional field and those in higher education who have the job of preparing them. Adapted Physical Education National Standards (APENS) were developed in 1995 to guide the certification of professionals in adapted physical education throughout the United States who successfully passed the national examination. In addition, the APEN standards have been infused into numerous teacher education programs at the undergraduate and master's levels as the foundation of preparation programs. Further, at some universities, the successful passing of the APENS examination has become an option in place of a thesis or professional paper for partial fulfillment of the requirements to graduate.

Since 2003 numerous professionals have worked to revise these standards to reflect current knowledge and practices and to present the information in a more user-friendly format. This book is the reflection of the revision.

The need for national adapted physical education standards and a national certification examination evolved approximately 30 years ago from the mandates of federal legislation, including the Individuals with Disabilities Education Act (IDEA) and the Individuals with Disabilities Education Improvement Act (IDEIA) (as amended on December 3, 2004). These mandates required that physical education services, specially designed if necessary, be made available to every student with a disability receiving a free and appropriate public education. These services should be provided by highly qualified teachers (IDEA, 2004; U.S. Department of Education, 2002).

The definition of who was highly "qualified" to provide physical education services to students with disabilities was left to the individual state certification requirements based on the assumption that these currently existed. Unfortunately, most states did not have defined certifications for adapted physical educators. Although 14 states subsequently implemented an endorsement or certification in adapted physical education, the majority of states and eight territories have not defined the qualifications teachers need to provide adapted physical education services to their students with disabilities (Cowden & Tymeson, 1984; Kelly, 1991a).

In 1991 the National Consortium for Physical Education and Recreation for Individuals with Disabilities (NCPERID), in conjunction with the National Association of State Directors of Special Education (NASDSE) and Special Olympics International, conducted an "Action Seminar" on adapted physical education for state directors of special education and leaders of advocacy groups for individuals with disabilities.

Although the group identified numerous barriers to providing appropriate physical education services to students with disabilities, the most significant barriers for state education leaders was the fact that they did not know what adapted physical education was, how individuals with disabilities could benefit from appropriate physical education programming, or what competencies teachers needed to deliver appropriate physical education services to students with disabilities. In response to these needs, the group recommended that NCPERID develop professional standards and a means for evaluating these standards (see Appendix A for background on this consortium). These standards could then be used by state and school administrators as well as parents to communicate the need for quality adapted physical education and to evaluate who was qualified to provide physical education services to students with disabilities.

The Action Seminar recommendations were presented to the NCPERID board in the summer of 1991. A NCPERID committee was formed and charged with creating a plan for developing national standards and a national certification examination. To this end, a special project proposal (Kelly, 1992) was submitted to the U.S. Department of Education (USDOE), Office of Special Education and Rehabilitative Services (OSERS), Division of Personnel Preparation (DPP) in the fall of 1991. This grant was funded in July of 1992 and provided funding for five years.

The purpose of this national standards project was to ensure that physical education instruction for students with disabilities is provided by qualified physical education instructors by (a) developing national standards for the field of adapted physical education and (b) developing a national certification examination to measure knowledge of the standards. The committees and procedures used to develop the national standards are presented in Appendix B. The results of these processes culminated in the establishment of a set of national standards, which are presented in this manual.

Standards

Based on the results of a national needs assessment (see Appendix B and Kelly & Gansneder, 1998), the content adapted physical educators needed to know was identified and divided into 15 broad standards areas. Following are brief descriptions of the specific standards.

Standard 1: Human Development

The foundation of proposed goals and activities for individuals with disabilities is grounded in a basic understanding of human development and its applications to those with various needs. For the adapted physical education teacher, this implies familiarity with theories and practices related to human development. This standard focuses on the knowledge and skills helpful in providing quality adapted physical education programs.

Standard 2: Motor Behavior

Teaching individuals with disabilities requires some knowledge of how individuals develop. In the case of adapted physical educators, it means having knowledge of typical physical and motor development as well as understanding the influence of developmental delays on these processes. It also means understanding how individuals learn motor skills and applying principles of motor learning during the planning and teaching of physical education to students with disabilities.

Standard 3: Exercise Science

Adapted physical educators must understand that modifications to the scientific principles of exercise and the application of these principles may be needed when teaching individuals with disabilities to ensure that all children with disabilities enjoy similar benefits of exercise. Although there is a wealth of information in the foundational sciences, this standard focuses on the principles that address the physiological and biomechanical applications encountered when working with diverse populations.

Standard 4: Measurement and Evaluation

Adapted physical educators must have a knowledge base in measurement and evaluation to comply with the mandates of legislation and meet the needs of students. Understanding the measurement of motor performance, to a large extent, is based on a good grasp of motor development and the acquisition of motor skills covered in other standards.

Standard 5: History and Philosophy

Legal and philosophical factors involved in current-day practices in adapted physical education are important to understand the changing contribution that physical education can make in the lives of students with disabilities. Major components of each law that related to education and physical activity are emphasized. This standard also offers a review of history and philosophy as they relate to special and general education.

Standard 6: Unique Attributes of Learners: Considerations for Professional Practice

Adapted physical educators must have a knowledge base of the disability areas identified in the Individuals with Disabilities Education Improvement Act (IDEA as amended in 2004). Material is categorically organized to present the information in a systematic manner. This organization is not intended to advocate a categorical approach to teaching children with disabilities. All children should be treated as individuals and assessed to determine their unique needs.

Standard 7: Curriculum Theory and Development

Those planning to teach physical education to students with disabilities should understand certain curriculum theory and development concepts, such as selecting goals based on relevant and appropriate assessments. Curriculum theory and development is more than writing unit and lesson plans. This is especially important when planning a program for a student with a disability.

Standard 8: Assessment

The process of assessment is commonly taught as part of the basic measurement and evaluation course in a physical education degree curriculum. Assessment goes beyond data gathering to include measurements for the purpose of making decisions about special services, placement, and program components for individuals with disabilities.

Standard 9: Instructional Design and Planning

Instructional design and planning must occur before an adapted physical educator can provide services to meet legal mandates, educational goals, and the unique needs of individuals with disabilities. Many of the principles addressed in other standards regarding human development, motor behavior, exercise science, and curriculum theory and development are needed to successfully design and plan adapted physical education programs.

Standard 10: Teaching

A major part of any adapted physical education position is teaching. In this standard many of the principles addressed earlier, such as human development, motor behavior, and exercise science, are applied to effectively provide quality physical education to individuals with disabilities.

Standard 11: Consultation and Staff Development

As more students with disabilities are included in the general education program, teachers will provide more consultation and staff development activities for colleagues. This will require sensitivity and excellent communication skills. Understanding the dynamics of interdisciplinary cooperation in the consultation process requires knowledge of several consultative models. This standard identifies key competencies that an adapted physical educator should have related to consultation and staff development.

Standard 12: Program Evaluation

Program evaluation is a process of which student assessment is only a part. It involves evaluation of the entire range of educational services. Because national standards for programs have only recently become available, few physical educators are formally trained for program evaluation. Therefore, most program evaluations that have been conducted are specific to the school or district or are limited to a small range of parameters such as the number of students scoring at a certain level of a physical fitness test. Adapted physical education programs or outcomes for students with disabilities are almost never considered in these program evaluations.

Standard 13: Continuing Education

Adapted physical educators must remain current in their field. A variety of opportunities for professional development are available. Course work at a local college or university is just one avenue. Adapted physical educators can take advantage of inservice workshops, seminars, and presentations at conferences and conventions. Distance learning opportunities are also becoming available.

Standard 14: Ethics

A fundamental premise within the APEN standards is that those who seek and meet the standards to be certified as adapted physical educators will strive at all times to adhere to the highest of ethical standards in providing programs and services for individuals with disabilities. This standard has been developed to ensure that adapted physical educators not only understand the importance of sound ethical practices, but also adhere to and advance such practices.

Standard 15: Communication

In recent years, the role of the professional in adapted physical education has evolved from that of a direct service provider to include communicating with families and other professionals to enhance program instruction for individuals with disabilities. This standard addressed the importance of adapted physical educators effectively communicating with families and other professionals using a team approach.

Each of the 15 standards is presented in a separate section in this book. Within each standard, the content adapted physical educators should know is presented in five levels (see table 1). The first three levels represent the content that all certified physical educators should know. The fourth level represents additional content knowledge adapted physical educators should know. The level five statements contain example applications of the level four content adapted physical educators should be able to demonstrate. The number and title of the standard is the Level 1 information centered at the top of the first page of each standard. Level 2 information, the major components of the standard, is bold and highlighted with lines above and below. Level 3 information, subcomponents of knowledge, is bold. Level 4 information, the unique adapted physical education content, is indented and italicized. Level 5 information, applications of the Level 4 content knowledge, is bulleted and indented under the Level 4 content.

TABLE 1 Example of the Five Levels of a Typical Standard

Level 1 Standard number and title	Standard 10: Teaching
Level 2 Major components of the standard	Teaching Styles: Demonstrate various teaching styles in order to promote learning in physical education
Level 3 Subcomponents and dependent pieces of knowledge of fact or principle related to the major component	Understand the command style of teaching
Level 4 Adapted physical education content—additional knowledge regarding the subcomponents that teachers working with individuals with disabilities need to know	Understand the effectiveness of using command style teaching with individuals with disabilities in order to promote learning in physical education 10.01.01.01
Level 5 Application of adapted physical education content knowledge from Level 4 to teaching individuals with disabilities	• Provide clear, concise, and simple language when needed • Use specific, clear, concise verbal cues to highlight points • Use total communication as needed • Use visual cues to demonstrate skill such as using a colored sock to show kicking foot

APENS and NASPE Standards

A basic philosophical tenet of APENS is that physical educators who teach students in integrated or segregated environments must be able to demonstrate basic instructional competencies. This is clearly reflected in the Level 1 through Level 3 competencies, which are the foundation of the Level 4 and Level 5 competencies specifically related to adapted physical education. APENS are logical extensions of the *Advanced Physical Educators Standards* (NASPE, 2001) as reflected in the APENS Levels 4 and 5. This comparison between APEN and NASPE/NCATE standards is presented in Table 2. It should be noted that the APEN standards, although developed *before* the NASPE standards, clearly reflect the content of the NASPE standards.

TABLE 2   Comparison of the NASPE Advanced Physical Education Standards to APENS

NASPE	APENS
1. Content Knowledge: Master physical educators have a command of the subject matter of physical education that reflects both breadth and depth that promotes lifetime physical activity.	1. Human Development 2. Motor Behavior 3. Exercise Science 4. Measurement and Evaluation 5. History and Philosophy 7. Curriculum Theory and Development 8. Assessment 9. Instructional Design and Planning 10. Teaching
2. Curricular Knowledge: Master physical educators consistently articulate a value base for selecting, planning, and evaluating their curriculum to meet student needs.	4. Measurement and Evaluation 7. Curriculum Theory and Development 9. Instructional Design and Planning 12. Program Evaluation
3. Equity/Fairness/Diversity: Master physical educators model and promote behavior appropriate in a diverse society by showing respect for and valuing all members of their communities and by having high expectations that their students will treat one another fairly and with dignity.	3. Exercise Science 6. Unique Attributes of Learners 11. Consultation and Staff Development 14. Ethics 15. Communication
4. Sound Teaching Practices: Master physical educators thoroughly comprehend the fundamental goals of physical education, blending relevant principles of pedagogical practice with the complex nature of the physical education content.	9. Instructional Design and Planning 10. Teaching
5. Assessment: Master physical educators consistently use a variety of authentic assessments aligned with national and state standards, state and local program goals, and student outcome goals to provide feedback to students, report student progress, shape instruction, and evaluate curriculum and program goals.	4. Measurement and Evaluation 8. Assessment 12. Program Evaluation
6. High Expectations for a Physically Active Lifestyle: Master physical educators maintain a stimulating, productive learning environment that holds all students to the highest expectations for a physically active lifestyle.	7. Curriculum Theory and Development 10. Teaching 15. Communication
7. Methods of Inquiry: Master physical educators know, understand, interpret, critique, and consistently use research to improve teaching practice.	8. Assessment 12. Program Evaluation 13. Continuing Education 14. Ethics
8. Collaboration, Reflection, Leadership, and Professionalism: Master physical educators are lifelong learners who collaborate as members of a larger learning community to improve school physical education for all students and enhance the professional culture of their field.	11. Consultation and Staff Development 13. Continuing Education 14. Ethics 15. Communication
9. Mentoring: Master physical educators contribute to the professional development and support of other current and/or future educators.	11. Consultation and Staff Development 15. Communication

How to Use This Manual

This manual may be used in different ways, depending on one's purpose for studying it.

Teachers Preparing for the APENS Examination

Teachers planning to take the APENS exam can use this manual to help prepare for the exam. First, they will need to distinguish between the content they already know and the content they need to review or learn. To start, teachers should read the Level 2 and Level 3 statements to understand the context. Next they should read the Level 4 statement and its applications, which are listed in the Level 5 statements. Once they understand the Level 4 and Level 5 statements, they can move on to the next Level 4 statement. If they do not know the Level 4 statement or only vaguely remember the content, they should mark it with a highlighter. Teachers should systematically repeat this process until they have reviewed all Level 4 statements for all 15 standards. Note that the numbers at the end of the Level 4 statements are codes used by NCPERID to link the statements to the study guide content (Kelly, 2006) and the exam questions.

Teachers working alone will need to look up this content in their college or university textbooks, in past class notes, or on the Web. This manual tells you the concepts you need to know, but it does not explain them. Teachers studying in groups can distribute some of the review work. First, they can meet as a group and review the Level 4 statements that each teacher has identified. In most cases, other members of the group will be able to review information on one or more of the Level 4 statements that other members do not know. After this review, there will probably still be some Level 4 statements that other members of the group do not know. These can be divided among the group members. Each member looks up the content of the Level 4 statement that he or she is assigned and then shares this information at the next group meeting.

University Faculty

Because the APENS are based on a needs assessment of what adapted physical educators need to know to do their jobs, they can also be used by faculty members at colleges and universities to evaluate their adapted physical education preparation programs. The APENS can be used much the way NCATE and the NASPE standards are used to evaluate teacher preparation programs in physical education. The APEN standards can be distributed to the faculty, with each faculty member being asked to review the standards in their area and indicate which ones are addressed in their courses. A simple process such as writing in the margin which course addresses each objective will suffice. One faculty member or faculty committee then summarizes which Level 3 and 4 standards are currently not being addressed in the curriculum. These can then be discussed at a future faculty meeting and distributed across the curriculum.

K-12 Administrators

All administrators share the goal of ensuring that all students with disabilities receive physical education taught by a qualified teacher. However, many may not be able to judge who is qualified. Administrators can use the APENS and the national exam as criteria when reviewing and hiring new teachers. Because the majority of students with disabilities are educated in the general physical education setting, ideally, all physical educators would be certified adapted physical educators (CAPEs). If it is not feasible or realistic to employ CAPEs for all general physical education positions, adapted physical education specialists who are CAPEs could be employed to work collaboratively with general physical educators to help them meet the physical education needs of the students with disabilities in their classes. If funding is not available to employ adapted physical education specialists, another option is to provide inservice training for the existing physical education staff so they can acquire the knowledge and skills needed to become CAPEs. The NCPERID can be contacted to identify local university faculty members who can provide both credit and noncredit options for preparing general physical educators to appropriately address the physical education needs of their students with disabilities. The Web site address is www. uwlax.edu/sah/ncperid.

Parents

Parents of students with disabilities should know that if their children require specially designed instruction in physical education, it should be designed and implemented by a qualified physical educator. To this end, parents should inquire at their child's IEP meeting who will provide the adapted physical education services and what qualifies this individual for this role. If the proposed teacher is a CAPE, the parents have some assurance that this teacher has met at least the minimal national standards established by the profession. If the proposed teacher is not a CAPE, the parents should request a written explanation stating why they are not employing a qualified teacher for this role and indicating that the school accepts responsibility and liability for any injuries or emotional distress their child may encounter that can be attributed to not being taught by a highly qualified educator.

Frequently Asked Questions

Based on numerous requests, an APENS Frequently Asked Questions section has been included in this edition. To review the questions and answers, see Appendix C.

Bibliography

Given the diversity of terms and the common use of abbreviations and acronyms in the field, a glossary has been provided at the end of the manual. Although not coded to each statement, a summative list of references that were used by the various committees in developing the standards is also included at the end of the manual.

ACKNOWLEDGMENTS

Many people and organizations contributed greatly to the development and maintenance of the APEN standards and exam. It goes without saying that individual support—such as the case of individual teaching—is the backbone of the adapted physical education profession. For every CAPE who is certified, there are many more individuals with disabilities who deserve the services of qualified professionals. The following people are acknowledged for their tremendous commitment to ensuring that the mission of APENS—"A CAPE in every school district in the country"—is one day realized.

Ron Davis, PhD, CAPE—Ball State University, Muncie, Indiana

Timothy D. Davis, PhD, CAPE—State University of New York, Cortland

Ron French, EdD, CAPE—Texas Woman's University, Denton

Hester L. Henderson, PhD, CAPE—University of Utah, Salt Lake City

Mike Loovis, PhD, CAPE—Cleveland State University, Cleveland, Ohio

Jan Seaman, EdD, CAPE—Executive Director, AAPAR/AAHPERD, Reston, Virginia

External assistance was provided by Dr. Dave Nichols, Texas Woman's University, and Dr. Katie Price, Angelo State University in Texas, who edited and reviewed the Exercise Science standard, and Dr. April Tripp from the University of Maryland at Townson, who edited and reviewed the Consultation and Staff Development standard.

We were also very grateful for the willingness of the following graduate students, who helped to edit and reformat all of the standards for clarity and uniformity: Valerie Hodge and Chad Wiet from the University of Utah and Tiffany Bowers and Colleen Koval from Texas Woman's University. Special thanks to Jim Melton for editing the final draft.

A special thanks to Tom Moran, the APENS administrative assistant from SUNY Cortland, for his assistance in including all of the revisions into the standards.

Secretarial assistance for this project was provided by Judy Melton, secretary at Texas Woman's University.

Human Development

Understand cognitive development

Explain the theory of cognitive development as proposed by Piaget

Understand the implications of Piaget's theory for the development of individuals with disabilities 1.01.01.01

- Apply Piaget's theory to the development of infants and individuals with various disabilities
- Recognize the strengths and limitations of Piaget's theory as applied to individuals with disabilities

Understand that perception, attention, and memory may impact the ability to effectively participate and learn in a physical education environment

Understand the impact cognitive disabilities have on perception, attention, and memory for learning in the physical education environment 1.01.02.01; 1.01.02.03; 1.01.02.04

- Develop programs that sequence materials appropriately for individuals with disabilities, recognizing unique attention deficits and perceptual disorders
- Create environments that enhance instruction in physical education by reducing external stimuli as needed

Understand the difference between short-term and long-term memory capacity as applied to individuals with selected disabilities (see Standard 2) 1.01.02.02

- Recognize the implications of short- and long-term memory in the learning process, specifically among individuals with disabilities
- Adapt the learning environment to compensate for short- or long-term memory deficits for individuals with disabilities such as mental retardation, traumatic brain injury

Understand the impact of physical and sensory disability on perception, attention, and memory for learning in physical education 1.01.02.03

- Adjust programs to respond to the challenges associated with the individual's perceptual skills (e.g., individuals with cerebral palsy or spina bifida may have other disabilities such as hearing disorder or mental retardation)
- Adjust programs to respond to the challenges associated with short attention spans and decreased memory

Understand the impact of emotional disability on perception, attention, and memory for learning in physical education 1.01.02.04

- Adapt programs to respond to the needs of individuals with various forms of emotional disturbance and behavior disorders including depression and mental illness
- Develop programs to respond to the unique needs of individuals with clinical mental disabilities including psychosis, neuroses, and personality disorders
- Recognize that some individuals with behavior disorders have the ability to excel in physical activity

Demonstrate knowledge of language and cognitive development through the lifespan

Describe the effect of limited verbal language on participation in physical education

Understand the impact of limited expressiveness and receptive language on participation in physical education 1.02.01.01

- Develop programs that respond to the expressive and receptive language needs of individuals with selected disabilities such as autism, congenitally deaf
- Provide programs that respond appropriately to the needs of individuals with language disorders

Understand the need to use alternative/augmentative communication in physical education (see Standard 9) 1.02.01.02

- Use alternative forms of communication such as American Sign Language, Signing Exact English
- Apply technology so that individuals with selected disabilities, such as visual disabilities, can successfully participate in physical education activity
- Recognize that the general physical educator must not only know how to express him/herself in the mode of communication utilized by his/her students, but must also know how to receive information from augmentative communication such as signs

Understand essential concepts related to social or affective development

Understand and define important terms such as *socialization, social roles,* and *social norms*

Know that individuals with disabilities are often excluded and/or inappropriately portrayed in discussions of social roles and social norms 1.03.01.01

- Advocate for individuals with disabilities and their right to be included in programs of physical education and sport sponsored by schools and communities
- Include individuals with disabilities in all appropriate aspects of physical education and sport programs
- Use examples of individuals with disabilities who are role models and highlight their successes in physical education and sport activities
- Recognize individuals with and without disabilities who do well in physical education settings

Appreciate the social influences present during infancy (e.g., attachment to objects, recognition of touch, and involvement with the environment)

Understand that some individuals with selected disabilities experience significant sensory deprivation 1.03.02.01

- Provide programs that emphasize the individuals' strength and limit situations that could cause frustration (e.g., individuals who are deaf/blind may be frustrated in large group activities)
- Utilize alternative forms of interaction to ensure that individuals with sensory disorders are not unnecessarily excluded

Recognize the role that the family plays in social development

Understand the stages of grief (denial, guilt, rejection, anger) experienced by parents at birth and the early stages of development of the child with a disability 1.03.03.01

- Develop programs and opportunities for parents and guardians and their infants and toddlers to participate in motor and physical activities
- Cooperate with other professionals in developing support programs and activities for parents and guardians of individuals with disabilities
- Continually inform parents and guardians of curricular innovations, special programs, and the progress of their child

Understand the impact of the presence of a child with a disability on the structure and function of the family 1.03.03.02

- Communicate with parents about the services provided in adapted physical education and the commitment to assist the development of their child (see Standard 15)
- Listen to parents and guardians, recognizing their needs to express concerns and frustrations about various issues, including the need for and value of physical activity involvement

Understand the unique needs, concerns, and worries experienced by many siblings of individuals with disabilities 1.03.03.03

- Provide opportunities for siblings to observe their brother or sister successfully participating in physical activity and sport-related movement experiences
- Share information, as appropriate, with siblings that helps to reduce anxiety and improve understanding about the long-term outlook for individuals with disabilities

Know the role that the family plays in promoting health and physical fitness throughout the lifespan of individuals with a disability 1.03.03.04

- Develop programs that promote social interaction between family members and the individual with a disability
- Structure programs to assist caregivers to play and interact with an individual with a disability

Know the behavioral indices of an individual with a history of abuse and neglect 1.03.03.05

- Structure programs to respond to the possible special health, fitness, movement, and play needs of individuals with a history of abuse and neglect
- Accept responsibility according to state and professional standards for reporting suspected cases of abuse and neglect

Demonstrate knowledge of diversity of families in the United States including child kinship patterns of never-married, single-parent families, remarried, and two-parent families

Know the impact of diverse child kinship patterns on the physical activity development of the child with a disability 1.03.04.01

- Develop programs that encourage parents, caregivers, and advocates to be involved in play and related movement experiences of their child without inhibition or concern for social norms
- Respect parents, caregivers, advocates, and others for their willingness to actively participate in physical activities with individuals with disabilities

Demonstrate knowledge of and appreciation for cultural diversity of families in the United States

Understand the importance of cultural heritage, including games and sports, toward development of the individual with a disability 1.03.05.01

- Use various forms of play, sport, and games enjoyed by individuals with diverse cultural backgrounds
- Adapt games that can be enjoyed by individuals with disabilities from various cultural backgrounds (see Standard 10)

Understand the important and unique role of play in the development of the individual

Know the various stages of play (i.e., independent, parallel, small group, large group) experienced by infants and children as they develop 1.03.06.01

- Plan programs that respond to the developmental play needs of infants, toddlers, and children
- Provide play experiences in which infants, toddlers, and children with disabilities have the opportunity to engage in positive social interaction

Understand the importance of group play to the process of socialization among individuals with and without disabilities 1.03.06.02

- Plan physical education programs that maximize opportunities for integrated group play
- Conduct physical education and sport programs that promote group interaction for individuals with and without disabilities

Understand the value of play interaction between and among individuals with and without disabilities 1.03.06.03

- Promote opportunities that support integrated play experiences
- Develop integrated play experiences based on the concept of inclusion

Understand the effect that various developmental delays and disabilities can have on the individual's successful participation in play activities 1.03.06.04

- Describe play behavior across the lifespan for individuals with disabilities
- Adapt programs so individuals with disabilities can be successful in play experiences
- Recognize that individuals with various disabilities may need modifications requiring teachers to individualize instruction

Understand theories of moral development in children and youth

Understand the role and impact of social institutions on the moral development of individuals with disabilities

Understand the unique opportunities within the physical education curriculum to promote appropriate values for individuals with disabilities 1.04.01.01

- Provide opportunities in the physical education curriculum that allow individuals with disabilities to exercise choice
- Use instructional strategies that emphasize the importance of fair play, sportsmanship, and teamwork

Appreciate the role of schools in the moral development of individuals with disabilities

Understand the sensitive nature of moral development and the vulnerability of some individuals with disabilities to exploitation 1.04.02.01

- Apply moral development concepts in the teaching of sport, play, and physical activity for individuals with disabilities
- Model acceptance of individuals with disabilities, emphasizing the person rather than the disability
- Emphasize that individuals with disabilities are to be treated respectfully and viewed as people rather than objects

Understand different personality theories as they relate to human behavior

Understand that field or ecological theory of personality describes the psychosocial interdependence of individuals in a community, taking into account the physical environment and the systems that operate in the environment

Understand that there is reciprocity between the actions of an individual with a disability and the actions of the other individuals participating in a physical education class 1.05.01.01

- Model acceptance and inclusion of the individual with a disability in the physical education class
- Develop physical education environments that emphasize the capability of the individual with a disability
- Include individuals with disabilities in planning physical education programs and related sport experiences

Understand the role of the physical environment (where they live, what school they attend) and the subsystems (social, economic, societal, home, day care) affecting the individual 1.05.01.02

- Review records and interview primary care providers to assist in creating successful physical education experiences
- Accept individuals with disabilities, recognizing that their prior experience and background may require a sensitive and empathetic teacher
- Avoid establishing predetermined limits on students because of background, culture, or socioeconomic status

Understand the importance of assessing individuals with disabilities by accounting for the environmental conditions under which activity can be performed, the attributes of the performer, and the interaction of that environment and the performer 1.05.01.03

- Use an ecological task analysis approach in teaching physical education activities
- Change the instructional environment, as appropriate, to ensure that the relationship among the performer, task, and conditions leads to success

Know how an individual's actions affect the environment and the environment affects the individual 1.05.01.04

- Obtain desired skill level and behavior performance by utilizing various approaches, including applied behavior analysis and task analysis
- Structure the environment so that it responds to the needs of selected individuals such as increase or decrease the amount of stimuli, size of movement space, or number of cues

Understand that self-actualization theory emphasizes that individuals are constantly striving to realize their full inherent potential

Understand the importance of meeting basic physiological, safety and security, love and belonging, and self-esteem needs before an individual can be self-actualized 1.05.02.01

- Plan programs in cooperation with others, including related personnel such as therapists, psychologists, parents, and individuals with disabilities
- Implement programs that focus on the complete individual, acknowledging the importance of incremental success

Understand the importance of unconditional positive regard of the individual with a disability 1.05.02.02

- Emphasize strengths of the individual in order to build on the needs that will generate self-actualization
- Develop a physical education environment that allows the individual with a disability to perceive the teacher and peers as supportive in the learning process

Understand that self-efficacy theory of personality development emphasizes the concept that belief in one's ability and personal resourcefulness will allow one to successfully achieve desired outcomes

Understand that an individual with a disability will experience a sense of personal mastery that can generalize to new situations 1.05.03.01

- Develop opportunities for individuals with disabilities to succeed using an incremental approach with positive reinforcement
- Encourage and facilitate individuals with disabilities to transfer skills learned during physical education class to other activities and life experiences

Understand levels of cues/prompts that will foster an individual with a disability learning new behaviors 1.05.03.02

- Utilize cues/prompts that are appropriate to the instructional and/or behavioral needs of the individual with a disability
- Recognize the importance of withdrawing cues/prompts to the least intrusive level for an individual with a disability
- Recognize that the individuals are learning about their own level of competence

Understand that normalization theory emphasizes that individuals with disabilities should live and function as closely as possible to the normal living, learning, and working conditions of people in society

Understand procedures and techniques in physical education classes that enhance the image of individuals with disabilities 1.05.04.01

- Structure the learning environment to create full integration of individuals with and without disabilities
- Incorporate examples of successful athletes with disabilities within the physical education environment

Understand the importance of selecting appropriate services to support inclusion of individuals with disabilities in general physical education settings 1.05.04.02

- Work cooperatively with other professionals to maximize integrated experiences for individuals with and without disabilities
- Support other professionals who provide motor experiences for individuals with disabilities

Demonstrate knowledge of factors influencing development

Understand that many disabilities are directly attributable to genetic, medical, and environmental factors

Understand that developmental disabilities may be caused by chromosomal aberrations; gestational disorders; degenerative disorders; mineral, nutritional, endocrine, and mineral dysfunction; infections and intoxicants; and environmental factors 1.06.01.01; 1.06.01.02; 1.06.01.03

- Check medical records and be aware of current medical status and medications and their impact on motor performance
- Collaborate with the appropriate school personnel related to placement and programming in physical education
- Plan proper safety precautions during physical activity based on the unique characteristics of the disability of the individual such as modifying activities for individuals with Down syndrome who have atlantoaxial instability

Understand that the cause of some disabilities is not well understood 1.06.01.04

- Consult with physicians and medical experts regarding such disabilities with unknown causes
- Identify local, state, and national agencies that may have information on the causes of these disabilities (see Standard 9)

Understand that development may be caused by chromosomal aberrations 1.06.01.05

- Explain the incidence of common chromosomal aberrations
- Explain the impact of common chromosomal aberrations, such as Down syndrome, on motor performance
- Collaborate with the appropriate school personnel related to placement and programming in physical education

Motor Behavior

Understand motor development

Understand neuromaturational/hierarchical models

Understand sensory integration 2.01.01.01
- Recognize the relationship between sensory integration and ataxia (motor awkwardness)
- Identify factors in intersensory and intrasensory integration related to movement control and coordination
- Select and design activities to stimulate and facilitate the development of intersensory and intrasensory integration

Understand neurodevelopmental theory 2.01.01.02
- Structure tasks and activities to inhibit abnormal movements
- Structure tasks and activities to stimulate and facilitate normal postural responses

Understand dynamic systems theory

Understand the diversity and influence of rate of performance and learning limiters such as body size and proportions, gravity, cognitive development, and biomechanical constraints on motor experiences of individuals with disabilities 2.01.02.01
- Apply knowledge of dynamic systems theory to program planning and implementation
- Develop individual program plans that diminish or accommodate for the effects of rate limiters

Understand factors (including prenatal and postnatal influences) affecting motor development such as nutritional status, genetic makeup, and environmental opportunities for practice and instruction

Understand how these factors could influence the rate and sequence of development for individuals with disabilities 2.01.03.01
- Identify characteristic behaviors related to factors that impact the rate and sequence of development
- Implement a program of activities specifically designed to minimize factors affecting motor development and to maximize developmental potential

Know the importance of synthesizing information on physical, cognitive, and psychological factors and their impact on skill acquisition for individuals with disabilities 2.01.03.02
- Develop programs that maximize individuals' strengths and diminish and/or accommodate for weaknesses in specific domains of motor behavior
- Maintain an integrated programmatic approach to instruction, based on the knowledge of the individual's cognitive and social development and its relationship to motor development

Understand normal sensory development related to the visual, auditory, tactile, vestibular, and kinesthetic systems

Understand common deviations in the development of the visual system among individuals with disabilities 2.01.04.01
- Recognize deficits in refractive and orthoptic vision including accommodation and tracking individuals with disabilities

- Describe the relationship between the development of visual functions such as constancy, figure-ground perception, and depth perception to movement control in motor activities
- Apply knowledge of visual functioning deficiencies in selecting and designing activities
- Develop and implement programs that strengthen orthoptic visual abilities such as visual fixation, pursuit, and search behaviors
- Modify activities to accommodate individuals with visual deficiencies

Understand common deviations in the development of the auditory system among individuals with disabilities 2.01.04.02

- Recognize and assess deficits in auditory recognition, discrimination, and localization
- Select and design activities to help accommodate deficits in auditory functioning
- Modify activities to accommodate auditory deficits

Understand common deviations in the development of the tactile system among individuals with disabilities 2.01.04.03

- Recognize behaviors associated with hyperresponsive (tactile defensive) and hyporesponsive (tactile seeking) tactile disorders
- Select and design activities to help remediate hyper- and hyporesponsive tactile disorders
- Develop and implement programs to enhance individuals' abilities to tolerate various levels of tactile stimuli
- Develop and implement programs that enhance individuals' abilities to accurately discriminate from among various tactile stimuli and use the information profitably

Understand common deviations in the development of the vestibular system among individuals with disabilities 2.01.04.04

- Recognize behaviors associated with vestibular functioning deficiencies
- Recognize signs of vestibular overstimulation
- Conduct basic screening to assess vestibular function
- Select and design activities to help remediate balance problems related to vestibular functioning
- Develop and implement programs that stimulate the vestibular system for integration with visual, kinesthetic, and tactile inputs

Understand common deviations in the development of the kinesthetic system among individuals with disabilities 2.01.04.05

- Recognize behaviors associated with deficiencies in the kinesthetic system
- Conduct basic screening to identify possible deficiencies in kinesthetic system functioning
- Select and design activities to help remediate deficiencies in kinesthetic system functioning
- Develop and implement programs that stimulate efficient use of kinesthetic inputs and integration with vestibular, visual, and tactile input systems

Understand patterns of cognitive, perceptual, and perceptual motor development and the factors that influence those patterns

Understand the influences of perceptual motor programs that emphasize cognitive and perceptual abilities among individuals with disabilities 2.01.05.01

- Develop and implement programs that afford individuals opportunities to formulate and execute motor plans

- Implement opportunities for augmented feedback when individuals are involved in activities that enhance motor planning abilities

Understand the development of postural control and relationship to the mechanisms of balance and equilibrium

Understand the significance of developmental delays throughout the lifespan on balance and related tasks 2.01.06.01

- Develop and implement programs that stimulate vestibular, visual, and proprioceptive senses
- Develop and implement programs that increase the strength and endurance of postural muscle groups

Understand the influence of the development of reflexes on normal motor development and the implications on skill acquisition

Understand the relationship between persistence of primitive reflexes and disabling conditions 2.01.07.01

- Identify the difference between primitive and postural reflexes
- Describe the influence of weak or persistent primitive reflexes on the rate and sequence of motor development as well as voluntary motor control in individuals with disabilities

Understand reflexes and reactions observed in individuals developing normally and abnormally 2.01.07.02

- Recognize the differing patterns of reflex behavior among individuals with disabilities such as persistent primitive reflexes in cerebral palsy
- Identify behaviors associated with persistent or weak primitive residual reflexes
- Select and design activities that inhibit primitive reflexes through positioning and stimulation of voluntary responses (see Standard 9)
- Select and design activities to help stimulate the development of postural and equilibrium reactions
- Modify activities to accommodate primitive reflexes

Understand the development and emergence of locomotion including prone progressions, assumption of an upright gait, and walking

Understand variance in "motor milestones" such as typical or average age of achievement for individuals with disabilities 2.01.08.01

- Identify behaviors associated with lack of attainment of "motor milestones"
- Implement activities that stimulate upright postures and control of head, neck, and trunk
- Implement activities that strengthen postural muscles and extremities necessary for locomotion

Understand the development and emergence of manipulation skills including reaching, grasping, and releasing

Understand variance in manipulation skills associated with individuals with disabilities 2.01.09.01

- Identify the impact of developmental delays in reaching, grasping, and releasing on the ability to perform functional motor skills, sport, and lifetime recreational activities
- Select and design activities that stimulate visual fixation and enable the visual-to-motor match needed to reach-grasp-release

Understand that there are differing patterns of manipulative skills among individuals with disabilities 2.01.09.02

- Modify activities to accommodate differing patterns of manipulative skills
- Implement activities to reach-grasp-release through the use of supportive assistive aids to enhance voluntary controls and means-end behaviors

Understand the development of fundamental motor skills and patterns

Understand variance in the progression of fundamental motor skill performance among individuals with disabilities 2.01.10.01

- Task analyze to determine the progression of fundamental motor skill acquisition according the area of the body (head, trunk, stance) or phase (preparation, action, and follow-through) of the skill
- Select and design activities to help stimulate fundamental motor skill development
- Modify activities to accommodate for differing patterns of fundamental motor skills exhibited by some individuals with disabilities

Understand how fundamental motor skills are refined and combined to produce sport skills

Understand how to adapt activities to promote development from the fundamental movement stage through the sport skill stage for individuals with disabilities 2.01.11.01

- Task analyze the sport-related movement according to the level of the fundamental motor skill exhibited
- Select and design activities to help stimulate the development of fundamental motor skills related to sport-related movements

Understand the relationship between mature fundamental motor skill development and performance of sport-related skill development

Understand how appropriate modifications of the physical environment enable individuals with disabilities to perform sport skills 2.01.12.01

- Modify sport-related activities to accommodate differing patterns of fundamental skills exhibited by some individuals with disabilities
- Change the structure and organization of sports and games to include diverse skill levels and performance indicators

Understand how motor development impacts the ability to engage in lifetime recreation and sport activities

Understand the influence of sport and leisure on the overall development of individuals with disabilities 2.01.13.01

- Use a functional model of skill development
- Use equipment that has been specifically designed to enhance participation by individuals with disabilities

Know when to adapt rules to accommodate participation by individuals with a disability in a sport or leisure activity of their choice 2.01.13.02

- Provide competitive sport opportunities for individuals with disabilities who are not currently served by an established organization
- Develop and implement leisure activities that meet the needs of individuals with disabilities who are not accommodated by existing sport offerings

Know how to modify activities and programs to enhance the cognitive, affective, and psychomotor development of individuals with disabilities (see Standard 10) 2.01.13.03

- Use knowledge about an individual's cognitive development to select tasks and activities that can be acquired, retained, and transferred to other related tasks and activities
- Use knowledge of an individual's social development to determine which tasks and activities will provide for maximum social integration and acceptance
- Use knowledge of an individual's psychomotor development to establish an integrated approach to program planning that includes cognitive and social development enhancement

Understand factors that contribute to positive and negative transfer such as the nature of the task, the goal of training, or the amount and type of practice

Understand the concepts of transfer and specificity when programming for individuals with disabilities 2.02.01.01

- Plan practice and learning tasks that will positively transfer to the next level of skill acquisition
- Use transfer to measure attainment of selected criterion skills
- Apply the concept of task specificity with the understanding that it presents certain problems for some persons with disabilities

Understand the stages of the different learning theories and models such as those of Fitts and Posner, Adams, and Gentile

Understand the implications of the stages of learning during skill acquisition for individuals with disabilities 2.02.02.01

- Plan and give feedback consistent with the knowledge needed at each stage of skill acquisition
- Structure practice and learning tasks to support individualizing within a class to match different rates of skill acquisition
- Plan for an increase in task complexity commensurate with individuals with various abilities
- Structure practice and learning tasks to move from a closed to an open skill such as from a ball on a batting tee to a pitched ball
- Make adjustments in teaching methods and instructions
- Use a variety of techniques to facilitate learning during the verbal-cognitive stage

Understand motor learning

Understand factors that positively and negatively affect retention such as practice schedules and failure to provide feedback

Understand the implications of overlearning on the retention of motor skills by individuals with disabilities 2.02.03.01

- Use practice variability to positively influence the retention of motor skills
- Analyze complex movements to determine which could benefit from randomly ordered practice
- Structure the duration of instructional units to facilitate retention of content

Understand prepractice considerations (e.g., motivation and goal setting)

Know techniques and procedures that can facilitate motivation and preparation for individuals with disabilities 2.02.04.01

- Plan practice and tasks with appropriate levels of novelty and complexity
- Set and present goals that are challenging but attainable with learner input
- Use performance standards to help individuals with disabilities set goals
- Modify activities as a means of achieving success

Understand principles of practice including how and when to use guidance techniques, mental practice, and whole versus part practice

Understand how practice principles can be used for individuals with disabilities 2.02.05.01

- Analyze skills to determine the most appropriate type of practice such as whole, whole-part, and part
- Use physical and verbal guidance to avoid errors early in learning
- Emphasize the use of mental practice
- Encourage the use of a combination of mental and physical practice to increase learning efficiency

Understand how massed and distributed practice are used for continuous and discrete tasks

Understand the concept of practice variability when promoting skill acquisition for individuals with disabilities 2.02.06.01

- Structure across and within practices so time spent on activities is divided into appropriate segments
- Recognize and classify tasks according to their energy cost (see Standard 3)
- Design practice sessions that include appropriate rest periods for discrete and continuous skills

Understand how to organize and schedule practice with emphasis on instructional efficiency

Understand how task variation complements skill acquisition in individuals with disabilities 2.02.07.01

- Vary practice schedules along various dimensions such as distance, speed, and time
- Use random practice selectively depending on the nature of the disability

Understand how random practice impacts on learning and retention of motor skills

Know how the effect of random practice may vary for individuals with disabilities 2.02.08.01

- Use random practice to aid task retention
- Construct variable practice sessions to incorporate a wide range of movement variations

Understand the factors that affect both transfer to training and the relationship between generalizability and specificity of learning such as automaticity, error detection, and transfer and generalization of learning

Know how these factors (i.e., automaticity, error detection, transfer, and generalization of learning) relate to error detection and generalizability of learning of individuals with disabilities 2.02.09.01

- Develop the ability to detect and correct errors among learners
- Analyze skills to determine which type of feedback is most useful in detecting errors and then direct learners' attention to it

Recognize characteristics of performance that accompany increased automaticity and error detection in individuals with disabilities 2.02.09.02

- Use a given stimulus pattern when practicing because it increases the probability of producing the specific response
- Design practice sessions to develop a high level of physical performance in both closed and open skills

Understand the importance of feedback to learning

Know how different types of feedback such as knowledge results, knowledge of performance, intrinsic, and augmented may be used to enhance performance of individuals with disabilities (see Standard 10) 2.02.10.01

- Use feedback to motivate learners
- Use feedback to reinforce appropriate movement patterns
- Use feedback to help learners detect and correct their own errors

Know how to vary methods of feedback delivery to enhance the performance of individuals with disabilities 2.02.10.02

- Select different types of feedback to enhance learning
- Determine which movement features are most critical for success
- Give feedback that is appropriate
- Use faded feedback and adjust schedules for fading to accommodate individual errors

Understand the relationship between altering the scheduling of feedback and guidance, reward, and motivation

Know how to use a system of least prompts, including when it is best to use verbal, visual, environmental, and physical prompts 2.02.11.01

- Use kinesthetic prompting to assist individuals with visual impairment
- Use appropriate visual, verbal, and physical prompts within a least-prompts instructional hierarchy
- Structure the physical environment to provide extrinsic feedback to learners

Understand how delays in knowledge of results during the intertrial interval and post knowledge of results delays affect skill acquisition

Understand how to manipulate the intertrial interval to enhance skill acquisition among individuals with disabilities 2.02.12.01

- Structure the internal interval to reduce the effects of delayed knowledge of results for individuals with visual disabilities
- Provide sufficient time after giving feedback for the learner to think about and understand errors
- Provide adequate postfeedback intervals for effective planning of the next movement

Understand motor control

Understand the stages of information processing (i.e., stimulus identification, response selection, and response programming)

Understand how the stages of information processing are affected by certain types of disabilities 2.03.01.01

- Modify tasks and instructions so that they are congruent with students' processing abilities

- Adjust strategies in gamelike situations to take into account delayed response processing

Understand the importance of attention and arousal in motor performance

Understand the concept of stimulus overselectivity and its effect on motor performance in individuals with disabilities 2.03.02.01

- Manipulate the environment or one's position in the environment for minimum infringement on the learner's attention
- When appropriate, structure and present tasks to elicit optimal arousal levels
- Structure activities involving the tracking of objects to account for certain types of disabilities

Understand the parts of the central nervous system responsible for motor control processes and their function and interaction with other systems

Understand how damage to various neurological structures affect motor performance in individuals with disabilities (see Standard 3) 2.03.03.01

- Structure tasks and activities to account for damage to the basal ganglion, which will influence coordinated movements such as throwing an object by some individuals with cerebral palsy
- Structure tasks and activities to account for cerebellar problems

Distinguish among simple, choice, and discrimination reaction time

Understand how certain types of disabilities may affect reaction time 2.03.04.01

- Modify activities to allow more or less processing time, as needed
- Structure tasks and activities to account for greater difficulty responding to multiple-choice situations such as in team activities

Distinguish among short-term sensory memory, short-term memory, and long-term memory

Understand how different types of memory problems may be influenced by an individual's disability 2.03.05.01

- Repeat previously experienced instructions or activities without negative effect
- Evaluate the effects of different types of kinesthetic and proprioceptive deficits on the ability to retain skills such as the way a bat is held

Understand how anticipation affects skill acquisition

Understand how spatial and temporal uncertainty can exacerbate movement difficulties in individuals with disabilities 2.03.06.01

- Structure tasks and activities to account for difficulty in anticipation for individuals with figure-ground problems involved in ball activities
- Structure tasks and activities involving the flight of objects to control for problems in timing that are evident in certain types of disabilities

Differentiate between controlled and automatic processes with emphasis on the response selection stage

Understand controlled and automatic processes in open and closed skills with individuals with disabilities 2.03.07.01

- Analyze skills in relation to interference resulting from the presence of primitive reflex behavior such as with some individuals with cerebral palsy executing a forehand in tennis
- Structure tasks and activities to account for reflex actions that may interfere with performance in a closed skill such as with some individuals with cerebral palsy swimming the front crawl stroke

Understand how feedback error and servomechanisms affect a closed loop system

Understand how positive and negative feedback systems may affect the closed motor skill performance of individuals with disabilities 2.03.08.01

- Structure activities for success to maximize the positive feedback associated with successful execution
- Reduce the frequency of highlighting errors in skill execution, which may adversely affect individuals with disabilities

Understand the elements in a closed loop system that may not be generated with rapid discrete actions (e.g., stages of information processing)

Understand how the stages of information processing impact the execution of a motor skill by individuals with disabilities 2.03.09.01

- Program activities that facilitate the use of proprioceptive feedback, which in certain types of disabilities may not be utilized effectively
- Develop short-term memory for the salient features of the task and activity to be executed

Understand the mechanisms of commonality and difference found both in open and closed loop models

Understand the concepts of the open loop system for programming activities for individuals with disabilities 2.03.10.01

- Use an open loop approach for certain types of disabilities such as autism
- Demonstrate care when preprogramming a series of actions for individuals with certain disabilities since the instructor may be limited to certain types of adjustments or improvements

Understand the concepts of the closed loop system for programming activities for individuals with disabilities 2.03.10.02

- Instruct and give augmented feedback to encourage learners to process intrinsic feedback
- Encourage the use of verbal rehearsal strategies to facilitate appropriate response selection

Understand the speed–accuracy trade-off (e.g., substituting accuracy for speed)

Understand how movement amplitude, the distance between two targets in an aiming task, is incorporated into the assessment process 2.03.011.01

- Determine the amount of emphasis placed on the velocity of movement such as how fast to stroke a tennis ball and realize that it differs with various types of disabilities
- Teach a skill with the required movement amplitude to avoid the individual relearning the skill

Understand how motor programs influence the execution of skilled movements

Understand individual abilities in the development of motor programs in individuals with disabilities 2.03.12.01

- Structure tasks and activities to account for marked variations in ability relative to how a person will learn and execute motor skills
- Structure tasks and activities to account for deficits in short-term and long-term memory in order to combine smaller elements of a skill into longer sequences that are controlled by a single motor program

Understand the mechanisms required to change motor programs (e.g., what defines the essential details of skilled action?)

Understand the implications of open and closed loop theories such as Schmidt's schema theory and Adams' closed loop theory to skill acquisition for individuals with disabilities 2.03.13.01

- Present tasks to learners so that the essential characteristics of the tasks are understandable
- Apply the open and closed loop theory to determine which skills or parts of skills are amenable to correction

Recognize individual differences and capabilities

Understand how to relate Henry's specificity hypothesis (tasks are composed of many unrelated abilities) to motor skill execution for individuals with disabilities 2.03.14.01

- Realize that the level of proficiency in one skill in a skill class such as underhand throwing may be different from another skill in the same class such as overhand throwing
- Structure activities to consider that the speed or motion of an agonistic muscle group may be faster or slower than that of the antagonistic muscle group

Exercise Science

Exercise Physiology Principles: Demonstrate knowledge of exercise physiology principles

Understand how to measure metabolism and work expenditure using indirect and direct calorimetry

Understand that measurement of energy expenditure may be affected by alterations in physiology or anatomy for individuals with disabilities 3.01.01.01

- Use modified protocols for measurement of energy expenditure with individuals with orthopedic disabilities such as spinal cord injury and multiple sclerosis
- Recognize that untrained individuals without disabilities who utilize upper extremities for exercise testing demonstrate lower energy expenditure levels than untrained individuals with disabilities
- Recognize that trained individuals who utilize upper extremities for exercise demonstrate higher energy expenditure levels than sedentary individuals
- Recognize that individuals with quadriplegia demonstrate lower levels of energy expenditure than individuals with paraplegia

Understand the effect of body mass on energy expenditure for individuals who are obese 3.01.01.02

- Recognize that weight-bearing activities such as running require more energy expenditure for those who are overweight
- Use non-weight-bearing or simplified weight-bearing activities initially such as walking

Understand metabolic rate at rest and during exercise

Understand that metabolic rates may be affected by various syndromes and metabolic and orthopedic disabilities 3.01.02.01

- Recognize that individuals with Down syndrome may have diminished metabolic rates, thus affecting their activity level and ability for weight management
- Recognize that individuals with Prader-Willi syndrome may have diminished metabolic rates, thus affecting their activity level and ability for weight management

Understand energy systems, sources, storage, mobilization, and roles in different activities (power, speed, endurance)

Understand that various disabilities may affect metabolism 3.01.03.01

- Accommodate individuals with McArdle's syndrome who are unable to utilize glycogen as a fuel source, thus limiting their ability to participate in short-term high-intensity activities
- Recognize that individuals with spinal cord injury such as quadriplegia may have a diminished ability to utilize fat as a fuel source, thus limiting their ability to participate in long-term endurance activities

Understand neural and endocrine control of metabolism at rest and during exercise and its relation to exercise intensity and duration

Understand that various disabilities may affect neural and endocrine control 3.01.04.01

- Accommodate individuals with uncontrolled diabetes who may have a diminished ability to synthesize fat and glycogen, thus limiting their ability to participate in physical activity

- Recognize that exercise can help an individual with diabetes who is stable by reducing the amount of insulin needed
- Appreciate that exercise can exacerbate ketosis and be deadly to an individual with diabetes who is unstable
- Realize that exercise can be deadly to an individual with diabetes who is unstable by causing excessive release of growth hormone, which may contribute to blood vessel disease

Neural Control: Demonstrate knowledge of muscular movement

Understand the neural and biomechanical control of movement from higher brain centers (anatomy and neural innervation of muscle, nerve transmission)

Understand how various disabilities may alter normal neural control of movement

- Recognize that multiple sclerosis will have delayed nerve transmissions affecting the ability to perform activities, particularly ambulation
- Acknowledge that spinal cord injuries have various levels of residual neural activity affecting ability to perform activities

Understand the difference between voluntary and involuntary movement

Understand that voluntary control of movement may be altered by various syndromes, as well as metabolic and orthopedic disabilities 3.02.02.01

- Recognize that deficiencies in voluntary control of movement due to cerebral palsy affect an individual's ability to perform free-weight lifting
- Acknowledge that use of upper extremities in manual wheelchair propulsion may result in extension of the lower extremities in individuals with cerebral palsy
- Place strapping in front of the legs during manual wheelchair propulsion to prevent knee extension for individuals with extensor pattern disorders

Understand the purpose of, processes of, and how to elicit reflexes (gamma loop, muscle spindles, Golgi tendon organs)

Understand that reflexes can be affected by various disabilities 3.02.03.01

- Acknowledge that neuromuscular disorders such as muscular dystrophy will have diminished reflexes that will hinder ability to perform certain activities
- Acknowledge that individuals with spinal abnormalities may have diminished reflexes due to neural impingement

Muscular Concepts: Demonstrate knowledge of various muscular concepts

Understand skeletal muscle structure and function

Understand that various syndromes, as well as metabolic and orthopedic disabilities, may alter skeletal muscle structure and function 3.03.01.01

- Acknowledge that individuals with spinal cord injuries may lose strength and functional ability
- Emphasize strength training programs for hypotonic individuals
- Emphasize non-weight-bearing activities for individuals with degenerative diseases such as muscular dystrophy

- Recognize that individuals with muscular dystrophy such as Duchenne are predisposed to skeletal muscle degeneration

Understand the interaction between metabolic and mechanical efficiency

Understand that various syndromes, as well as metabolic and orthopedic disabilities, may alter metabolic and mechanical efficiency 3.03.02.01
- Accommodate individuals who display motor patterns resulting from mechanical inefficiency
- Accommodate individuals who display motor patterns resulting from metabolic inefficiency

Understand muscular strength and muscular endurance

Understand that various syndromes, as well as metabolic and orthopedic disabilities, may affect muscular strength and function 3.03.03.01
- Acknowledge that individuals with progressive neuromuscular conditions will lose strength
- Acknowledge that individuals with spastic cerebral palsy will have a muscular imbalance between flexor and extensor muscles

Understand the concepts of overload, specificity, and muscular adaptations when developing weight training programs

Understand that the overload and specificity principles apply to individuals with disabilities 3.03.04.01
- Recognize that individuals with disabilities that result in hypotonia such as Down syndrome may demonstrate a delayed response to muscular training
- Recognize that individuals with degenerative muscular diseases may not develop benefits from muscular training

Understand aspects of flexibility

Understand that flexibility training applies to individuals with disabilities 3.03.05.01
- Recognize that individuals with hypotonic conditions such as Down syndrome do not need flexibility emphasized in their fitness programs
- Emphasize flexibility exercise for individuals with hypertonic conditions such as cerebral palsy

Cardiorespiratory Factors: Demonstrate knowledge of various cardiorespiratory factors

Understand the anatomy and function of the cardiorespiratory system

Understand that congenital defects or syndromes such as congenital heart defects, aortic stenosis, atrial septal defects, and Marfan syndrome may alter the anatomy and function of the cardiovascular system 3.04.01.01
- Limit the duration and intensity of exercise for individuals with impaired cardiac function
- Maintain close contact with the physician for individuals with impaired cardiac function
- Recognize the cardiovascular training limitation of individuals with heart disease

Understand the electrical and circulatory processes of the cardiac cycle, control of the heart, and basic anatomy of the circulatory system

Understand how the variability of the cardiac cycle applies to individuals with congenital defects, syndromes, or orthopedic disabilities 3.04.02.01

- Recognize that individuals with congenital heart defects may have limited aerobic capacity due to an inadequate amount of oxygenated blood or an inability to eliminate an adequate amount of carbon dioxide
- Contact physician before engaging individuals with coronary defects in an exercise program
- Define an appropriate level of exercise intensity for individuals with congenital heart defects

Understand oxygen consumption ($\dot{V}O_2$) at rest and during exercise

Understand that oxygen consumption may be different between individuals with disabilities and individuals without disabilities 3.04.03.01

- Recognize that individuals with spinal cord injuries including spina bifida will have lower oxygen consumption levels due to use of small muscle mass
- Describe the differences in maximum heart rate (HR) between hand and/or arm ergometry and wheelchair ergometry

Understand the determinants and control of circulation at rest and during exercise

Understand that various orthopedic disabilities and metabolic disease such as diabetes result in neural and vascular damage that may affect circulation 3.04.04.01

- Recognize that individuals with spinal cord injuries have impaired hemodynamic responses (such as reduced blood flow and lowered blood pressure) and thermoregulation
- Recognize that individuals with spinal cord injuries have impaired vasoconstriction and vasodilation

Understand cardiorespiratory dynamics (cardiac output, stroke volume, contractility, heart rate, blood pressure, synergy of contraction, distensibility of ventricles, oxygen transport) at rest and during exercise

Understand that congenital defects, syndromes, and orthopedic disabilities may interfere with cardiorespiratory dynamics 3.04.05.01

- Recognize that individuals with spinal cord injury, quadriplegia, and Down syndrome have reduced heart rates
- Acknowledge that the use of standard heart rate values for the determination of exercise intensity is not applicable

Understand the effects and risk factors of coronary heart disease

Understand that individuals with disabilities are often at a higher risk for cardiovascular heart disease 3.04.06.01

- Recognize that high blood cholesterol levels are more prevalent in individuals with disabilities
- Review medical records for individuals with disabilities for elevated total cholesterol levels

Respiratory Factors: Demonstrate knowledge of respiratory system

Understand the purpose of ventilation and respiration, oxygen exchange and transport, acid–base regulation, and partial pressures of gases

Understand that orthopedic or chronic obstructive pulmonary disease conditions can interfere with the function of the respiratory system 3.05.01.01

- Recognize that exercise may precipitate an asthma attack
- Promote desirable exercise conditions such as allergen-free and stress-free environments
- Describe techniques to control ventilation and respiration during an asthma attack
- Work with the individual and caregivers on regulating medication
- Use the proper warm-up activities prior to exercise for individuals with chronic obstructive pulmonary disease

Understand the anatomy of the pulmonary system, dynamic and static lung volumes, mechanics of ventilation, ventilatory parameters (maximum voluntary ventilation, breathing frequency, tidal volume) and training adaptations

Understand that chronic obstructive pulmonary disease and orthopedic disabilities, particularly those that cause ventilatory muscle dysfunction, may interfere with the respiratory system function 3.05.02.01

- Be aware that individuals with asthma may panic because they feel they are not receiving enough air
- Practice safety precautions and relaxation techniques to control breathing

Understand the control of ventilation at rest and during exercise

Understand that chronic obstructive pulmonary disease and orthopedic disabilities may restrict ventilation 3.05.03.01

- Recognize that individuals with higher level spinal injuries often lack the muscle control for ventilation thus limiting strenuous activity
- Develop intact accessory muscles through physical activity and respiratory training

Nutrition: Demonstrate knowledge of nutritional concepts

Understand nutritional concepts (fat, carbohydrate, protein), nutritional supplements (vitamins and minerals), and concept of a balanced diet

Understand that individuals with disabilities may have specific nutritional needs 3.06.01.01

- Provide guidance regarding proper nutrition for individuals with disabilities
- Monitor sugar intake for individuals with diabetes
- Monitor food intake for individuals with Prader-Willi syndrome
- Monitor aspartame intake in individuals with phenylketonuria

Body Composition: Demonstrate knowledge of body composition

Understand the components of body composition

Understand the differences in the percentage of body fat in individuals with disabilities 3.07.01.01

- Utilize Kelly-Rimmer equation for computing percent body fat for individuals with mental retardation
- Recognize that lean body mass is higher in individuals with paraplegia than in those with quadriplegia

Understand the differences among underweight, overweight, overfat, and obese

Know which individuals with disabilities in general are underweight, overweight, overfat, or obese 3.07.02.01

- Demonstrate how to use height and weight tables to classify a person with a disability as overweight, using small, medium, and large frames
- Refrain from using skinfold calipers over paralyzed muscle groups and scar tissue

Understand the factors that are associated with the treatment of obesity

Understand the factors that are associated with the treatment of obesity in individuals with disabilities such as exercise, nutrition, and behavioral intervention

- Develop a weight reduction program that emphasizes exercise
- Develop a weight reduction program that emphasizes nutrition
- Develop a weight reduction program that emphasizes behavioral intervention

Environmental Effects: Demonstrate knowledge of environmental effects on performance

Understand the adaptations to thermal stress (hot, cold), what constitutes thermal stress, and the symptoms of thermal injury

Understand that individuals with disabilities such as asthma or orthopedic involvement may be susceptible to thermal change conditions 3.08.01.01

- Recognize that the body's ability to thermoregulate is increasingly compromised, the higher the spinal cord injury
- Recognize that individuals with spinal injuries, muscular dystrophy, and multiple sclerosis are particularly prone to thermal injuries and must be well hydrated and monitored when performing activity

Understand the impact of high- and low-pressure environments on individuals with disabilities 3.08.01.02

- Monitor respiration rates of individuals with asthma at high altitudes due to reduced oxygen pressure
- Monitor respiration rates of individuals with cystic fibrosis at high altitudes due to reduced oxygen pressure

Exercise Prescription and Training: Demonstrate knowledge of exercise prescription and training

Understand the physiological benefits and adaptations of exercise (decreased blood pressure, decreased submaximal heart rate, improved endurance)

Know the benefits of exercise training for individuals with exercise-induced asthma 3.09.01.01

- Recognize the effects of exercise response and training for individuals with exercise-induced asthma

- Recognize the effects of medication for individuals with exercise-induced asthma
- Design exercise programs that are safe and effective for individuals with exercise-induced asthma
- Design conditioning programs for individuals who are wheelchair users

Understand the differences between fitness, physical activity, and rehabilitation

Know the differences between fitness, physical activity, and rehabilitation programs for individuals with disabilities 3.09.02.01

- Assign homework for individuals with disabilities that increases activity levels
- Develop a rehabilitation program for individuals with disabilities with the assistance of team members from allied medicine

Understand the current American College of Sports Medicine recommendations for exercise prescription

Understand that heart rate depends on the injury levels of individuals with disabilities such as spinal cord injuries 3.09.03.01

- Use ratings of perceived exertion (RPE) to determine exercise intensity level when heart rate is difficult to obtain
- Emphasize duration of activity rather than activity intensity for individuals with obesity. After the exercise program has been ongoing, emphasize that the greater the intensity, the better

Understand the concept and use of metabolic equivalent (MET)

Understand the difference in maximum MET levels between individuals with and without disabilities 3.09.04.01

- Use the metabolic equivalent (MET) as a method of classifying fitness levels
- Compare and contrast METs with other methods of classifying individuals with special needs such as $\dot{V}O_2$max, watts, etc.

Understand the Karvonen formula for estimation of maximal and training heart rate zone

Understand that the Karvonen formula may be ineffective for individuals with disabilities such as Down syndrome who may have chronotropic incompetence 3.09.05.01

- Calculate training heart rate using the Karvonen formula for individuals with disabilities
- Use conservative training heart rates for individuals who are severely deconditioned

Understand the concept and use of the rate of perceived exertion (RPE)

Understand the importance of RPE when gauging exercise intensity in individuals with disabilities such as type 1 diabetes mellitus and individuals on beta blockers 3.09.06.01

- Teach individuals with exercise-induced asthma how to utilize ratings of perceived exertion (RPE)
- Use prior RPEs to design new exercise programs for individuals with exercise-induced asthma

Understand the different types of maximal and submaximal methods of determining cardiovascular fitness

Understand the different testing protocols for persons with disabilities 3.09.07.01

- Use the Pacer shuttle run for individuals with disabilities such as mental retardation or partially sighted

- Use wheelchair ergometers (rollers) or arm crank ergometers (Monark) to determine submaximal test for individuals using manual wheelchairs

Understand the different types of direct and indirect determinations of muscular strength, endurance, and flexibility

Understand the types of muscular strength, endurance, and flexibility tests used for individuals with disabilities 3.09.08.01

- Use appropriate test of muscular strength and endurance for individuals who use wheelchairs
- Use an appropriate flexibility test (goniometer) for individuals who use wheelchairs

Understand the principles of the general adaptation system reaction, resistance, exhaustion, overload, specificity, reversibility, and individuality and how they relate to exercise prescription

Understand the concept of reversibility and how it applies to individuals with disabilities such as spinal cord injury 3.09.09.01

- Design cardiorespiratory training programs utilizing specificity of exercise such as wheelchair ergometers
- Accommodate for the concept of reversibility for an individual with a disability who has been removed from school for an extended period of time due to surgery

Understand the physiological differences between genders related to exercise performance

Understand the physiological differences of the aerobic capacity and body composition between males and females with disabilities 3.09.10.01

- Recognize that females have lower $\dot{V}O_2$max than males
- Recognize that females, in general, are in need of a more intensive exercise intervention than males

Biomechanics/Kinesiology: Demonstrate knowledge of basic biomechanical and kinesiological concepts and principles

Understand kinesiology

Understand pathokinesiology and its relationship to altered human movement patterns caused by disabilities 3.10.01.01

- Explain basic changes in movements or joint positions
- Use appropriate activities and equipment that alter movements or accommodate abnormal joint positions

Understand biomechanics

Understand pathobiomechanics and its relationship to kinesiological movement in individuals with disabilities 3.10.02.01

- Explain basic changes in biomechanical movements of joint positions
- Use appropriate activities and equipment that alter movement patterns or accommodate abnormal joint positions

Understand statics

Understand specific biomechanical and kinesiological properties such as static tension, static stretch, and equilibrium and their relationship to physical and motor performance for individuals with disabilities 3.10.03.01

- Recognize that individuals with disabilities such as deafness, developmental delays, some forms of cerebral palsy (ataxia and spasticity), and other neurosomal disorders have impaired static balance skills
- Accommodate individuals exhibiting exaggerated stretch reflexes with abnormally high muscle tone such as spastic cerebral palsy

Understand dynamics

Understand the mechanics of dynamic movement, equilibrium, dynamic stretch, and dynamic tension and their relationship to physical and motor performance for individuals with disabilities 3.10.04.01

- Recognize that individuals with disabilities such as deafness, developmental delays, cerebral palsy, learning disabilities, and other neurosomal disorders often have impaired dynamic balance
- Accommodate individuals with disabilities such as athetoid or ataxic cerebral palsy who demonstrate uncoordinated and unintegrated movements

Understand kinematics

Understand the relationship of time and space on motion and calculations of mechanical efficiency on physical and motor performance for individuals with disabilities 3.10.05.01

- Demonstrate an understanding of individuals with disabilities who take more time to effect a desired motor response
- Recognize that some physical impairments such as amputations change the mechanics of an activity or skill
- Recognize that individuals with disabilities may perform skills with less velocity and acceleration influencing the outcome of the skill

Understand kinetics

Understand forces that affect movement and motion and their relationship to physical and motor performance for individuals with disabilities 3.10.06.01

- Demonstrate kinetic open and closed chains as well as kinetic principles in instructing a variety of activities
- Recognize that individuals with neuromuscular disabilities may take longer to start or stop a movement

Understand the anatomical reference position as it is associated with body movement

Understand the anatomical positions of the body and how these positions are used for studying movement of individuals with disabilities 3.10.07.01

- Describe body and joint positions that are lateral, medial, dorsal, ventral, cephal, or caudal to each other
- Describe movements that are lateral, medial, dorsal, ventral, cephal, or caudal to each other

Understand planes associated with body movement

Understand frontal, transverse, and sagittal planes and axes as well as the relationship to movement for individuals with disabilities 3.10.08.01

- Recognize that shoulder or hip abduction and adduction take place in the frontal plane, rotation occurs in the transverse (or horizontal) plane, and flexion and extension occur in the sagittal plane

- Recognize that individuals with orthopedic disabilities may have pathokinesiological joint positions that cause excursion or placement of the joints in other planes such as varum or valgum
- Recognize that Newton's laws affect movement and how the application of forces influence the skill

Understand the relationship of the axes to corresponding planes of the human body

Understand instances where anatomical constraints of individuals with disabilities may cause movement to be in different axes of rotation 3.10.09.01

- Realize that individuals with cerebral palsy use different muscles or joints due to contractures
- Describe how individuals with joint fusion due to surgery or arthritis may need to initiate movements in different axes

Understand movement analysis

Understand the use of statics, dynamics, kinematics, kinetics, body axes, planes, balance, and equilibrium for studying and planning movement activities for individuals with disabilities 3.10.10.01

- Demonstrate ability to perform a movement analysis and plan instruction for individuals with disabilities
- Observe abnormal positions of joints or body parts and how these may affect movements
- Demonstrate ability to task analyze a skill into smaller achievable parts
- Develop a systematic observation strategy to perform a quality analysis

Understand fundamental mechanical concepts

Understand Newton's laws, levers, vectors, force, pulley system, mass/weight, stability, gravity, inertia, momentum, torque, velocity, and acceleration and their relationship to movement for individuals with disabilities 3.10.11.01

- Accommodate individuals who are obese by providing extra time to initiate and cease their motions
- Recognize that individuals who are obese will need more strength to start and stop
- Describe the differences in wheelchair design for sports such as tennis or basketball vs. track or road racing vs. medical use
- Recognize that changing body position or equipment may change the mechanical advantage of a lever system

Understand balance, equilibrium, and stability

Understand the concepts of balance, equilibrium, and stability in planning activity programs for individuals with disabilities 3.10.12.01

- Demonstrate use of concepts of balance, equilibrium, and stability in planning and instructing movement activities such as teaching individuals how they can lower their center of gravity to increase their stability
- Acknowledge that individuals with cerebral palsy, amputations, and neuromuscular disorders may need special instruction in areas of balance and equilibrium
- Describe the factors that contribute to balance and stability including mass, center of gravity, line of gravity, friction, and changing the base of support

Understand force production and absorption

Understand aerodynamics, lift, drag, inertia, movement of inertia, velocity, spin/rotation, centrifugal, centripetal, lever, force arm, resistance force, and speed and their relationship to movement and motor performance for individuals with disabilities 3.10.13.01

- Describe effects of primitive reflexes in individuals with disabilities when producing too much or too little force
- Describe effects on anatomical structures in individuals with disabilities when producing too much force
- Describe mechanical differences between everyday (medical), sport, and track/racing wheelchairs
- Describe wheelchair propulsion (torque production) and recovery techniques for sport and track/racing wheelchairs

Understand basic fluid mechanics

Understand fluid mechanics principles of buoyancy in relation to individuals with specific disabilities 3.10.14.01

- Recognize that individuals with paralysis will have some body parts more buoyant due to atrophy of muscle tissue and increased fatty tissue
- Accommodate individuals with paralysis or contractures who cannot demonstrate a horizontal body position resulting in increased drag because lower extremities may decrease buoyancy
- Accommodate individuals with muscular dystrophy who demonstrate increased buoyancy due to atrophy of muscle tissue and increased fatty tissue

Bone Growth and Development: Demonstrate knowledge of the biomechanics of bone growth and development

Understand that Wolff's law implies that bones develop and change according to mechanical loads such as compression and tension

Understand that individuals with disabilities such as scoliosis demonstrate abnormal orthopedic development 3.11.01.01

- Recognize that unequal muscular development will result in abnormal bone growth such as limb deformities
- Recognize that individuals who remain sedentary will undergo bone demineralization and may develop osteoporosis

Understand that processes such as cartilaginous hyperplasia, hypertrophy, and calcification may interfere with normal growth and maturation of bone

Understand that certain characteristics of disabilities associated with abnormal bone growth make individuals prone to injury 3.11.02.01

- Recognize that contraindications such as high-impact activities and high-resistance weight training may be associated with abnormal bone growth and conditions
- Prescribe exercises and activities that encourage healthy bone growth

Understand the effects of decreased activity or lack of exercise on bone mineralization

Know the effects of decreased activity or lack of exercise on bone mineralization of individuals with disabilities associated with growth problems and/or deformities 3.11.03.01

- Realize that time spent while bedridden or immobilized results in weakened bone anatomy
- Systematically increase an individual's physical activity time

Understand types of bone fractures

Understand common causes of various types of bone fractures such as greenstick, avulsion, longitudinal, and transverse in individuals with disabilities 3.11.04.01

- Avoid contact sports and high-impact activities for individuals who are at risk for fractures
- Develop a referral policy for individuals who are suspected of being at risk of a fracture

Neuromuscular Function: Demonstrate knowledge of the biomechanical aspects of neuromuscular function

Understand the basic properties of muscle tissues such as irritability, extensibility, elasticity, and contractility

Understand general deviations in basic properties of muscle tissue among individuals with disabilities such as hypotonicity 3.12.01.01

- Recognize specific deviations in basic properties of muscle tissue found with disabilities such as spasticity or contractures
- Describe specific deviations in the basic properties of muscle tissue found in individuals with disabilities such as muscular dystrophy

Understand the force–velocity relationships of muscle tissue

Understand the relationship between force and muscle tissue in individuals with disabilities such as cerebral palsy, degenerative muscle conditions, and spina bifida 3.12.01.01

- Recognize that more time is needed to generate muscular force for a given movement in individuals with disabilities
- Recognize that more time is needed to generate desired motor action in individuals with disabilities such as cerebral palsy
- Recognize that it is more difficult for individuals with disabilities such as cerebral palsy and degenerative muscle conditions to generate faster purposeful movements

Understand force–length relationships with muscle tissue

Understand force–length relationship (isometric) with individuals with disabilities such as cerebral palsy, degenerative muscle conditions, and spina bifida 3.12.03.01

- Recognize the optimal muscle length to generate the most force in an individual with disabilities
- Identify how power can be improved in these individuals

Understand force–time relationships with muscle tissue

Understand force–time relationship with individuals with disabilities such as cerebral palsy, degenerative muscle conditions, spina bifida, and mental retardation 3.12.04.01

- Recognize that powerful and forceful movements will be more difficult for individuals with disabilities that include degenerative muscle conditions
- Identify how power can be improved in these individuals

Understand the concept of strength from a biomechanical perspective

Understand that improper biomechanics adversely impacts the strength of some individuals with disabilities 3.12.05.01

- Recognize that the individual may be influenced by posture and spinal deformities
- Recognize that decreased range of motion affects force production

Understand the concept of power from a biomechanical perspective

Understand that the ability of some individuals with disabilities to generate power is compromised due to improper mechanics 3.12.06.01

- Adapt activities for some individuals with disabilities to allow for additional time to effectively generate power
- Use lightweight equipment to increase strength and power

Understand the biomechanics of endurance

Understand that improper biomechanics adversely impacts the endurance of some individuals with disabilities 3.12.07.01

- Recognize that alterations in movement such as gait and range of motion may interfere with the ability of some individuals with disabilities to sustain activity
- Modify activity to recognize the endurance needs of some individuals with disabilities such as hand/arm ergometry

Understand how sensory receptors in muscles (muscle spindles) contribute to neuromuscular control

Understand sensory receptors in muscles (muscle spindles) for individuals with disabilities such as cerebral palsy, Down syndrome, and muscular dystrophy 3.12.08.01

- Describe contraindicated movements for individuals with cerebral palsy that would stimulate the stretch reflex and result in increased hypertonicity (spasticity)
- Describe exercise that stimulates the stretch reflex that helps enhance power in individuals with Down syndrome

Understand how sensory receptors in tendons (Golgi tendon organs) contribute to neuromuscular control of human movement

Understand differences in sensory receptors of tendons among individuals with disabilities such as cerebral palsy and muscular dystrophy 3.12.09.01

- Use proprioceptive neuromuscular facilitation exercises to enhance range of motion
- Use proprioceptive neuromuscular facilitation exercises to enhance strength

Understand how sensory receptors in other body tissues contribute to neuromuscular control of human movement

Understand structure and functions of vestibular, cutaneous, visual, and auditory receptors in individuals with disabilities 3.12.10.01

- Recognize that individuals with sensorineural hearing impairments may demonstrate balance problems or vestibular dysfunction
- Recognize that individuals with visual impairments may demonstrate diminished balance skills
- Recognize that individuals with sensory losses demonstrate impaired kinesthetic awareness

Human Skeletal Articulations: Demonstrate knowledge of biomechanics of human skeletal articulations

Understand the characteristics of joints based on structure and movement

Understand joint anomalies in individuals with disabilities such as arthritis and cerebral palsy 3.13.01.01

- Use aquatics as a mode for physical activity
- Schedule physical education later in the day for individuals with rheumatoid arthritis
- Schedule physical education earlier in the day for individuals with osteoporosis

Understand that the three sources of joint stability are the structures of bony, ligamentous, and muscular arrangements

Understand specific disabilities associated with hyper joint flexibility, such as cerebral palsy, juvenile arthritis, osteoarthritis, rheumatoid arthritis, osteogenesis imperfecta, lax ligaments, and neuromuscular conditions 3.13.02.01

- Describe strength and muscular endurance exercises that enhance specific motor control and movement functions
- Design an activity program to ensure safe strength development

Understand the concept of joint flexibility or range of motion (ROM)

Understand specific disabilities associated with hyper joint flexibility such as cerebral palsy and Down syndrome 3.13.03.01

- Describe programming needs of individuals with hypo and hyper joint flexibility such as cerebral palsy and Down syndrome
- Describe specific proprioceptive neuromuscular facilitation exercises utilizing the stretch reflex to enhance the ROM of individuals with cerebral palsy and arthritis

Understand that individuals with specific disabilities may develop varying degrees of contractures and antagonistic stretching resulting in loss of flexibility 3.13.03.02

- Restore joint flexibility and balance by stretching contracted muscle and strengthening stretched muscle
- Use a warm-up that stretches agonists and strengthens antagonists in involved muscles
- Incorporate assistive stretching activities of affected musculature indicated for individuals with flaccid paralysis
- Prevent contractures using a balance training program within the tolerance of the individual
- Use multidisciplinary approach with the physical therapist and the occupational therapist (see Standard 15)

Understand the advantages of the different approaches such as sustained stretching and proprioceptive neuromuscular facilitation to increasing flexibility

Understand various approaches such as passive stretching, active static stretching, and proprioceptive neuromuscular facilitation to increasing flexibility of individuals with disabilities 3.13.04.01

- Apply various approaches to increasing flexibility of individuals with specific disabilities known to have low flexibility levels such as cerebral palsy
- Use rhythms as a mode for performing flexibility exercises for individuals with disabilities

Understand the benefits and harmful effects of different approaches such as dynamic or ballistic stretching

Understand how individuals with disabilities are affected by both active and passive stretching techniques 3.13.05.01

- Acknowledge that after warm-up, therapeutic stretching aids in injury prevention and relaxes joints and muscles
- Use a balanced program of activities that allows stretching of contracted muscles and strengthening of weakened (stretched) muscles
- Realize that dynamic (ballistic) stretching exercises for contracted muscles are contraindicated for all individuals
- Adapt flexibility exercise program based on therapeutic assessment performed by multidisciplinary team

Neck and Upper Extremity Movement: Demonstrate knowledge of the biomechanics of neck and upper extremity movement

Understand the anatomical structure of neck and upper extremity articulations

Understand how deviations such as atlantoaxial instability, scoliosis, lordosis, kyphosis, and growth plate irregularities such as Scheuermann's disease affect anatomical structure and movement capabilities of the neck and upper extremities 3.14.01.01

- Avoid activities that compress or hyperflex the neck such as back rolls and headstands for individuals with atlantoaxial instability
- Use exercises that mobilize the spine in extension for individuals with spinal curvatures

Understand the functions of the neck and upper extremities

Understand that restrictions such as limited range of motion can affect basic functions of the neck and upper extremities 3.14.02.01

- Avoid contraindicated exercises such as neck bridges
- Seek medical advice when working with individuals with neck pain or motor limitations

Understand ways in which the spine and pelvic girdle are adapted to carry out functions such as shock absorption and ambulation

Understand neck and upper extremity function in terms of disc size, disc arrangement, compression/tensile/shear force, and structure in relation to neck and upper extremity movements in individuals with disabilities 3.14.03.01

- Recognize that individuals with fused spines will lack the mobility and shock absorption characteristic of those without fusions
- Refer individuals with herniated disc to physician for exercises that can help relieve the pain and swelling
- Prohibit activity that places stress on the neck of individuals with atlantoaxial instability

Understand the muscle groups that are active during specific neck and upper extremity movement

Understand problems such as hypertonic muscles associated with activity during neck and upper extremity movement 3.14.04.01

- Use therapeutic stretching of internal rotators and strengthening of external rotators at shoulder joint for individuals with disabilities such as spastic cerebral palsy
- Encourage individuals to utilize remaining functional capacity such as an individual with flaccid paralysis resulting from spinal cord injuries

Understand the biomechanical factors contributing to injuries of the neck and upper extremities

Understand causes and characteristics of neck and upper extremity injuries such as soft tissue injuries, ruptured/herniated disc, fractures, dislocations, and tendonitis 3.14.05.01

- Discuss structural and functional deviations with members of the multidisciplinary assessment team
- Describe the mechanical deviations of the various neuromuscular and orthopedic conditions and their effect on movement and program considerations
- Apply mechanical principles to solutions and/or modifications of movement problems
- Use orthotics such as wheelchairs, canes, braces to improve functional movement for skill and physical fitness acquisition
- Recognize adaptations and modifications of movement patterns via mechanical principles to ambulatory individuals to increase physical fitness and skill acquisition
- Use basic mechanical principles such as low center of gravity, laws of levers, and motion to minimize injury
- Use proper transfer techniques

Spine and Pelvis Movement: Demonstrate knowledge of the biomechanics of spine and pelvis movement

Understand how anatomical structure affects movement capabilities of the spine

Understand how deviations such as scoliosis, lordosis, anterior pelvic tilt, kyphosis, and growth plate irregularities such as Scheuermann's disease affect load-bearing and movement capabilities of the spine and pelvic girdle 3.15.01.01

- Assess movement capacity based on type and degree of deformity
- Use treatment and indicated activities for the deviations of the spine and pelvic girdle for individuals with scoliosis and lordosis
- Assess movement capacity based on type and degree of condition, and prescribe activities, including adaptations and modifications based on evaluation
- Incorporate prescribed orthotic devices into activities based on type and degree of condition

Understand functions of the spine and pelvic girdle

Understand restrictions that can affect basic functions such as compression, flexion, extension, hyperextension, lateral flexion, and rotation of the spine and pelvic girdle for individuals with disabilities 3.15.02.01

- Recognize that individuals with upper and lower level spinal paresis lose functional support, stability, and mobility below level of lesion
- Recognize that functional and skillful movement of the trunk, pelvis, and lower extremity will be considerably diminished relative to type, degree, and location of spinal injury
- Recognize limitations to functional maintenance of posture and consequent trunk and pelvic stability, balance, and symmetry
- Use flexibility training for the lower body

Understand ways the spine and pelvic girdle are adapted to carry out functions such as vertical posture and ambulation

Understand vertebral structure in terms of size, disc, compression, shear forces, and pelvic girdle structure in relationship to spinal and lower extremity movements for individuals with disabilities 3.15.03.01

- Identify problems that can affect basic functions of the spine and pelvic girdle
- Discuss contraindications that can lead to or exacerbate disc problems

Understand the relationship between muscle location and the effectiveness of muscle action in the trunk

Understand actions of muscles in upper and lower extremities, spine, and abdomen in trunk action for individuals with disabilities 3.15.04.01

- Describe restricted movements of upper and lower extremity muscles
- Recognize that muscle size and strength are relative to the degree of spasticity and that contracture, flaccidity, paralysis, or general paresis will cause limitations in trunk movement
- Conduct postural screening early to identify spinal curvatures to prevent further deformity

Understand the biomechanical contributors to injuries of the spine

Understand causes and characteristics of spinal injuries such as soft tissue injuries, herniated disc, and fractures 3.15.05.01

- Describe treatment for spinal injuries such as soft tissue injuries, herniated disc, and fractures
- Describe contraindicated activities for spinal injuries such as soft tissue injuries, herniated disc, and fractures

---

Lower Extremity Movement: Demonstrate knowledge of the biomechanics of lower extremity movement

---

Understand how anatomical structure affects the movement capabilities of lower extremity articulations

Understand how deviations in anatomical structure affect movement capabilities of the pelvis, hip joint, and ankle joint for individuals with disabilities 3.16.01.01

- Recognize that deviations such as coxa valga and coxa vara in anatomical structure affect the movement capabilities of the hip joint
- Recognize that deviations in anatomical structure such as genu valgum, varum, and recurvatum affect the movement capabilities of the knee joint
- Use strength and flexibility training for muscle contracture in hip and pelvic region
- Use strength and flexibility training for muscle contractures around the knee joint
- Implement flexibility training for flaccidity of muscles around the knee and compensatory strength and endurance training for involved muscles
- Implement strength and flexibility training for muscle contracture around the ankle and foot

Understand how the lower extremity is adapted to weight-bearing functions

Understand how deviations in alignment of the lower extremity can affect both lower and upper extremities for individuals with disabilities 3.16.02.01

- Describe the stance and gait of individuals with coxa valga and vara; genu valgum, varum, and recurvatum; and foot pronation and supination
- Use various methods of measurement and appraisal of postural deviation, such as plumb line, posture grids, and goniometers
- Recognize structural and functional mechanics of various postural deviations and their implications for exercise and sport
- Assess the stance and gait of individuals with postured deviations (see Standard 8)
- Accommodate structural and functional mechanics as they affect gait
- Design programs, use equipment, and modify activities for individuals with postural deviations
- Use physical fitness activities in conjunction with therapists for functional postural deviations
- Use orthotic devices for individuals with severe postural deformity

Understand muscle groups that are active during specific lower extremity movements

Understand how weight-bearing stance and gait are affected when some muscle groups are too active in individuals with disabilities 3.16.03.01

- Describe muscle groups and possible stretching exercises for hip abnormalities such as coxa valga and vara; genu valgum, varum, and recurvatum; and ankle and foot abnormalities such as pronation and supination
- Use orthotic devices for individuals with severe foot deformities

Understand the biomechanical factors contributing to injuries of the lower extremity

Understand causes and characteristics of lower extremity injuries such as soft tissue injuries, fractures, dislocations, and tendonitis for individuals with disabilities 3.16.04.01

- Describe treatment for lower extremity injuries such as soft tissue injuries, fractures, dislocations, and tendonitis
- Describe contraindicated activities, including inappropriate footwear, for lower extremity injuries, such as soft tissue injuries, fractures, dislocations, and tendonitis

Measurement
and Evaluation

Standardized Procedures: Demonstrate knowledge of a set of conditions, equipment, and instructions to which data collection must conform to assure validity

Demonstrate knowledge of standardized instruments and procedures for use in determining current level of motor performance such as fitness tests, motor development profiles, motor skills tests, reflex and perceptual motor inventories as well as direct measures

Understand instruments and procedures for measuring physical and motor fitness of individuals with disabilities 4.01.01.01

- Use standardized instruments and procedures for measuring and evaluating physical fitness such as AAHPERD Health Related Fitness Test, Prudential Fitnessgram, and the Brockport Test for Individuals with Physical and Sensory Impairments
- Measure physical fitness using methods such as skinfold calipers for body composition and goniometers for range of motion with individuals with disabilities

Understand instruments and procedures for measuring motor skills of individuals with disabilities 4.01.01.02

- Use standardized instruments or procedures for measuring and evaluating motor skill acquisition such as The Ohio State University Scale of Intra-Gross Motor Assessment (SIGMA), Project ACTIVE, and the Test of Gross Motor Development (TGMD II)
- Measure the acquisition of motor skills among individuals with disabilities using curriculum-based procedures such as Everyone-CAN, Data-Based Gymnasium, and achievement-based curriculum (ABC)

Understand instruments and procedures for measuring motor development in individuals with disabilities 4.01.01.03

- Use instruments such as the Brigance Diagnostic Inventory of Early Development, Denver Developmental Screening Test, and Peabody Developmental Motor Scales II with individuals with disabilities
- Measure motor development using direct measures such as reflex testing, results of caloric tests, or Apgar scores

Understand the use of instruments and procedures that have implications for aspects of performance such as components of language tests and perceptual motor tests 4.01.01.04

- Interpret the motor demands of standardized instruments measuring language and cognitive function
- Observe procedures used by other professionals to evaluate movement including reflex testing, mobility, flexibility, sensory motor strengths and weaknesses, gross and fine motor skills, positioning/handling techniques, leisure skills, and postural analysis
- Interpret the effects of culture on the motor demands made by motor performance instruments

Use instruments to determine eligibility for adapted physical education and individualized program planning in the local education agency (LEA) 4.01.01.05

- Use measurement and evaluation procedures prescribed
- Use specific standardized instruments or procedures for determining the need for related services such as checklists, rubrics, or observation techniques as suggested by other professionals

Demonstrate knowledge of how to locate and obtain standardized instruments and procedures for use

Access resources for measuring motor performance of individuals with disabilities in the LEA 4.01.02.01

- Use resource centers for test instruments
- Use the *Buros Mental Measurement Yearbook* to identify tests

Demonstrate knowledge of teachers/staff who could assist in locating resources in the LEA 4.01.02.02

- Meet the resource specialists available
- Communicate with other adapted physical educators regarding the availability of resources for measurement

Evaluate the quality of available standardized instruments

Understand the test characteristics such as measures of central tendency and variability that describe the nature of the instrument/procedure as it pertains to individuals with disabilities 4.01.03.01

- Explain the difference between the mean and median on standardized instruments
- Explain the standard deviation and what it means in the interpretation of test scores

Know information sources for evaluating tests for individuals with disabilities 4.01.03.02

- Use information published on standardized instruments to determine use with individuals with disabilities
- Describe test characteristics used in the selection of standardized instruments and procedures such as validity and reliability

Recognize potential limitations and problems related to the use of standardized instruments and procedures

Understand the limitations of using standardized test instruments with different disabilities 4.01.04.01

- Determine appropriate tests for specific types of disabilities such as the *Brockport Test for Individuals with Physical and Sensory Impairments*
- Recognize when the use of standardized instruments is inappropriate for use with individuals with disabilities
- Demonstrate appropriate use of authentic test instruments

Understand the problems of using standardized instruments with individuals with various disabilities 4.01.04.02

- Modify standardized test instructions to accommodate language problems
- Select appropriate alternative test items
- Develop an authentic test instrument

Recognize the necessity to construct instruments and/or modify procedures to measure the current level of motor performance of individuals

Understand the effect of modifying a standardized test on the reliability and validity of the test and the results 4.01.05.01

- Modify testing procedures and/or instruments to accommodate individuals with disabilities
- Identify and utilize appropriate test items for measuring parameters of interest

Understand the process of developing a teacher-made test

Know the basis for identifying and selecting performances to be measured that are appropriate to the needs, capacities, and limitations of individuals with disabilities 4.01.06.01

- Select test items reflecting the major instructional areas identified in federal law
- Select test items reflecting school, local, or state curriculum guidelines that reflect an authentic, community-based, functional test

Types of Scores: Demonstrate knowledge of the nature of scores, which determines their use (e.g., interpretation, improvement, comparison with standards, achievement, manipulation)

Demonstrate knowledge of continuous, discrete, dichotomous, interval, ordinal, and nominal scores

Demonstrate knowledge of the types of scores generated by standardized instruments/ procedures commonly used to measure individuals with disabilities 4.02.01.01

- Use dichotomous, ordinal, and nominal scores when explaining student progress or class standing
- Use continuous, discrete, and interval scores when determining eligibility for special class placement

Understand the use of various types of scores for use in determining current levels of performance of individuals with disabilities 4.02.01.02

- Explain the characteristics of the different types of scores for determining the current level of performance of individuals with disabilities
- Utilize different types of scores for determining the current level of performance of individuals with disabilities
- Compare the relative values of the different types of scores for determining the current level of performance of individuals with disabilities
- Explain the limitations of the different types of scores for determining the current level of performance of individuals with disabilities

Standard Scores: Demonstrate knowledge of scores on a scale that have been generated by transforming a set of raw scores to a common unit of measure using the mean and standard deviation

Understand the concept of conversion from raw scores to standard scores such as T and z scores

Use standard scores in reporting current level of performance of individuals with disabilities 4.03.01.01

- Interpret T and z scores in terms of the mean of each scale on tests for individuals with disabilities
- Interpret T and z scores in terms of the standard deviation of each scale on tests for individuals with disabilities

Understand the value of standard scores in communicating test results

Know the importance of communicating test results to parents or guardians of individuals with disabilities and to other professionals 4.03.02.01

- Convert class raw scores on other performances to standard scores to enhance comparison and communication
- Explain standard scores used in expressing motor performance to parents and guardians of individuals with disabilities and other professionals

Know the importance of being able to communicate test results expressed in age equivalencies or motor quotients for individuals with disabilities 4.03.02.02

- Explain developmental motor quotient and age equivalent scores of individuals with disabilities to other professionals
- Correlate developmental motor quotients and age equivalent scores to standard scores or scores expressing position in a group such as percentile ranks

Understand established standards for referring students for special services such as adapted physical education and related services

Understand eligibility criteria for adapted physical education in terms of standard scores 4.03.03.01

- Explain eligibility criteria for adapted physical education services
- Determine eligibility for adapted physical education (see Standard 8)

Indicators of Relationship Between Performances: Demonstrate an understanding of relationships of measurements gathered on varied performances by one individual

Understand how performance on one test or test item may relate to performance on another test or test item

Understand that relationships may exist among scores gathered on individuals with disabilities 4.04.01.01

- Draw conclusions on the present level of performance of individuals with disabilities utilizing scores expressed in different units of measure, standard score, or position in a group
- Draw conclusions on the present level of performance of individuals with disabilities utilizing scores made on one performance to explain scores made on another performance

Normal Curve: Demonstrate knowledge of a symmetrical curve centered on a point that is the mean score; also called a bell-shaped curve

Understand the concept of a normal distribution of scores

Understand that individuals with disabilities will usually obtain scores at the low end of a normal distribution of scores 4.05.01.01

- Compare a raw score on a distribution of scores obtained on individuals without disabilities with a distribution of scores obtained on individuals with disabilities
- Explain the relationship between percentile rank and the normal curve

Know that tests usually exclude individuals with disabilities 4.05.01.02

- Qualify statements when reporting the performance of individuals
- Explain that scores compared to individuals without disabilities appear lower than scores compared to individuals with disabilities

Understand the scores in a normal distribution cluster near the mean

Understand the meaning of obtained test scores that range two or more standard deviations below the mean as related to individuals with disabilities 4.05.02.01

- Explain that scores two or more standard deviations below the mean are significantly outside the normal range
- Prioritize needs of individuals with disabilities based on their deviation from the mean

Understand that a normal distribution is not always obtained unless a large number of scores are plotted including high scores obtained by individuals who are gifted as well as low scores obtained by individuals with disabilities 4.05.02.02

- Interpret the distribution of scores obtained in a single class in terms of heterogeneity of performance
- Interpret the distribution of scores obtained in a single class in terms of homogeneity of performance

Descriptive Values: Demonstrate knowledge of results of score analysis that bring meaning to a set of scores

Understand the concepts involved in measures of central tendency such as the influence of extreme scores or a small number of scores on the mean and median

Understand when to use the median as a reference for comparing a raw score with group performance of individuals with disabilities 4.06.01.01

- Explain an individual's score relative to the median when a few scores skew the distribution of a single class
- Explain how the number of scores affects the differential between the median and the mean

Understand when to use the mean as a reference for comparing a raw score with group performance of individuals with disabilities 4.06.01.02

- Explain an individual's score relative to the mean when a few scores skew the distribution of a single class
- Explain how the number of scores affects the differential between the mean and the median

Understand the concepts involved in measures of variability such as the reflection of the homogeneity or heterogeneity of a group of scores

Understand when to use standard deviation for comparing a raw score with group performance of individuals with disabilities 4.06.02.01

- Explain an individual's score in terms of standard deviations
- Explain how the number of scores affects the standard deviation of a set of scores from a single class

Understand when to use variance for comparing a raw score with group performance of individuals with disabilities 4.06.02.02

- Explain the variance of a set of scores when reporting the median
- Determine the variance of a set of scores for use in determining eligibility for special services

Understand the use of measures of central tendency and variability to gain a perspective of obtained scores for individuals with disabilities 4.06.02.03

- Explain an individual's score relative to the mean and standard deviation of a set of scores
- Explain an individual's score relative to the mean and standard deviation of a standardized instrument

Measures of Position: Demonstrate knowledge of a score that has a specified proportion of the population below it in a distribution thereby defining its position in the distribution

Understand the concept of conversion from raw scores to measures of group position such as percentile ranks, quartiles, and stanines

Know the use of percentiles, quartiles, or stanines when reporting current level of performance of individuals with disabilities 4.07.01.01

- Express an individual's scores in terms of percentiles and explain their meaning
- Express an individual's scores in terms of quartiles and explain their meaning
- Express an individual's scores in terms of stanines and explain their meaning

Recognize the relative value of percentiles, percentile ranks, quartiles, and stanines for communicating test results

Understand how measures of position compare the raw score of an individual with a disability with its position in a larger distribution 4.07.02.01

- Explain the position of an individual's raw score that converts to a given percentile
- Explain the position of an individual's raw score that converts to a given quartile
- Explain the position of an individual's raw score that converts to a given stanine

Understand that percentiles and quartiles work from a base of 10 and therefore may be easier to interpret for individuals with disabilities 4.07.02.02

- Explain that the percentile or quartile reflects the point below which the percentage of others who took the test have scored
- Explain that a percentile or quartile score is not the percentage correct on the test

Test Characteristics: Demonstrate knowledge of the qualities of a test such as reliability, validity, and objectivity that make it functional for a given purpose such as placement, diagnosis, evaluation of achievement, prediction, program evaluation, or motivation

Understand the relationship between the purpose for testing and characteristics of the test

Understand the desirable characteristics of tests used for screening individuals with disabilities 4.08.01.01

- Explain the administrative feasibility of a selected screening device
- Explain the economy of a screening instrument

Understand the desirable characteristics of tests used for placement decisions for individuals with disabilities 4.08.01.02

- Describe the discrimination ability of tests used for placement
- Explain how norm-referenced standards assist with placement decisions

Understand the desirable characteristics of tests used for developing individualized educational, family, or transitional plans for individuals with disabilities 4.08.01.03

- Explain test validity
- Use norm-referenced standards for establishing performance criteria when writing goals for individualized education programs (IEPs)
- Develop an authentic, community-based, functional test

Understand the most important characteristics of motor performance tests such as reliability, validity, objectivity, and utility

Understand standard error of measurement and its common sources especially with individuals with disabilities 4.08.02.01

- Understand standard error of measurement and how it affects the reliability and validity of a test score
- Understand what standard error of measurement means relative to a single test score

Understand the multicultural and linguistic issues affecting the valid and reliable measurement of motor performance among individuals with disabilities 4.08.02.02

- Encourage dress codes that maximize motor performance while being sensitive to cultural practices of dress
- Limit the amount of competition during measurement as some cultural mores preclude competition

Understand additional desirable characteristics of tests used in adapted physical education (administrative feasibility, economy of time, order effect, utility, etc.) 4.08.02.03

- Recognize the characteristics of various disabilities that can adversely affect the test-retest reliability of assessment results
- Recognize the characteristics of various disabilities that can adversely affect the content, concurrent, and face validity of an assessment instrument
- Recognize the attributes of various disabilities that can adversely affect the objectivity (interrater reliability) of the test results
- Evaluate a measurement instrument or procedure for its appropriateness for individuals with disabilities

Select appropriate test instruments and procedures based on intended purpose, test characteristics, attributes, and characteristics of the population to be tested

Understand that instruments selected must be validated for use with individuals having disabilities recognized by federal law (IDEA, 2004) 4.08.03.01

- Determine the cost, ease of administration, training time, and type of scores of selected tests
- Ensure that selected instruments meet all mandated criteria for individuals with disabilities

Understand measurement terminology such as reliability, validity, administrative feasibility, and objectivity when selecting measurement instruments for testing individuals with disabilities 4.08.03.02

- Select administratively feasible tests for placement, reporting progress, and measuring achievement of individuals with disabilities
- Select instruments that are objective, reliable, and valid for various purposes

Pretest Planning: Demonstrate knowledge of preparation that occurs before test administration

Understand the purposes for testing in physical education

Understand screening, diagnostic testing, assessment, and evaluation relative to individuals with disabilities 4.09.01.01

- Coordinate the testing of motor performance from screening to program evaluation
- Establish criteria for screening that can be implemented consistently

Know the unique roles of instructional assessment, diagnostic testing, and monitoring progress in programs for individuals with disabilities 4.09.01.02

- Understand and describe the purposes for testing at each stage of the assessment process
- Explain the purpose of different types of instruments used at each stage of the assessment process

Plan prior to testing

Understand the importance of planning a testing program for individuals with disabilities 4.09.02.01

- Establish a plan for testing individuals with disabilities on a regular basis
- Select appropriate times, facilities, and instruments or procedures for testing a variety of individuals with disabilities
- Identify and use appropriate communication techniques required by some individuals with disabilities

Understand what equipment is needed for administering the selected instruments or procedures to individuals with disabilities 4.09.02.02

- Obtain equipment necessary for testing apart from the test itself
- Maintain consistency in testing conditions such as same equipment, facility, and instructions

Standards: Demonstrate knowledge of levels of achievement that reflect a desirable level of performance based on health or other movement-related benefits

Compare and contrast norm-referenced, criterion-referenced, and content-referenced standards

Understand that content-referenced standards have criteria embedded in a domain, community program, or curriculum for individuals with disabilities 4.10.01.01

- Use content-referenced, domain-referenced, community-based, and curriculum-based instruments such as I-CAN, ABC, or Data-Based Gymnasium
- Use content-referenced, domain-referenced, community-based, and functional curriculum-based instruments for individuals with specific disabilities

Understand the relative value of norm-referenced, content-referenced, and criterion-referenced instruments for testing individuals with disabilities 4.10.01.02

- Use norm-referenced standards in making placement decisions
- Use content-referenced standards in planning IEPs
- Use criterion-referenced standards in establishing annual goals

Demonstrate an understanding of the construction of norm-referenced and criterion-referenced instruments

Understand the differences between norm-referenced and criterion-referenced standards for individuals with disabilities 4.10.02.01

- Explain the comparison of individuals with a given population when using norm-referenced standards
- Explain the comparison of a performance with a target performance when using criterion-referenced standards

Understand the similarities between norm-referenced and criterion-referenced standards for individuals with disabilities 4.10.02.02

- Describe the segment of the population on whom the criterion-referenced standards are based in terms of percentage
- Use criterion-referenced tests when clear criteria can be determined

---

Data Gathering: Demonstrate knowledge that the process of gathering information on students for the purpose of assessment may take the form of formal or informal testing or objective or subjective testing and may use criterion-, content-, or norm-referenced standards

---

Utilize informal procedures such as checklists, task analysis, rubrics, curriculum-embedded measures, and behavioral observation (see Standard 10)

Understand the use of unobtrusive measures such as rating scales, case studies, and anecdotal records with individuals with disabilities 4.11.01.01

- Maintain anecdotal records related to a student's IEP
- Observe a student's motor behavior during unstructured and unplanned play

Understand the use of systematic observational techniques such as academic learning time (ALT) and opportunity to respond for individuals with disabilities 4.11.01.02

- Use event recording techniques to observe behavior
- Use duration recording techniques to observe behavior
- Use interval recording techniques to observe behavior

Understand the use of individual reports in the process of gathering data on individuals with disabilities 4.11.01.03

- Use student self-report evaluation when appropriate
- Use peer evaluation when appropriate

Understand various protocols used in administration of tests such as performance testing, direct measures, formal standardized procedures, informal unstructured activity, etc.

Understand various testing protocols, forms of data gathering, environmental settings, and organizational structures used in physical education and the effects of these on the performance of individuals with disabilities 4.11.02.01

- Describe various testing protocols for measuring motor development, physical fitness, motor skill acquisition, and sensory motor function
- Describe various forms of data gathering for individuals with disabilities such as parent report, standardized testing, self-report, observation, task analysis, and direct measures

Understand the difference between coaching and encouraging an individual while administering a test to individuals with disabilities 4.11.02.02

- Determine the amount of time needed to administer selected tests
- Understand the effect of knowledge of results on performance

Understand the effects of medication on attention, coordination, and responsiveness when administering tests to individuals with disabilities 4.11.02.03

- Note the presence of psychotropic drugs in individuals with disabilities during testing
- Observe the motor behavior of an individual taking medication at various times during the day

Recognize the value of establishing rapport with individuals with disabilities prior to testing 4.11.02.04

- Demonstrate the ability to establish rapport
- Validate the comfort level of individuals with the examiner by observing their interactions with other teachers

Understand the basic principles of subjective data gathering in contrast to objective testing protocols

Understand the essential functional gross and fine motor performances marking significant motor milestones throughout the lifespan 4.11.03.01

- Adapt test items to accommodate limited motor development
- Observe infants engaged in motor activity and report observations

Understand the biomechanical elements expected in fundamental motor patterns and skills for individuals without disabilities before testing individuals with disabilities 4.11.03.02

- Describe when biomechanical elements of movement are absent, substituted, or changed by individuals with disabilities
- Explain the differences between observed biomechanical elements of movement and expected biomechanical elements

Understand data gathering through curriculum-embedded features of movement for individuals with disabilities 4.11.03.03

- Explain the curricular elements (features) describing the student's current level of performance
- Select curricular activities based on current level of performance

Understand the value of conducting play-based assessment with individuals with disabilities 4.11.03.04

- Create a play-based environment for observing play behaviors and motor performances
- Use a variety of environments or settings in which to observe play behaviors and motor performance
- Gather interview data from the significant others regarding play behaviors and individual and/or family preferences and practices relative to physical activity
- Gather data from the multidisciplinary team members regarding play behaviors and individual and/or family preferences and practices relative to physical activity

- Obtain measurements through video recording
- Obtain measurements using ecological inventories

Understand the value of a task analysis of motor skills for gathering data on individuals with disabilities 4.11.03.05

- Use task analysis to develop criterion-referenced tests for measuring instructional content
- Use task analysis for defining instructional sequences

Understand how to gather data through review of written reports and medical records of individuals with disabilities 4.11.03.06

- Read written reports from other professionals and correlate with findings in motor performance testing
- Read medical records and correlate with findings in motor performance testing

Understand direct measures for gathering data other than through motor performance such as dynamometry, telemetry, and goniometry

Know the need to use direct measures instead of performance measures of individuals with disabilities 4.11.04.01

- Use skinfold calipers for measuring body composition
- Use dynamometry for measuring strength
- Use goniometry for measuring range of motion

Understand the use of screening methods

Know the legislative restrictions on the use of screening individuals with disabilities 4.11.05.01

- Use screening methods as an informal procedure to gather initial data
- Limit screening to the requirements of legislation and the guidelines for the local educational agency

Understand how screening methods can be used as an informal procedure to validate other data on individuals with disabilities or when other procedures are untenable 4.11.05.02

- Use a checklist or rubric of behaviors that validate formally obtained data
- Write a descriptive narrative of the motor behavior of individuals considered untestable

Understand the advantages of individual versus mass organizational testing such as reliability and validity of scores, consistency of motivation, and precision of performance

Know the types of testing environments appropriate to the characteristics of individuals with disabilities 4.11.06.01

- Arrange the testing environment appropriate to the characteristics
- Provide a distraction-free testing environment for individuals with attention disorders

Understand the effects of mass versus individual testing on individuals with specific disabilities 4.11.06.02

- Determine which type of testing is appropriate based on the characteristics of an individual with disabilities
- Provide opportunities for practice trials in a mass testing environment when appropriate

Understand the limitations of individual versus mass organizational testing of classes of individuals with disabilities 4.11.06.03

- Describe the competencies needed by individuals with disabilities in a mass testing environment
- Verify the validity of test results obtained from an individual assessment of a student with a disability versus results from a mass testing environment

Performance Sampling: The practice of measuring representative factors of motor performance as a means of obtaining an overview of an individual's true ability

Understand the concept of performance sampling using objective and subjective testing

Understand the use of performance sampling in determining a student's eligibility for adapted physical education 4.12.01.01

- Identify motor parameters to be sampled when considering eligibility for adapted physical education services
- Determine an efficient and effective sampling procedure to use in an adapted physical education environment

Understand the use of baseline data collection for program development for individuals with disabilities 4.12.01.02

- Use multiple trials to establish baseline performance
- Preestablish baseline performance at each annual review
- Use baseline data to write annual goals and objectives

Understand the concept of performance generalization across contexts for individuals with disabilities 4.12.01.03

- Provide opportunities for motor performance of a given skill in a variety of contexts
- Use the individual's ability to generalize to community-based activities

History and Philosophy

Trends in Education: Knowledge of trends in education of individuals with disabilities

Understand evolution of educational reform in relation to individuals with disabilities

Understand era of the lack of education and emotional-social or medical treatment provided to individuals with disabilities 5.01.01.01
- Explain persecution of individuals with disabilities in society before the 1800s
- Explain neglect of individuals with disabilities with regard to education prior to the 1800s

Understand segregated educational placements for individuals with disabilities 5.01.01.02
- Explain strengths of segregated educational placements
- Explain weaknesses of segregated educational placements

Understand least restrictive environment 5.01.01.03
- Discuss continuum of placement alternatives
- Identify the characteristics of each placement as it relates to individual needs

Understand regular education initiative/total inclusion 5.01.01.04
- Explain regular education initiative/total inclusion from a positive position
- Explain regular education initiative/total inclusion from a negative position

Understand evolution of physical education for individuals with disabilities

Understand trend of physical education in separate schools and classes 5.01.02.01
- Explain the pros of separate physical education classes
- Explain the cons of separate physical education classes

Understand trend of least restrictive environment for individuals with disabilities in the physical education setting 5.01.02.02
- Explain least restrictive environment in physical education
- Explain continuum of placement alternatives in relation to least restrictive environment in physical education

Understand evolution of multidisciplinary concepts in education

Understand multidisciplinary approach with regard to adapted physical education (see Standard 15) 5.01.03.01
- Explain the role of the adapted physical educator in the multidisciplinary team
- Explain the importance of the adapted physical educator collaborating with the multidisciplinary team

Understand interdisciplinary approach with regard to adapted physical education services 5.01.03.02
- Explain the role of the adapted physical educator in the interdisciplinary team
- Explain the importance of the adapted physical educator collaborating with the interdisciplinary team

Understand crossdisciplinary/transdisciplinary approach with regard to adapted physical education services 5.01.03.03
- Explain the role of the adapted physical educator in the crossdisciplinary/transdisciplinary team

- Explain the importance of the adapted physical educator collaborating as part of the crossdisciplinary/transdisciplinary team
- Contrast multidisciplinary, interdisciplinary, and crossdisciplinary/transdisciplinary

Understand evolution of funding education for individuals with disabilities

Understand funding terminology in relation to individuals with disabilities legislation 5.01.04.01

- Explain authorization of funds in relation to legislation for individuals with disabilities
- Explain appropriation of funds in relation to legislation for individuals with disabilities
- Explain discretionary funds in relation to legislation for individuals with disabilities

Law: Knowledge of public laws that affect physical education and sport for individuals with disabilities

Understand major components of these laws in relation to education and physical activity

Understand nondiscrimination clause (Section 504 and ADA) 5.02.01.01

- Advocate for qualified individuals with disabilities to participate in interscholastic athletics and extra class activities
- Advocate for activities to be conducted in architecturally accessible structures
- Advocate for program accessibility

Understand major components of the Individuals with Disabilities Education Act (IDEA, 2004) in relation to education and physical activity

Understand free, appropriate education in the least restrictive environment for individuals with disabilities 5.03.01.01

- Explain individualized education program (IEP)
- Explain least restrictive environment

Understand the meaning of direct services in the law 5.03.01.02

- Explain the legal definition of special education
- Explain the legal definition of physical education

Understand the meaning of related services for individuals with disabilities 5.03.01.03

- Suggest related services, such as physical and occupational therapy, when needed to succeed in physical education
- Explain the scope and content of related services

Understand categories of disabilities listed in the law 5.03.01.04

- List examples of who is qualified by law to receive adapted physical education services based on state and federal qualifications
- Explain definition of disabilities

Understand parental involvement in the education of all children and youth with disabilities 5.03.01.05

- Discuss parent and guardian role in the IEP process
- Discuss parent and guardian input in the adapted physical education process
- Explain due process in relation to parent and guardian involvement

Understand major components of the Individuals with Disabilities Education Act (IDEA, 2004) in relation to physical activity

Understand the clause describing the inclusion of athletes with disabilities in relation to the Rehabilitation Act and the Americans with Disabilities Act as amended 5.04.01.01

- Advocate for individuals with disabilities in integrated and segregated sports programs
- Read current literature related to the United States Olympic Committee on disability sport organizations (DSOs)

Understand implications for education and physical activity

Understand change in age for services for individuals with disabilities 5.05.01.01

- Advocate for infant and toddler motor activities
- Explain state age requirements related to services available to individuals with disabilities

Understand the individual family service plan in relation to families and individuals with disabilities (see Standard 9) 5.05.01.02

- Explain components of the individualized family service plan such as family needs and resources
- Explain how physical activities are a part of the individualized family service plan

Understand what types of individuals with disabilities are served by IDEIA, 2004 5.05.01.03

- Explain developmentally delayed
- Explain at risk for developmental delay
- Explain identified disabilities

Understand implications for physical activity

Understand public accommodation and access 5.06.01.01

- Advocate for physical activity sites to become accessible
- Describe program accommodation

Understand age change for individuals with disabilities 5.07.01.01

- Advocate for physical activities for individuals birth through 21
- Advocate for community resources for physical activities for infants, toddlers, and their parents and guardians

Understand transition services 5.07.01.02

- Describe adapted physical educator's role in the transition from home to school
- Describe adapted physical educator's role in transition from school to vocation and community

Understand the addition of the disability categories 5.07.01.03

- Explain autism as a separate category
- Explain traumatic brain injury as a separate category

Understand the implications of the No Child Left Behind Act 5.07.01.04

- Explain this Act in relationship to employing qualified school personnel
- Explain the Act in relationship to state testing
- Apply the requirements in this law to adapted physical education

History: Knowledge of history of physical education for individuals with disabilities

Understand medical model

Understand medical gymnastics and its early role in the adapted physical education movement 5.08.01.01

- Identify individuals associated with the medical gymnastics movement
- Explain components of medical gymnastics that have had an impact on current adapted physical activity practices such as individually prescribed exercises

Understand corrective/remedial physical education

Understand corrective/remedial physical education and its impact on early adapted physical education services 5.08.02.01

- Explain components of corrective/remedial physical education such as orthopedic and structural remediation that have an impact on current practices in adapted physical education
- Identify individuals associated with corrective/remedial physical education

Understand movement from adapted physical education as a separate service to the broader concept of continuum of service delivery into the mainstream

Understand adapted physical education as a program 5.08.03.01

- Identify components of adapted physical education as a program such as assessment, placement, and evaluation
- Explain the adapted physical education placement and programming process

Understand adapted physical education as a service delivery system continuum 5.08.03.02

- Explain continuum of placements in adapted physical education
- Advocate for most appropriate placement

Philosophy: Knowledge of physical education, recreation, and sport

Understand the role of physical education in the school curriculum

Understand how physical education contributes to the total development of individuals with disabilities 5.09.01.01

- Advocate for physical education in the total curriculum of individuals with disabilities
- Advocate for physical education in the IEP and the IFSP (see Standard 9)

Understand the philosophy of physical education as education "of the physical"

Understand the importance of physical and motor fitness such as flexibility, agility, and strength as it relates to individuals with disabilities 5.09.02.01

- Explain the importance of physical fitness in the life of an individual with disabilities
- Explain the importance of motor skills in the life of an individual with disabilities

Understand the philosophy of physical education as education "through the physical"

Understand physical, cognitive, and affective outcomes in adapted physical education 5.09.03.01

- Explain physical outcomes of physical education with individuals who have a disability to other educators and parents and guardians
- Explain cognitive outcomes of physical education with individuals who have a disability to other educators and parents and guardians
- Explain affective outcomes of physical education with individuals who have a disability to other educators and parents and guardians

Understand the role of sport in the total curriculum

Understand sport opportunities for individuals with disabilities 5.09.04.01

- Advocate for adapted (segregated) sport opportunities within the physical education curriculum
- Advocate for inclusive sport opportunities within the physical education curriculum

Understand the role of recreation in the life of an individual with a disability

Understand physical recreation opportunities for individuals with disabilities (see Standard 15) 5.09.05.01

- Advocate for physical recreation activities within the physical education curriculum
- Advocate for appropriate physical recreation activities in transition planning

Understand the relationship between therapeutic recreation and adapted physical education 5.09.05.02

- Explain leisure counseling and its application to adapted physical education
- Explain therapeutic recreation as a related service

Philosophy: Special education

Understand multidisciplinary functioning

Understand coordination of resources for individuals with disabilities 5.10.01.01

- Use philosophy that supports cooperation
- Share resources to optimize educational goals
- Develop partnerships to maximize the use of resources for individuals with disabilities

Understand transition process philosophy

Understand transition services 5.10.02.01

- Explain adapted physical educator's role in the transition process
- Advocate for adapted physical educator's role in the transition process

Understand least restrictive environment from a philosophical standpoint

Understand least restrictive and most restrictive environments in physical education for individuals with disabilities 5.10.03.01

- Explain the least restrictive environment for an individual with a disability
- Advocate for a variety of placements in physical education for individuals with disabilities
- Advocate for a variety of supports in the general physical education setting

Understand inclusion from a philosophical standpoint

Understand inclusion as it relates to physical education for individuals with disabilities 5.10.04.01

- Explain criteria for exclusion from general physical education
- Explain split placement (part general physical education/part adapted physical education)

Understand rationale for educating children from birth to three years of age

Understand rationale for providing physical and motor activities to young children with disabilities 5.10.05.01

- Advocate for physical activity for young children with disabilities
- Advocate for an adapted physical education specialist to consult and assist in providing physical activity for young children with disabilities

Unique Attributes of Learners
Considerations for Professional Practice

Mental Retardation: Understand unique attributes of individuals with mental retardation

Understand motor attributes such as low levels of health-related physical fitness and motor ability

Understand the problems in achieving health-related physical fitness for individuals with specific medical conditions 6.01.01.01
- Establish appropriate expectations and goals
- Adapt fitness activities to individuals with low motor skills
- Adapt physical activities to be within the medical margin of safety

Understand the possible motor skill performance and learning problems such as difficulty acquiring locomotor and object control skills 6.01.01.02
- Repeat fundamental motor skills and patterns in a variety of activities
- Incorporate individuals into a general physical education program with developmentally appropriate peers
- Modify activities only as needed to allow for maximum participation
- Adapt activities for individuals with specific motor problems such as running and throwing

Understand cognitive attributes such as low cognitive ability

Know the various levels of cognitive ability 6.01.02.01
- Adapt activities for individuals with various levels of mental retardation
- Evaluate the effectiveness of the adapted activities

Understand the implications of low cognitive ability to the understanding of directions 6.01.02.02
- Use various modalities for instruction
- Use continuum of prompts and cues
- Use alternative methods of communication (see Standard 9)
- Adapt directions to appropriate mental age/ability
- Task analyze motor skills into small learning steps

Understand the implications of low cognitive ability on motivation 6.01.02.03
- Motivate with age-appropriate, relevant reinforcers
- Make the purpose of the activity known
- Set realistic goals
- Provide ongoing, immediate feedback

Understand the implications of low cognitive ability on attention span 6.01.02.04
- Plan multitude of activities
- Demonstrate the ability to effectively repeat directions
- Structure the environment for maximal attention
- Provide reinforcement for staying on task
- Use other teachers and paraprofessionals to provide a lower student–teacher ratio (see Standards 9 and 10)

Understand implications of low cognitive ability on social behavior such as poor group cooperation or behavioral outbursts 6.01.02.05
- Identify inappropriate social behavior
- Identify antecedent to poor social behavior
- Use behavior management techniques (see Standard 10)
- Collaborate with psychologist and/or behavior specialist

Understand health and medical attributes of individuals with mental retardation such as secondary or multiple disabilities

Know the incidence of atlantoaxial instability syndrome (AAIS) among individuals with Down syndrome 6.01.03.01

- Check medical records for results of cervical X-rays before starting program
- Avoid activities that place the neck in extreme flexion, such as tumbling, in individuals who test positive for AAIS

Know the incidence of susceptibility to respiratory infections in individuals with Down syndrome and other conditions such as secondary disabilities 6.01.03.02

- Avoid activities that may reduce resistance
- Coordinate with medical community to determine contraindicated physical and motor activities

Know the incidence of heart conditions among individuals with mental retardation such as those with Down syndrome 6.01.03.03

- Check for written and signed medical release forms prior to beginning a physical education program
- Adapt cardiorespiratory activities

Know the incidence of hypotonus among individuals with mental retardation such as Down syndrome

- Discourage hyperflexible postures
- Encourage muscular strengthening especially around the joints
- Adapt activities involving movement on uneven surfaces
- Adapt activities involving agility and changing directions

Know the propensity toward being overweight in individuals with mental retardation 6.01.03.05

- Determine cause of problem with other health professionals
- Incorporate family into solution
- Provide calorie-burning activities
- Incorporate nutritional information into the physical education lesson

Know the incidence of poor eyesight in individuals with Down syndrome 6.01.03.06

- Adapt catching and throwing activities
- Modify activity (i.e., contact) that may be unsafe for an individual who wears glasses

Know the incidence of poor hearing in individuals with Down syndrome 6.01.03.07

- Use visual and/or tactile demonstrations
- Determine if there are any activities in which an individual should not participate

Deafness and Hard of Hearing: Understand unique attributes of individuals who are deaf or hard of hearing

Understand motor attributes such as vestibular considerations

Know implications of an impaired vestibular system for individuals who are deaf or hard of hearing 6.02.01.01

- Use appropriate tests for balance
- Teach compensation such as using vision and proprioception
- Emphasize principles of equilibrium such as a wide base of support and low center of gravity

Understand cognitive attributes such as the use of vision as primary input for learning

Know methods of presenting information other than auditory (see Standard 9) 6.02.02.01
- Use visual and/or tactile demonstrations
- Use task cards

Understand communication attributes such as nonverbal communication and use of hearing aids

Know techniques to enhance communication (see Standard 9) 6.02.03.01
- Use sign language
- Provide a safe place to put hearing aids during aquatics and contact sports
- Use handouts and chalk or white board for learning enhancement
- Talk to individuals, not to interpreters
- Use enhancements for speech reading such as placing student in good visual positioning and standing in well-lighted area

Know the impact of instruction on individuals with various levels of hearing ability 6.02.03.02
- Adapt teaching methods to individuals who are hard of hearing and deaf
- Use assistive devices such as auditory trainers, and wearing a microphone

Understand implications of unique methods of communication on safety in physical activity 6.02.03.03
- Use visual signals to request attention (stop, start, etc.)
- Use buddy system
- Provide written handouts or posters for key rules and strategies
- Meet with students before class to discuss any concerns
- Check with individuals for understanding of rules and concepts
- Use sign language
- Make sure an individual can see signs, lips, and other visual cues
- Use tactile cues such as floor vibrations

Understand the philosophy of the individual's family for communication, such as signing, oral, or total communication 6.02.03.04
- Respect philosophy of communication mode
- Use student/family preferred communication mode

Speech and Language Disorders: Understand unique attributes of individuals with speech and language disorders

Understand receptive language disorders such as receptive aphasia

Understand implications of various methods of receiving messages in physical activity 6.03.01.01
- Use sign or pantomime
- Use pictures or symbols
- Use nonverbal games
- Encourage others in class or on a team to adapt communication
- Use consistent language
- Consult with speech and language therapist for additional strategies to optimize communication

Understand expressive language disorders such as mechanical disorders and expressive aphasia

Understand the implications of various methods of expressive communication in physical activity 6.03.02.01

- Encourage the use of communication devices
- Adapt communication devices to various physical activity settings such as aquatics
- Allow time for an individual to respond
- Ask open-ended questions as well as yes–no questions
- Protect communication devices from damage
- Cooperate with interpreter
- Provide individual with a signal to alert an emergency
- Validate individual's frustration when a message is hard to communicate
- Show individual appropriate ways to show frustration

Blindness and Visual Impairments: Understand the unique attributes of individuals who are blind or visually impaired

Understand the implications of blindness and visual impairment for motor skill acquisition

Know the problems with body image and awareness 6.04.01.01

- Conduct body part identification and body part movement assessment
- Conduct posture assessment
- Use variety of tactile cues to elicit proper body mechanics
- Use imagery and nonvisual cues
- Teach self-monitoring of movement
- Provide stretching activities for tight muscle groups
- Provide strengthening activities for weak muscles
- Coordinate program with physical and/or occupational therapist when appropriate

Know about the poor movement potential in individuals who are blind or visually impaired 6.04.01.02

- Provide opportunity to explore movement potential
- Use a variety of movement experiences
- Use sound to enhance the desire to try new experiences
- Use hands-on assistance
- Use success tasks to gain the trust of an individual
- Consider safety when planning activities (see Standard 9)
- Provide spatial awareness activities

Know that low levels of fitness may negatively impact movement skill performance and learning by some individuals who are blind or visually impaired 6.04.01.03

- Focus on orientation and mobility activities during fitness activities
- Give individual orientation to the activity environment
- Provide individuals with feedback about their performance and the performance of others
- Use different textures or ropes for guides and boundaries
- Use auditory devices for directional orientation
- Teach others in class to aid in orientation and mobility
- Develop landmarks in instructional areas
- Work with orientation and mobility specialist to determine the proper use of canes and dogs as well as proper mobility when participating in activities and games
- Teach activities that can be performed without dependence on others such as riding a stationary bike or using a treadmill

Understand implications of blindness and visual disability for cognitive processing

Know that learning is not primarily through the visual sense 6.04.02.01

- Provide Braille, or large print tests and handouts, or oral tests when necessary
- Teach individual the types of things that other individuals learn by sight and by watching others such as strategies, innovative moves, and rules
- Teach using verbal and tactile demonstrations

Understand medical and health considerations of various types and causes of blindness and visual impairments

Understand that retinal detachment has implications for contact activities and jarring 6.04.03.01

- Adapt activities to reduce/eliminate head bumping
- Report signs of retinal detachment

Understand that glaucoma may have implications on physical activity choices 6.04.03.02

- Plan activities that do not cause increased eye pressure
- Consult physician when providing underwater activities

Know the various types of visual impairments and blindness 6.04.03.03

- Collaborate with other professionals to plan a physical activity program for individuals with various types of visual impairments and blindness
- Adapt activities for individuals with total blindness, tunnel vision, or various types of partial sight

Understand the various conditions that include blindness such as retinitis pigmentosa 6.04.03.04

- Collaborate with medical personnel when an individual has a condition that includes blindness
- Adapt activities for accompanying conditions such as mental retardation, deafness, and neurological impairment

Behavioral Conditions: Understand the unique attributes of individuals with behavioral disorders

Understand the impact of behavioral disorders on learning motor skills

Know that there is a multitude of behaviors that an individual may exhibit when diagnosed as having a behavioral disorder such as seriously emotionally disturbed and the impact of each on learning motor skills 6.05.01.01

- Collaborate with other professionals when developing and implementing an effective physical and motor skill activity program
- Adapt physical and emotional environment and teaching strategies for individuals with various behavioral disorders
- Adapt teaching strategies for individuals with various behavioral disorders

Understand the impact of behavioral disorders on medical/health issues

Know the implications of medication (drug therapy) that may be used for various behavioral disorders on motor performance and learning 6.05.02.01

- Use the *Physician's Desk Reference* for medication information
- Consult with school medical personnel on the side effects and contraindications of specific medications

Understand the impact of behavioral conditions on safety in physical activities

Understand that certain behavior problems may lead to safety problems such as impulsivity and noncompliance 6.05.03.01

- Provide a definite routine to be followed, clear limits, and rules individuals can achieve
- Use applied behavior analysis principles (see Standard 10)
- Display appropriate authority
- Develop consistent rules with consequences
- Provide heavily structured environments when necessary

Learning Disabilities: Understand the unique attributes of individuals with learning disabilities

Understand aspects of motor dysfunction

Understand the implications of a general body coordination dysfunction 6.06.01.01

- Assess the individual to determine possible existence of a coordination problem (see Standard 8)
- Use different size and weight balls
- Use simple to complex skills
- Provide for extra practice
- Adapt rules for success

Understand the implications of a visual motor dysfunction 6.06.01.02

- Adapt equipment
- Provide for extra practice
- Consult with vision specialist about a possible visual dysfunction

Understand the implications of a balance dysfunction 6.06.01.03

- Use a gradual balance progression from static to dynamic
- Teach the use of a wide base of support and low center of gravity
- Use caution with risky balance tasks such as high balance beam

Understand the implications of a spatial awareness dysfunction 6.06.01.04

- Use floor spots for "home base"
- Provide high color contrast of boundary lines
- Use multisensory approach such as tactile, kinesthetic, and vestibular input at the same time

Understand the implications of a laterality dysfunction 6.06.01.05

- Use mirroring techniques for increased visual feedback
- Use footprints on floor
- Constantly reinforce the left and right concept in games, motor patterns, and exercises
- Use cueing techniques such as colored bracelets, ankle bands, and uneven wrist weights

Understand the implications of a body image dysfunction 6.06.01.06

- Use mirroring for increased visual feedback
- Use activities where maximal tactile input is achieved such as aquatics, wrestling, and log rolls

Understand the implications of a sensory system dysfunction 6.06.01.07
- Adapt environment to individuals who are tactile defensive
- Provide a variety of equipment in various shapes, textures, and weights

Understand the implications of kinesthetic awareness problems 6.06.01.08
- Provide activities that increase pressure on body surfaces, joints, and muscles such as pushing and pulling
- Provide activities that use quick change of direction and uneven surfaces to stimulate proprioceptors
- Use visual feedback such as mirrors during movement activities
- Provide games that involve body imitation

Understand the implications of a continuum of responsivity such as hyperresponsivity or hyporesponsivity 6.06.01.09
- Adapt physical and emotional-social environment for individuals with hyperresponsivity, hyporesponsivity, or vacillating responsivity (varying activity levels)
- Adapt the teaching strategies to individuals with hyperresponsivity, hyporesponsivity, or vacillating responsivity (varying activity levels)

Understand cognitive difficulties

Know the implications of attention span problems 6.06.02.01
- Provide for smooth and timely transitions from one activity to another
- Plan numerous different activities for each session
- Minimize distractions
- Gradually increase the duration of time in an activity

Know the implications of disorders of written language 6.06.02.02
- Use alternative means to give written tests
- Read written material aloud or tape the instructions

Describe disorder of auditory processing 6.06.02.03
- Simplify language
- Reinforce auditory directions with visual cues
- Use consistent language

Understand social difficulties

Describe the implications of social imperception 6.06.03.01
- Use activities that encourage peer interaction in small groups
- Identify nonverbal communication to individual

Understand the implications of perseveration 6.06.03.02
- Avoid activities that cause perseveration
- Provide a high contrast between activities

Cerebral Palsy: Understand the unique attributes of individuals with cerebral palsy

Understand motor attributes of individuals with cerebral palsy

Know the "types" of cerebral palsy 6.07.01.01
- Adapt physical environment for individuals with various types of cerebral palsy
- Adapt instructional strategies for individuals with various types of cerebral palsy

Know the implications of hypertonus on motor performance 6.07.01.02

- Adapt activities for limited range of motion
- Discuss strength training with physical therapists and physicians
- Avoid activities that will increase tone substantially such as quick jumping movements
- Teach relaxation activities

Know the implications of hyperactive stretch reflex on motor performance 6.07.01.03

- Adapt activity for movement limitations
- Use slow, static stretches
- Position individual for maximal movement

Understand the implications of primitive reflex patterns on motor performance 6.07.01.04

- Adapt activities to avoid unwanted reflexes
- Position students to avoid unwanted reflex patterns
- Avoid sudden noises and touches

Understand the implications of abnormal motor development 6.07.01.05

- Adapt for problems working against gravity
- Adapt activities to account for splinter skills

Understand the mobility aids used to improve motor activity function (see Standard 9) 6.07.01.06

- Adapt activities for users of orthotics, wheelchairs, walkers, and crutches
- Provide a safe environment for individuals who do and do not use mobility aids when in group situations
- Consult with an occupational therapist for adaptations to physical education equipment

Understand cognitive attributes of individuals with cerebral palsy

Know the incidence of secondary disabilities in individuals with cerebral palsy such as mental retardation, learning disabilities, and visual perceptual problems 6.07.02.01

- Adapt activities to meet the needs of secondary disabilities
- Collaborate with special educator to use a similar reinforcement plan

Understand health and medical considerations of individuals with cerebral palsy

Understand types of medical conditions of individuals with cerebral palsy 6.07.03.01

- Collaborate with the medical community about postsurgical activity programs
- Communicate with the medical community about individuals with seizure disorders

Understand the communication considerations of individuals with cerebral palsy

Know the types of communication disorders of individuals with cerebral palsy 6.07.04.01

- Consult with speech and language pathologist
- Reinforce language and speech during physical activity
- Adapt activity to encourage use of communication devices

Muscular Dystrophy: Understand the unique considerations of individuals with muscular dystrophy

Understand the motor considerations of individuals with muscular dystrophy

Understand various types of muscular dystrophy such as Duchenne 6.08.01.01
- Adapt activity to the specific type and severity of muscular dystrophy
- Communicate with parents and guardians and multidisciplinary team members about any contraindicated activities of their child when participating in physical activities (see Standard 15)

Understand the implications of gait problems during physical activities 6.08.01.02
- Adapt activities involving locomotor skills such as running, jumping, and climbing stairs
- Use proper assistance in the recovery from falls

Understand the implications of muscle atrophy for performing specific physical and motor skills 6.08.01.03
- Adapt activity for posture problems due to muscle imbalance from atrophy
- Avoid activities that may cause dislocations due to poor muscle tone
- Provide activities that maintain current level of muscular strength and endurance

Understand health and medical considerations of individuals with muscular dystrophy such as respiratory involvement

Understand the implications of respiratory fatigue for performing motor skills and physical fitness activities 6.08.02.01
- Limit length and intensity of activity
- Provide interval work with rest periods
- Emphasize maintenance of fitness
- Use breath control activities such as aquatics
- Avoid areas where air quality is poor such as damp areas

Know the emotional effects of muscular dystrophy on the individual

Describe the emotional effect of a progressive disability on learning motor skills 6.08.03.01
- Focus on an individual's enjoyment in participating in physical education activities
- Use out-of-wheelchair activities
- Encourage participation in general physical education as long as possible

Spina Bifida: Understand the unique attributes of individuals with spina bifida

Understand motor attributes of individuals with spina bifida

Understand the implications of the various levels of motor involvement 6.09.01.01
- Adapt physical environment because of the motor involvement due to myelomeningocele, meningocele, or occulta
- Adapt instructional activities for motor involvement due to myelomeningocele, meningocele, or occulta

Understand the implications of mobility impairment and limitations in individuals with spina bifida 6.09.01.02

- Incorporate mobility aids into activities
- Utilize upper body activities
- Provide an introduction to wheelchair sports

Understand the implications of orthopedic dysfunction common in spina bifida 6.09.01.03

- Adapt physical environment for those individuals with bone fractures, paraplegia, or club foot and other foot deformities
- Adapt instructional strategies for those individuals with bone fractures, paraplegia, or club foot and other foot deformities

Understand health and medical considerations

Understand the implications of hydrocephalus 6.09.02.01

- Avoid contraindicated activities for individuals with shunts
- Avoid upside-down positions for long periods of time
- Avoid deep pressure on the shunt or head
- Discuss possible high-risk activities such as headstands, forward rolls, and soccer heading with medical personnel before incorporating them into physical education programs

Understand the implications of limited skin sensation 6.09.02.02

- Adapt activities to encourage change of positions
- Encourage self-monitoring of bruises and cuts
- Use care in transferring and in using physical assistance

Understand the implications of obesity as a complication 6.09.02.03

- Provide activities for calorie burning
- Infuse nutritional information into the physical activity program

Understand the implications of bowel and bladder dysfunction 6.09.02.04

- Remind individual to empty bag before physical activities
- Provide a privacy area for dressing and toileting

Amputations: Understand the unique attributes of individuals with amputations

Understand various levels of amputations

Understand the implications of lower body amputation on motor function 6.10.01.01

- Adapt activity to increased energy requirements due to upper body being solely used
- Plan strengthening activities for atrophy in surrounding muscles to the stump
- Provide stationary activities such as arm ergometry for individuals with mobility restrictions

Understand the implications of upper body amputations on motor functions 6.10.01.02

- Provide adapted equipment
- Teach safe falling techniques

Understand health and medical considerations that may be present in individuals with amputations

Understand the implications of increased perspiration due to reduced cooling surfaces 6.10.02.01

- Advise individuals on appropriate exercise clothing
- Keep water available for hydration
- Monitor individual for heat-related illness

Understand the incidence of obesity due to inactivity 6.10.02.02

- Advocate for physical activity opportunities
- Use effective motivators for participation (see Standard 10)
- Provide adaptations to calorie-burning activities

Understand implications of skin irritations and skin breakdown on the stump 6.10.02.03

- Encourage stump care
- Adapt activities when skin breakdown occurs on the stump

Spinal Cord Injury: Understand the unique attributes of individuals with spinal cord injuries

Understand motor attributes at various levels of spinal injury

Understand the implications of paraplegia 6.11.01.01

- Teach upper body activities
- Adapt activities for use with mobility aids (see Standard 9)
- Plan activities to avoid overuse injuries to arms and hands

Understand the implications of quadriplegia 6.11.01.02

- Plan activities for limited mobility such as quad rugby
- Plan activities with wheelchair use in mind

Understand medical and health considerations

Understand the implications of bowel and bladder dysfunction 6.11.02.01

- Provide area for privacy in toileting and dressing
- Remind individual to empty external collection bag

Understand the implications of skin abrasions and ulcers 6.11.02.02

- Check skin frequently
- Encourage weight shifting and position changes
- Educate individual about proper hygiene such as showering after physical activity and wearing proper workout clothing

Understand the implications of body regulation dysfunction 6.11.02.03

- Make appropriate heart rate modifications to calculate target heart rate based on lesion level
- Monitor blood pressure during initial exercise sessions
- Monitor individual for temperature-related illnesses
- Check extremities during temperature extremes
- Keep individual hydrated

Posture Disorders: Understand the unique considerations of individuals with posture problems

Understand various forms of posture disorders in individuals with disabilities

Understand the implications of scoliosis 6.12.01.01

- Secure medical clearance for activities
- Provide symmetrical activities
- Remove jackets or braces for swimming
- Monitor skin for breakdowns

Understand the implications of lordosis 6.12.01.02

- Teach correct postural alignment
- Teach lower back stretches such as sit and reach
- Teach abdominal strengthening exercises such as crunches

Understand the implications of kyphosis 6.12.01.03

- Incorporate chest muscle stretches
- Incorporate upper back extension exercises

Understand the implications of foot deformities 6.12.01.04

- Refer individuals with suspected foot problems to appropriate school/medical personnel
- Collaborate with physical or occupational therapists and/or physician for activities to promote proper foot alignment

Juvenile Rheumatoid Arthritis: Understand the unique attributes of individuals with juvenile rheumatoid arthritis (JRA)

Understand physical attributes of JRA

Understand the implications of limited range of motion (ROM) 6.13.01.01

- Provide daily ROM exercises
- Use warm water aquatics exercises
- Adapt activities for limited ROM

Understand the implications of chronic pain 6.13.01.02

- Provide other less strenuous activities during flare-ups of the condition
- Monitor postactivity condition to plan for next class
- Use isometric activities

Understand psychological attributes of JRA

Understand the implications of changing symptoms on physical activity participation 6.13.02.01

- Communicate with individual daily
- Communicate with medical personnel and parent/guardian
- Adapt attitude to meet the changing needs of the individual with JRA

Understand the implications of sedentary lifestyle 6.13.02.02

- Emotionally support the individual who is afraid to perform physical activities due to anticipation of pain
- Advocate for aquatics exercises as part of the IEP

Understand medical and health considerations of JRA

Understand the implications of joint instability 6.13.03.01
- Use knowledge of individual symptoms in providing weight-bearing activities
- Use caution in contact activities
- Use caution in activities where falls are common, such as skating
- Consult with medical personnel about contraindications

Dwarfism: Understand the unique attributes of individuals with short stature

Understand physical attributes of achondroplasia

Understand the implications of spinal anomalies 6.14.01.01
- Provide posture screening
- Check medical records for activity contraindications
- Use caution in contact sports and high-impact aerobics

Understand the implications of lower body limitations such as bowed legs and decreased leg length 6.14.01.02
- Adapt activities involving locomotor efficiency
- Adapt distances to travel

Understand the implications of upper body limitations such as restricted elbow range of motion and decreased arm length 6.14.01.03
- Adapt equipment size
- Adapt distance to target
- Adapt activities that use weight bearing on arms

Understand medical and health considerations of dwarfism

Understand the implications of small chest size and narrow nasal passages 6.14.02.01
- Adapt cardiorespiratory endurance activities
- Check with a physical or occupational therapist, as well as physician, for indicated and contraindicated activities

Understand the implications of frequent hip and knee dislocations 6.14.02.02
- Adapt activity to postsurgical limitations
- Adapt activities for individuals who need to avoid contact sports and lateral movements

Osteogenesis Imperfecta: Understand the unique attributes of individuals with osteogenesis imperfecta

Understand physical attributes of osteogenesis imperfecta

Understand the implications of brittle bones 6.15.01.01
- Adapt activities for wheelchair users
- Use soft equipment such as yarn balls
- Adapt possible high-risk activities such as jumping, high-impact activities, contact sports, twisting and turning

- Encourage opportunities for aquatic activity participation
- Use continuous, smooth-moving activities versus quick, start-and-stop movements

Understand the implications of chest deformities such as funnel chest 6.15.01.02

- Adapt cardiorespiratory fitness activities
- Adapt activities for limited trunk range of motion

Understand the implications of spinal anomalies 6.15.01.03

- Obtain medical clearance to determine contraindicated activities
- Provide posture screening

Autism: Understand the unique considerations of individuals with autism

Understand unique cognitive considerations

Understand the implications of perseveration 6.16.01.01

- Provide clear closure of lessons and activities
- Redirect inappropriate behavior

Understand the implications of poor eye contact 6.16.01.02

- Use verbal cues to direct attention
- Perform demonstrations several times

Understand unique communication considerations

Understand the implications of speech and language disorders 6.16.02.01

- Use sign language when appropriate
- Interpret gestures used by the individual such as pointing and leading an individual to an area
- Encourage speech and speech sounds when appropriate

Understand unique social interaction considerations

Understand the implications of poor group interaction 6.16.03.01

- Use one-to-one instruction
- Use peer tutors
- Use small group interaction at first

Understand health and medical issues

Understand the implications of the lack of danger awareness 6.16.04.01

- Monitor for safety
- Work in areas that are secure and free from potential hazards
- Provide small student–teacher ratio
- Provide adequate supervision

Understand the implications of self-stimulatory and self-injurious behavior 6.16.04.02

- Provide careful supervision
- Provide small student–teacher ratio
- Cooperate with multidisciplinary team recommendations for behavior management program (see Standard 10)
- Provide feedback to multidisciplinary team about behavior in physical education class (see Standard 15)
- Provide opportunity for regular, vigorous activity

Traumatic Brain Injury: Understand unique considerations of individuals with traumatic brain injury

Understand motor considerations

Understand the implications of excessive muscle tone 6.17.01.01

- Emphasize stretching
- Coordinate strength training program with a physical/occupational therapist and/or physician
- Avoid activities that will increase tone substantially such as quick jumping movements
- Teach relaxation activities
- Adapt activities
- Plan for extra time for agility activities

Understand the implications of hemiplegia 6.17.01.02

- Adapt activities for balance problems
- Adapt activities for one-hand usage
- Adapt equipment

Understand the implications of ataxia 6.17.01.03

- Use a wider area for activities such as for an agility run
- Use caution with activities involving balance
- Modify activities that depend on agility
- Provide area for safe landing and stopping points such as a finish line
- Provide protective equipment such as elbow pads and helmets for those who are prone to falls

Understand the implications of visual motor dysfunction 6.17.01.04

- Adapt activities using high-speed projectiles
- Adapt activities where depth perception is needed
- Plan activities using bright and contrasting objects and targets

Understand the implications of poor body awareness 6.17.01.05

- Use visual demonstrations
- Use verbal cues
- Use physical prompts
- Plan for specific body awareness activities

Understand cognitive attributes

Understand the implications of cognitive deficiencies in learning a new activity 6.17.02.01

- Use repetition
- Use task analysis

Understand the implications of problems with short-term memory 6.17.02.02

- Link verbal explanation with physical "walk through"
- Use repetition
- Use cue words and key terms
- Use handouts for studying rules

Understand social attributes

Understand the implications of poor social skills 6.17.03.01

- Use success-oriented activities to decrease fear of failure
- Use small group or dual activities
- Use proper reinforcement for correct social behavior
- Point out inappropriate social skills

Understand speech and language disorders

Understand the implications of receptive language disorders 6.17.04.01

- Consult with speech and language specialist
- Use sign and pantomime
- Use pictures or symbols
- Use nonverbal games
- Encourage other individuals involved in a physical activity to be patient and helpful
- Use consistent language

Understand the implications of expressive language disorders (see Standard 9) 6.17.04.02

- Encourage use of communication boards
- Adapt communication boards to various settings such as aquatics
- Allow time for responses
- Ask open-ended questions as well as yes–no questions
- Protect communication devices from damage
- Cooperate with interpreter
- Provide student with signal to alert teacher to emergency
- Validate individual's frustration when message is difficult to communicate
- Show individual appropriate ways to show frustration
- Persist in finding out what is said when it is difficult to understand

Understand behavioral attributes

Understand the implications of lack of initiation 6.17.05.01

- Plan for movement exploration to discover potential
- Plan success-oriented activities
- Use hierarchy of cues that allow for increased self-direction

Understand the implications of impulsivity 6.17.05.02

- Provide structured environment
- Anticipate impulsive behavior
- Set behavioral limits
- Teach self-monitoring techniques

Understand the implications of lack of appropriate judgment 6.17.05.03

- Provide specific choices
- Monitor for safety
- Use questioning for review of rules

Understand health and safety considerations

Understand implications of thermoregulation disorders 6.17.06.01

- Plan for time needed to go slowly from one temperature extreme to another
- Avoid contraindicated activities, if advised, such as a sauna and hot tub
- Monitor individual for illnesses resulting from excessive heat and cold

Understand the implications of seizure disorders 6.17.06.02

- Devise an emergency plan in the event of a seizure
- Collaborate with parents and medical personnel to determine an individual's indicated and contraindicated activities

Heart Conditions: Understand unique consideration of individuals with heart conditions

Understand physical considerations

Understand the implications of acquired and congenital heart conditions 6.18.01.01
- Adapt activities for individuals with low exercise tolerance
- Obtain written medical clearance
- Teach self-monitoring of exertion level
- Monitor individual's heart rate
- Recognize warning signs such as blue tinge to lips and nail beds
- Use results of stress testing to plan an individual program

Understand the implications of heart conditions such as secondary disorders 6.18.01.02
- Read medical records of individuals with syndromes that have a high incidence of heart conditions as secondary disorders
- Adapt activities to exercise tolerance that is within the medical margin of safety

Tuberculosis: Understand unique considerations of individuals with tuberculosis

Understand physical considerations of tuberculosis of the spine (Pott's disease)

Understand the implications of tuberculosis spondylitis 6.19.01.01
- Adapt activities for low fitness level
- Adapt activities for pain level
- Encourage individual to work up to potential

Nephritis: Understand unique considerations of individuals with nephritis

Understand elevated blood pressure

Understand the precautions that must be taken during specific fitness activities 6.20.01.01
- Avoid fitness activities when infection is present
- Monitor blood pressure

Understand anemia

Understand the limited amount of oxygen available to cells 6.20.02.01
- Plan for rest periods
- Use caution/avoid cardiorespiratory tests and activities that may not be within a medical margin of safety

Understand problems with poor fitness

Understand the increased heart rate and breathing rate 6.20.03.01
- Adapt aerobic exercise to work in lower target heart rate zones
- Plan for rest periods

Asthma: Understand unique considerations of individuals with asthma

Understand physical considerations

Understand the implications of intrinsic asthma 6.21.01.01

- Provide slow, long warm-up
- Provide information for an individual to self-monitor
- Adapt cardiorespiratory fitness activities

Understand implications of extrinsic asthma 6.21.01.02

- Provide alternative activities to aerobic exercise on hot and humid days
- Avoid placing individual near allergens such as dust, fresh-cut grass, and smog
- Use individual medical history when providing outside activities on windy and polluted days
- Avoid exposing an individual to sudden temperature changes
- Encourage aquatics as the activity of choice

Understand the implications of signs and symptoms 6.21.01.03

- Respond to an individual with rounded shoulders (as an indicator of an asthma problem)
- Provide exercises for stretching of pectorals due to hunched shoulder syndrome
- Begin emergency procedures in response to wheezing
- Encourage the individual to drink plenty of water in response to increased mucus production
- Allow inhalers to be available before, during, and after exercise

Understand health and medical considerations

Understand the implications of an asthma episode 6.21.02.01

- Identify early signs and symptoms
- Provide quiet area to perform a breathing exercise routine
- Provide area for inhaler use
- Follow preestablished emergency procedures

Understand the implications of medication 6.21.02.02

- Refer to the *Physician's Desk Reference* for possible side effects of a medication
- Communicate concerns to parents and medical personnel

Sickle Cell Anemia: Understand unique considerations of individuals with sickle cell anemia

Understand physical considerations

Understand the implications of anemia 6.22.01.01

- Use caution or avoid cardiorespiratory tests and activities unless within the medical margin of safety
- Provide rest intervals

Understand medical and health attributes

Understand the implications of heat intolerance 6.22.02.01

- Recognize symptoms such as heat headaches, listlessness, and exhaustion
- Avoid overheating

Understand emotional attributes

Understand the implications of erratic nature of symptoms 6.22.03.01
- Communicate with the individual prior to each instructional session to ascertain condition
- Communicate with the caretakers and medical personnel

Lead Poisoning: Understand unique considerations of individuals who have lead poisoning

Understand physical considerations

Understand the implications of clumsiness 6.23.01.01
- Adapt activities for appropriate level of motor ability
- Provide activities that are achievable and challenging
- Provide activities that increase quality of movement

Understand health and medical attributes

Understand the implications of seizure involvement 6.23.02.01
- Consult with physician and parents for indicated and contraindicated activities
- Have medical first aid treatment for seizures posted

Understand the implications of limited amount of oxygen available to cells 6.23.02.02
- Plan rest periods
- Adhere to indications and contraindications in medical records

Understand emotional considerations

Understand the implications of irritability 6.23.03.01
- Respond to the irritable nature of individual
- Adjust disciplinary measures appropriately to the level of irritability

Hemophilia: Understand unique considerations of individuals with hemophilia

Understand physical considerations

Understand hemarthrosis 6.24.01.01
- Avoid activities involving contact/bumping
- Use caution in incorporating activities involving high impact such as jumping and catching fast, hard projectiles
- Teach the individual how to self-monitor physical limits
- Incorporate strength training for muscles around joint with physician's written permission
- Use caution in quick start-and-stop activities

Understand health and medical considerations

Understand the implications of bleeding 6.24.02.01
- Identify early signs of internal bleeding such as swelling and heat in a joint
- Follow preestablished emergency procedures
- Apply cold compress to affected joint

- Ask individual to elevate affected part
- Avoid giving aspirin

Understand emotional issues

Understand the implications of having a life-threatening disability 6.24.03.01
- Offer support
- Avoid emotional manipulation by the individual
- Integrate as much as possible into the general physical education program

Seizure Disorders: Understand unique considerations of individuals with seizure disorders

Understand health and medical considerations

Understand the implications of partial seizures 6.25.01.01
- Report sudden behavior change to medical staff
- Adapt activities that may be unsafe due to sudden partial seizure

Understand the implications of generalized seizures 6.25.01.02
- Provide plan of action for others in the activity during the care of the individual with a generalized seizure
- Protect from injury by placing soft materials under/near any moving body parts
- Do not place anything in mouth
- Check for breathing following seizure
- Provide place for rest following seizure
- Complete appropriate incident/accident forms

Understand the implications of the specific factors that may precipitate seizures 6.25.01.03
- Avoid situations such as stress that may trigger a seizure
- Know individual precautions

Understand the implications of identified high-risk activities 6.25.01.04
- Provide additional staff during high-risk activities
- Use caution in activities such as scuba diving
- Use caution in activities with heights due to the possibility of falls during a seizure
- Consult with a physician before doing contact and collision sports

Understand the implications of medication 6.25.01.05
- Be aware of common side effects of anticonvulsant medication
- Refer individual who is medicated to appropriate school personnel for medical care for atypical behavior such as irritability, drowsiness, increase in clumsiness, blurred vision, etc.

Leukemia: Understand unique considerations of individuals with leukemia

Understand health and medical considerations of individuals with leukemia

Understand the implications of chemotherapy 6.26.01.01
- Adapt activities for individuals with anemia
- Adapt activities for decreased resistance to infections

Diabetes: Understand unique considerations of individuals with type 1 diabetes

Understand health and medical considerations of individuals with diabetes

Understand the implications of varying sugar/insulin levels 6.27.01.01

- Supervise blood sugar test before and after class, if indicated
- Communicate with parents and medical staff
- Keep sugar drinks or glucose gel in office
- Avoid conducting all the items of a physical fitness test in one session if individual is unaccustomed to such activities
- Follow predetermined emergency plan
- Monitor adjustments to diet/insulin administration with respect to physical activity based on physician's instructions
- Identify signs of hypoglycemia and hyperglycemia

Understand implications of brittle diabetes 6.27.01.02

- Help student care for skin abrasions
- Encourage proper foot care
- Encourage peripheral skin checks
- Report any change in vision

Multiple Disabilities: Understand unique considerations of individuals with multiple disabilities

Understand physical and motor considerations

Understand the implications of gross motor problems 6.28.01.01

- Adapt activities for movement limitations
- Adapt activities to incorporate individuals who use various assistive devices such as wheelchairs or walkers

Understand the implications of fine motor problems 6.28.01.02

- Adapt activities involving grasping
- Adapt activities involving releasing objects

Understand cognitive attributes

Know the range of cognitive levels in individuals with multiple disabilities 6.28.02.01

- Inquire about mental age
- Present information according to mental age
- Use age-appropriate activities

Understand the multidisciplinary approach to educating individuals with multiple disabilities 6.28.02.02

- Cooperate with multidisciplinary team
- Reinforce goals of classroom teacher, special education teacher, and related service providers

Understand speech and language attributes

Understand the implications of alternative communication modes (see Standard 9) 6.28.03.01

- Use any means to encourage communication such as communication boards, signing, and pointing
- Collaborate with classroom teacher and speech and language specialist

Understand health and medical issues

Know the appropriate precautions and instructional procedures to teach appropriate behaviors related to body secretion dysfunction such as drooling and incontinence 6.28.04.01

- Follow preestablished routine for handling body secretions when changing diapers and caring for injuries involving body fluids
- Reinforce independent behaviors such as wiping own mouth

Know the appropriate precautions related to appliance use such as gastrointestinal tubes 6.28.04.02

- Use caution with trunk exercises for those who are tube fed as indicated by medical personnel
- Consult physician about contraindications for individuals who are ventilator-dependent
- Adapt activities for those with a tracheotomy

Deaf/Blind: Understand the unique considerations of individuals who are deaf/blind

Understand physical and motor considerations

Understand implications of mobility impairment 6.29.01.01

- Incorporate activities to enhance orientation and mobility
- Allow individual to explore surroundings
- Encourage individual to feel position and movement of your body whenever possible

Understand cognitive attributes

Understand the implications of tactile and kinesthetic senses as the modes of learning 6.29.02.01

- Use physical guidance and prompts
- Use tactile markers for boundaries
- Provide a variety of movement experiences
- Use consistent organization of space and equipment

Understand communication considerations

Understand the implications of an auditory and visual communication impairment 6.29.03.01

- Use tactile signing and finger spelling in hand
- Use residual hearing and sight
- Use multiple cues
- Minimize extraneous visual and auditory stimuli
- Use tactile cues to indicate upcoming events

Understand health and medical considerations

Understand the implications of secondary disabilities 6.29.04.01

- Adhere to individual indications and contraindications in medical records
- Adapt activities to the individual's medical profile

Attention-Deficit/Hyperactivity Disorder: Under the unique considerations of individuals with attention-deficit/hyperactivity disorder

Understand the difference between attention-deficit and hyperactivity disorder

Know the characteristics of individuals with attention-deficit/hyperactivity disorder (combined type) 6.30.01.01

- Adapt environment and teaching strategies for inattentive behaviors
- Adapt environment and teaching strategies for hyperactivity behaviors

Know the characteristics of individuals with attention-deficit/hyperactivity disorder (predominately inattentive type) 6.30.01.02

- Adapt environment and teaching strategies for inattentive behaviors
- Can develop and implement a program based on any contraindicated activities related to a prescribed medication
- Know the characteristics of individuals with attention-deficit/hyperactivity disorder, predominately hyperactive-impulsivity type
- Adapt environment and teaching strategies for hyperactive behaviors
- Adapt environment and teaching strategies for impulsive behaviors

Acquired Immune Deficiency Syndrome (AIDS): Understand unique considerations of individuals with AIDS

Understand health and medical considerations

Understand the implications of fatigue 6.31.01.01

- Plan rest periods
- Provide adequate but not overtaxing physical activities

Understand the susceptibility to infections 6.31.01.02

- Avoid close contact with an individual who has a cold or communicable disease
- Consult with physician for indicated and contraindicated activities

Understand the modes of transmission 6.31.01.03

- Use gloves when handling blood and body fluids
- Follow preestablished plan for handling body fluid waste and cleaning up mats and gymnasium floors

Understand psychosocial issues

Understand the prejudice and stigmatization of the individual 6.31.02.01

- Prepare others in class with facts about AIDS
- Use information about current status of confidentiality laws to guide behavior
- Model an attitude of acceptance

Congenital Effects of Drug Dependency: Understand unique considerations of children who were born to individuals addicted to drugs or alcohol

Understand physical considerations

Understand the implications of abnormal movement patterns 6.32.01.01
- Adapt activities for individuals with tremors
- Adapt activities for individuals with muscle spasms

Understand the implications of developmental delays 6.32.01.02
- Plan activities that are developmentally appropriate
- When appropriate, include individuals with developmental delays with peers in general physical education class

Understand the implications of abnormal muscle tone 6.32.01.03
- Consult with a physical therapist
- Adapt activities to an individual's poor muscle control

Understand cognitive attributes

Understand the implications of abnormalities in alertness 6.32.02.01
- Plan activities that command attention
- Use individuals' names to gain attention
- Provide incentives to maintain attention

Understand health and medical considerations

Understand the implications of congenital heart defects 6.32.03.01
- Consult with physician for limitations
- Adapt activities for exercise tolerance limitations

Developmental Coordination Disorder: Understand the unique considerations of individuals with developmental coordination disorder

Understand how to plan instructions

Understand the implications of motor planning and perceptual motor disorders 6.33.01.01
- Recognize the need to provide specific motor planning activities
- Collaborate with adapted physical educators and occupational therapists to design a motor planning lesson
- Provide appropriate motor planning activities

Understand how to implement instructions

Understand the implication of perceptual motor practice (i.e., throwing, catching, kicking, striking) 6.33.02.01
- During practice, use simple language, reinforce auditory directions, and use consistent language for an individual with an auditory processing problem
- During practice, teach using verbal and tactile demonstrations for an individual with visual processing problems
- Provide numerous opportunities to explore movement potential, use a variety of movement experiences, and use a gradual balance progression from static to dynamic

Curriculum Theory and Development

Understand that organizing centers (i.e., frames of reference, themes, or emphases) are the focus for curriculum design

Understand the influence of educational trends such as culturally responsive pedagogy, inclusive education, knowledge-based approaches, and outcome-based education on physical education curriculum

Understand the adapted physical educator's role in an inclusive physical education curriculum 7.01.01.01

- Collaborate with the general physical education teacher about the progress and participation of the individuals with disabilities
- Teach fundamental motor and play skills to enable individuals with and without disabilities to participate together in an inclusive physical education program
- Develop and assist in implementing a plan to enable an individual's successful and maximum participation
- Develop curricula that are accessible and that build on the concept of the least restrictive environment (LRE)

Recognize the existence of curricular models in physical education such as movement education, fitness, developmental, activity-based, humanistic/social development, and personal meaning

Know the pros and cons of various curricular models designed specifically for adapted physical education such as achievement-based curriculum, Smart Start, I-CAN, and Data-Based Gymnasium 7.01.02.01

- Write IEP and lesson plan objectives compatible with curricular models such as Smart Start, Everyone CAN, and Data-Based Gymnasium
- Implement curricular objectives consistent with an individual's current levels of educational performance

Understand how information from society, learner needs and interests (including strengths and abilities), and physical education subject matter relate in the identification of organizing centers

Understand how to operationalize the concept of "reasonable accommodation" within the curriculum design process for individuals with disabilities 7.01.03.01

- Individualize learning objectives to facilitate inclusion of individuals into the instructional activities of the general class
- Adapt activities/skills based on the individual's abilities

Understand how philosophical and psychological concerns influence selection of organizing centers

Understand the implications of social views and values in selection of organizing centers for individuals with disabilities 7.01.04.01

- Plan for and adapt organizing centers that are accessible
- Prepare all individuals without disabilities for inclusion of individuals with disabilities in a general physical education class

Understand the implications of relevant assessment data in identification of organizing centers for individuals with disabilities 7.01.04.02

- Account for all individuals' abilities when organizing the curriculum
- Plan for the successful and maximum participation of individuals with disabilities

Generate alternative organizing centers as the focus for the physical education curriculum

Understand implications of specific concepts related to individuals with disabilities, such as least restrictive environment (LRE), regular education initiative (REI), full inclusion, and No Child Left Behind Act 7.01.05.01

- Implement organizing centers that meet the needs of individuals with disabilities
- Collaborate with the IEP team and include the general physical educator, if relevant, to determine program placement
- Defend the selection of organizing centers based on implementation of either LRE or full inclusion concepts
- Explain the importance of employing and retaining quality personnel

Understand how to select content goals based on relevant and appropriate assessment

Understand how to specify content using approaches such as structure-of-content, objective-taxonomic, and task descriptive

Know the difference between the developmental and functional approaches to curriculum design for individuals with disabilities 7.02.01.01

- Devise goals that are developmental and age appropriate
- Plan for goals using a task-specific or developmental approach depending on learner needs

Understand how to conduct a learner analysis

Understand the purpose of pretest data for selection of relevant and appropriate assessment tools

Understand the requirement for establishing the present level of performance in individuals with disabilities 7.03.01.01

- Assess present level of educational performance in physical education
- Analyze results of tests used to establish an individual's present level of performance in physical education

Understand how pretest data are factored into the IEP process 7.03.01.02

- Interpret the results of assessment used to establish the individual's present level of performance
- Use assessment results to write objectives that are related to the individual's present level of performance
- Present the results of the assessment process at the IEP meeting

Interpret pretest data as a basis for placement and instruction

Understand how placement decisions are made as a function of the IEP process 7.03.02.01

- Discuss assessment results with the IEP team prior to program placement decisions
- Consider all factors (motor, social, behavioral) when making a placement decision

Understand how to devise a process for collecting pretest data that reveals entry learning levels related to the individual's strengths and weaknesses

Understand the requirement for using valid and reliable tests to measure the physical and motor attributes of individuals with disabilities prior to development of the IEP 7.03.03.01

- Identify the strengths and weaknesses of the major assessment instruments used in adapted physical education (see Standard 4)
- Conduct assessments in accordance with the procedures established for administration of the instrument selected

Understand the distinction between informal assessment techniques such as rubrics and checklists and formal techniques such as norm-referenced tests (see Standard 8) 7.03.03.02

- Use informal assessment procedures to screen for areas of strength and weakness in physical education to determine need for further testing prior to IEP development
- Use formal assessment measures to determine areas of strength and weakness in physical education to determine program placement and IEP development

Understand how to derive learning objectives based on relevant and appropriate assessment

Understand how to specify learning objectives that are congruent with the underlying goals of the curriculum

Know that learning objectives must be congruent with the definition of physical education as it appears in the Individuals with Disabilities Education Improvement Act (IDEA, 2004) 7.04.01.01

- Use assessment results to develop instructional objectives that are congruent with the definition of physical education for each individual
- Devise appropriate objective criteria and evaluation procedures to determine the achievement of the instructional objectives

Understand how to develop precise, measurable learning objectives

Understand the criteria required for writing measurable objectives as specified for the IEP 7.04.02.01

- Write objectives that relate directly to the individual's needs as determined by the physical and motor assessment
- Write objectives that are observable and measurable (see Standard 9)

Understand how to develop a task analysis for the purpose of ordering learning objectives

Know that a task analysis can illuminate the essential ecological components of skill acquisition for individuals with disabilities 7.04.03.01

- Teach to the levels of the ecological task analysis that are appropriate for each individual
- Use an ecological task analysis to establish appropriate skill sequences for each individual

Understand how to conduct an activity analysis for the purpose of ordering learning objectives

Understand the impact of cognitive, affective, and psychomotor development of individuals with a disability on the selection of an activity in which they will participate 7.04.04.01

- Modify activities to meet the individual's needs
- Modify activities to complement the individual's strengths

Understand how to devise learning experiences

Understand how to substantiate the selection of learning experiences

Understand the cyclical nature of the IEP process and how content can be revised based on the achievement of short-term instructional objectives 7.05.01.01

- Write short-term instructional objectives designed to meet long-term goals (see Standard 9)
- Use the appropriate developmental sequence of motor skills
- Revise, at least on an annual basis, goals and objectives commensurate with the individual's achievement

Understand how to utilize individualization (such as learning style options, pacing, and level of difficulty) as a basis for implementing learning experiences

Understand how to organize practice in a manner that capitalizes on the learning styles of individuals with disabilities (see Standard 10) 7.05.02.01

- Use paraprofessionals and peer tutors to enable maximum participation of individuals with disabilities
- Teach paraprofessionals and peer tutors how to interact in a positive manner and give reinforcement to individuals with disabilities
- Teach paraprofessionals and peer tutors how to effectively instruct, give feedback, and assess individuals with disabilities

Assessment

Legislative Issues: Legislation in regard to assessment of individuals with disabilities throughout the lifespan (see Standard 5)

Know federal and state legislation for assessment of individuals with disabilities

Understand personnel requirements for assessment under federal and state law 8.01.01.01

- Demonstrate adequate training for valid test administration
- Explain requirements of federal and state law to parents relative to motor assessment

Understand the criteria that the instrument(s) used must meet to be considered acceptable under the law in terms of validity and reliability 8.01.01.02

- Use instruments that meet criteria acceptable under the law
- Identify characteristics of instruments used that comply with federal law

Understand the process of assessment under the law 8.01.01.03

- Conduct assessment in a nondiscriminatory manner
- Assess according to the frequency required by law

Understand the difference between instructional services and related services for individuals with disabilities 8.01.01.04

- Explain the differences between instructional services and related services for individuals with disabilities to parents and guardians
- Recommend related services to parents and guardians as appropriate

Know state and school district regulations/guidelines for assessment of individuals with disabilities

Know LEA eligibility criteria for adapted physical education 8.01.02.01

- Communicate the rationale and use of eligibility criteria for adapted physical education
- Implement eligibility criteria for placing students into adapted physical education

Know the referral process

Understand the processes involved in referring and assessing individuals with disabilities for special education services 8.01.03.01

- Comply with the timelines for responsiveness to a referral
- Complete assessment process within the specified time under the law

Understand the physical educator's responsibilities in the referral process relative to physical and motor performance 8.01.03.02

- Explain the responsibilities in the referral process related to physical education for individuals with disabilities
- Initiate and support referrals to appropriate professionals for assessment

Understand appropriate procedures for data gathering based on referral information and suspected areas of motor disability 8.01.03.03

- Conduct appropriate screening for individuals with suspected motor disabilities
- Relate areas of screening with parameters measured in the assessment process

Understand the roles of other professionals 8.01.03.04

- Refer individuals with disabilities to related services personnel, such as physical, occupational, and speech therapists
- Explain to parents and guardians the role and purpose(s) of various related services professionals

Understand the ethical issues of assessment such as nonbiased assessment and the use of individual's native language or commonly used form of communication (see Standard 5)

Understand what is meant by informed consent of parents and guardians 8.01.04.01

- Obtain informed consent for assessment process
- Explain a student's need for adapted physical education assessment to parents and guardians who are hesitant to give consent for assessment

Understand due process and its ethical implications 8.01.04.02

- Comply with the due process procedures for all physical education services
- Explain due process to parents and guardians as needed

Understand how different cultures and languages can affect the assessment process 8.01.04.03

- Apply necessary modifications in the assessment process for any influences due to culture and language
- Use an interpreter in instances in which individuals do not speak English as their primary language

Understand the need for confidentiality of records 8.01.04.04

- Read appropriate records for an individual prior to gathering assessment data
- Obtain information discretely from the classroom teacher and other professionals prior to gathering data

Acknowledge the rights of parents or guardians to obtain an appropriate and objective evaluation of performance by personnel outside the educational agency

Understand the relationship between the results of an outside evaluation and the results of motor assessment conducted by appropriately trained professionals under the law 8.01.05.01

- Communicate, when appropriate, with outside personnel who conducted the evaluations
- Resolve or validate the results of motor assessment with the results of assessment by outside personnel

Terminology: The nomenclature used in the specialized field of motor assessment of individuals with disabilities

Awareness of the differences among screening, assessment, measurement, and evaluation

Understand the purpose of screening 8.02.01.01

- Conduct appropriate screening
- Articulate the findings of the screening process to other professionals, parents, and guardians

Understand the purpose of assessment 8.02.01.02

- Explain the various purposes for which assessment data are collected
- Describe the primary purposes for which assessment data are used in adapted physical education

Understand the purpose of measurement 8.02.01.03

- Distinguish between the purposes of measurement of individuals with disabilities and measurement of individuals without disabilities
- Describe how measurements are used in adapted physical education

Understand the purpose of program evaluation 8.02.01.04

- Compare and contrast the purposes of program evaluation for individuals with disabilities and individuals without disabilities
- Explain how program evaluation can be used for comparing adapted physical education to general physical education programs

Know formal and informal methods for gathering qualitative as well as quantitative data on motor performance

Understand how to use the various forms of data collected related to individuals with disabilities 8.02.02.01

- Use diagnostic evaluations, instructional assessment, and program evaluation for monitoring progress
- Integrate information obtained from parent and guardian reports and other informal measures with formally obtained performance measures

Know curriculum-embedded methods of gathering data

Understand the process of gathering data on play behavior 8.02.03.01

- Administer one or more curriculum-based evaluation procedures such as Smart Start, I-CAN, Data-Based Gymnasium, and ABC
- Use data gathered on play behavior in reporting present levels of performance of individuals with disabilities

Know terminology such as eligibility criteria, individualized education program, and current level of performance

Know the terminology related to motor assessment 8.02.04.01

- Communicate utilizing terminology unique to assessment of individuals with disabilities
- Teach colleagues appropriate terminology for movement parameters

Understand reasons for discrepancies between performance on standardized tests and curriculum-embedded performance

Know how performance score discrepancies relate to individuals with disabilities 8.02.05.01

- Defend or refute scores on standardized tests against performance-based observations of an individual's present level of performance
- Use appropriate assessment procedures such as age-appropriate evaluation, functional skills assessment, life-skills measurement, developmentally appropriate, and bottom-up and top-down approaches
- Integrate motor performance data with behaviors reported by other professionals and caregivers

Administration: Knowledge of various instruments measuring human performance related to physical education

Know instruments that measure the qualities necessary for physical and motor fitness: fundamental motor skills and patterns; skills in aquatics, dance, and individual and group games and sports; as well as functional living skills

Know how to administer curriculum-based assessment procedures such as Smart Start, Everyone CAN, Data-Based Gymnasium, and ABC 8.03.01.01

- Use at least one curriculum-based assessment procedure
- Describe some of the administrative advantages of curriculum-based assessment procedures

Know the instruments most commonly used by adapted physical educators 8.03.01.02

- Use tests measuring physical fitness such as the Prudential Fitnessgram, Brockport Physical Fitness Test
- Use tests measuring the acquisition of motor skills such as Bruininks-Oseretsky Test of Motor Proficiency (BOT II), Test of Gross Motor Development (TGMD II)
- Use tests measuring motor development such as Brigance Diagnostic Inventory of Early Development, Denver Developmental Screening Test, Peabody Developmental Motor Scale II, and Project MOVE

Know other measurement and evaluation procedures prescribed by the local education agency (LEA) 8.03.01.03

- Use the measurement and evaluation procedures used by the LEA when appropriate
- Explain advantages of the LEA's prescribed measurement and evaluation procedures to other professionals

Understand how to use specific standardized instruments or procedures for determining needs in related services such as checklists or observation techniques suggested by other specialists 8.03.01.04

- Explain motor demands made by instruments measuring language and cognitive function
- Explain procedures used by other professionals to evaluate movement including reflex, mobility, and flexibility testing; sensory motor, gross motor, and fine motor skills testing; positioning/handling techniques; and leisure skills education

Know other measurement and evaluation procedures used by related services personnel 8.03.01.05

- Distinguish interrelationship of motor skills with related services such as speech and language and occupational and physical therapy
- Recognize the variety of motor skills and abilities assessed by other professionals on the multidisciplinary team

Administration: Demonstrate knowledge of an assortment of instruments measuring all aspects of human performance

Recognize the need for staff training, additional administrative support, and reallocation of resources in utilizing a diversity of instruments

Understand how to determine the level of need for inservices on test administration for individuals with disabilities 8.03.02.01

- Provide an inservice to general physical educators related to test administration based on the data gathered through a needs assessment survey
- Provide inservice to general physical educators on screening procedures for making appropriate referrals for adapted physical education based on data gathered through a needs assessment survey and interview with the district director of special education

Interpretation: Gaining clarification and meaning of measurement results

Understand the use of measurement results for the purpose of identifying educational needs

Understand how to interpret measurement results of screening and diagnosis 8.04.01.01

- Use the measurement results of screening and diagnosis to refer individuals with disabilities for further assessment
- Use the measurement results of screening and diagnosis to write annual instructional goals

Understand how to interpret norm-referenced, criterion-referenced, and content-referenced results for individuals with disabilities 8.04.01.02

- Use the results of norm-referenced, criterion-referenced, and content-referenced instruments in determining annual instructional goals and short-term objectives
- Use the results of norm-referenced, criterion-referenced, and content-referenced instruments in prescribing programs for individuals with disabilities

Understand how to establish norm-referenced and criterion-referenced standards for qualifying students for placement in adapted physical education 8.04.01.03

- Use the entrance standards established to recommend adapted physical education services for individuals with disabilities
- Explain the entrance standards to caregivers and other professionals during the IEP meeting

Understand the use of measurement results for instructional planning

Understand how to interpret measurement results and use them in the instructional planning 8.04.02.01

- Show evidence of using measurement results in the development of the instructional plans
- Modify expectations for student performance based on measurement results

Understand how to interpret measurement results for monitoring progress of individuals with disabilities 8.04.02.02

- Incorporate the measurement results when monitoring the program evaluation progress of individuals with disabilities
- Use measurement results to give individuals feedback in the learning process
- Use measurement results to develop progress reports for the individual and the parents
- Use measurement results in the summative evaluation

Understand the relationships among measures of physical and motor fitness; fundamental motor skills and patterns; and skills in aquatics, dance, and individual and group games and sports as well as functional living skills

Understand how to incorporate integrated activities into the instructional plan 8.04.03.01

- Incorporate activities addressing reflex behavior, sensorimotor function, leisure skills, and functional skills into the educational plan (see Standard 9)
- Include lifetime activities in the instructional plan based on the results of assessment

Understand the importance of providing feedback for social, behavioral, and language skills as they relate to, and are demonstrated in, a motor performance context 8.04.03.02

- Incorporate the necessary feedback concerning social, behavioral, and language skills into the student's overall physical education plan
- Use both general and specific feedback when implementing the physical education plan

Understand the connection between motor performance measures and self-help and mobility skills 8.04.03.03

- Incorporate self-help and mobility skills into the individual's physical education program when appropriate
- Identify self-help and mobility skill programs

Understand the importance of parental or guardians' input in the assessment process 8.04.03.04

- Actively seek parental or guardian input
- Include parents or guardians in the delivery of services by encouraging family activities

Understand the importance of effectively communicating the results of assessment

Understand how to communicate motor performance scores to parents or guardians 8.04.04.01

- Interpret motor performance scores to parents or guardians
- Explain the relationship between motor performance scores and play behavior observed by parents or guardians

Understand how to communicate motor performance scores to classroom teachers and other professionals 8.04.04.02

- Interpret motor performance scores to classroom teachers and other professionals
- Work cooperatively with other professionals to determine the need to refer for further testing for additional instructional or related services
- Explain the importance of providing general, specific, and corrective feedback for motor performance

Understand how to communicate motor performance scores to individuals with disabilities as appropriate 8.04.04.03

- Interpret motor performance scores to individuals with disabilities as appropriate
- Question individuals with disabilities on how they might improve their performance over the next review period

Understand that measurement results must reach a criterion in order to be determined eligible for adapted physical education

Understand the local measurement criteria for determining eligibility for adapted physical education 8.04.05.01

- Interpret local criteria for determining eligibility for adapted physical education
- Explain the difference between qualifying and nonqualifying performances relative to eligibility for adapted physical education

Understand the choices of services available to students with disabilities in the school district or local educational agency

Understand service delivery options for physical education in cooperation with a multidisciplinary team 8.04.06.01

- Suggest the optimal service delivery option for physical education in cooperation with the multidisciplinary team
- Agree on the service delivery options for physical education in cooperation with the multidisciplinary team

Understand adaptations or modifications of activities based on the student's identified needs 8.04.06.02

- Provide suggestions for adaptation or modifications of activities based on the individual's identified needs
- Modify facilities and equipment as needed to accommodate the individual's identified needs (see Standard 9)

Recognize the need for staff training, additional administrative support, and reallocation of resources for effective administration of physical fitness and motor performance instruments and the interpretation of assessment results

Understand how to provide inservice training for general physical educators on measurement and interpretation of motor performance assessment 8.04.07.01

- Provide inservice on assessment to general physical educators on an ongoing basis
- Attend inservices and workshops to keep current with assessment issues (see Standard 13)

Understand the need for classroom teacher involvement in physical and motor performance assessment interpretation 8.04.07.02

- Offer inservice to classroom teachers about measurement and interpretation of physical and motor performance assessment results as needed
- Provide guidelines for referral to adapted physical education

Decision Making: The process of making choices from alternatives

Knowledge of a theoretical framework with which to make comprehensive assessment decisions

Understand the nature of decisions to be made such as placement, diagnosis, and the prescription of programs for individuals with disabilities 8.05.01.01

- Use the appropriate assessment instruments when making placement or diagnosis decisions
- Use the appropriate assessment instruments to obtain data to prescribe appropriate program effectiveness

Understand the value of assessment as an ongoing process

Understand how ongoing assessment relates to programming decisions for individuals with disabilities 8.05.02.01

- Use ongoing assessment in prescribing programs
- Use ongoing assessment of annual goals and objectives as a means to determine program effectiveness

Understand instructional decisions based on assessment results

Understand how to plan teaching based on assessment results 8.05.03.01

- Provide evidence of the effects of assessment on instructional decisions by changing teaching plans
- Demonstrate that expectations for performance of individuals is based on the results of assessment

Understand the difference between a full range of physical education services and essential physical education service options for individuals with disabilities 8.05.03.02

- Explain the difference between the two service options to parents, guardians, and other professionals
- Provide essential physical education services for individuals with disabilities

Know motor assessment resources available in the field

Understand how to locate names of local/state/regional resources for assistance with motor assessment issues 8.05.04.01

- Provide parents, guardians, and other professionals with names of local/state/ regional resources for assistance with motor assessment issues
- Explain to parents or guardians their rights to obtain assistance with motor assessment from sources outside the school environment

Skills Required of the Assessment Team: The ability to work together with other professionals in a multidisciplinary team (see Standard 15)

Report the assessment results to parents, guardians, and other professionals

Understand how to use the appropriate statements with regard to the individual with a disability when reporting assessment results 8.06.01.01
- Make statements of fact, inference, and probability and distinguish among them
- Use previous experience for establishing a context of reporting assessment results

Record assessment results for use by members of the multidisciplinary team

Understand the essential components of a comprehensive assessment report for use in making recommendations for programming 8.06.02.01
- State the essential dimensions of a summary report including demographics, overall summary of assessment results, specific behavioral observations during testing, specific subtest performances, and general recommendations regarding eligibility for services
- Discriminate between supportive data and opinion

Understand how to interface the report of physical fitness and motor performance assessment and programming recommendations with the reports, and programming of other team members

Understand the potential for developing collaborative lesson plans using assessment results provided by team members for general physical education classes and other inclusionary experiences 8.06.03.01
- Write rubrics in collaboration with the general physical educator
- Team teach with the general physical educator using a collaborative lesson plan
- Demonstrate the use of a task analysis when teaching as it relates to assessment results

Collaborate with team members to understand how to develop instructional strategies based on the team report that facilitate self-directed and independent participation of individuals with disabilities within the movement environment 8.06.03.02
- Develop transition goals in physical activity to integrate the individual in community-based activities
- Teach necessary skills to achieve transition goals
- Plan community-based physical activity experiences
- Coordinate community-based physical activity experiences with other professionals such as a therapeutic recreator or personal trainer

Understand how to collaborate with and support other team members 8.06.03.03
- Engage other team members in discussion of the progress of individuals with disabilities at times other than formalized, planned meetings
- Use multidisciplinary strategies as appropriate

Instructional Design and Planning

Curriculum Plan: Understand the factors needed to develop a systematic overall curriculum plan of instruction

Analyze individual strengths/needs, goals, and priorities

Understand individual needs, goals, and priorities specific to individuals with disabilities 9.01.01.01

- Determine long-term goals suitable for instruction given individual's potential and time available to implement instructional programs, such as the school year, as well as considering such factors as equipment, space, and number of individuals per class
- Determine the prerequisite behaviors and ancillary behaviors needed to complete the goals targeted for instruction
- Consider individual's ability in the physical, cognitive, and social domains based on the individual's assessment and evaluation of long-term annual goals and behavioral objectives
- Determine individual's preferences for activities
- Consider individual's various learning modalities such as visual, kinesthetic, or auditory
- Establish and promote behaviors with the most immediate value, such as those that allow individuals to function as independently as possible in the community and later in life
- Identify behaviors that offer long-term support and lifetime application

Analyze resources, constraints, and alternative delivery systems

Understand resources, constraints, and alternative delivery systems and strategies specific to meeting the needs of individuals with disabilities (see Standards 7 and 15) 9.01.02.01

- Collaborate with support personnel such as paraprofessionals and peer tutors to assist in planning for instruction (see Standard 15)
- Collaborate with community support services such as Special Olympics and YMCA for developing instructional programs for individuals with disabilities
- Use existing resources in adapted physical education such as the ABC for instructional planning (see Standard 7)
- Advocate for accessibility to facilities and teaching areas such as ramps for individuals who are in wheelchairs as well as accessibility to playground equipment
- Advocate for alternative placement in the least restrictive environment
- Advocate for participation in intramural and interscholastic sport programs

Determine scope (goals and objectives) and sequence (when they will be taught) of the curriculum based on long-term goals, which will serve as the basis for the IEP and IFSP

Understand the concept of "planning down" to establish long-term goals for individuals with disabilities 9.01.03.01

- Select goals based on projected employment, living situation, leisure preferences, and skill potential
- Select goals based on access to facilities and equipment
- Collaborate with other professionals to project long-term, community-based sport and physical recreation goals

Understand the concept of instructional time and how it relates to planning functional curricula for individuals with disabilities 9.01.03.02

- Calculate the total time available in the program
- Adjust the amount of time based on access to facilities and equipment, on student–teacher ratio, on teacher competency, and on outside practice opportunities

Understand how to delimit the number of goals that can be achieved in the program by individuals with disabilities based on the amount of instructional time and the resources available 9.01.03.03

- Determine goal emphasis
- Establish time needed to achieve mastery of objectives
- Plan time needed for retention and maintenance

Understand how to delineate and sequence the objectives across the years of the program, based on the attributes of the learner's disability, so that the program goals can be achieved in the time available 9.01.03.04

- Sequence objectives based on age appropriateness, developmental level, and social ability such as interacting with others
- Determine when instruction should begin, when achievement is expected, and what objectives should be included in the IEP

Understand how to use the scope and sequence of the objectives in the curriculum as the basis for program evaluation of individuals with a disability (see Standard 12) 9.01.03.05

- Based on assessment data, determine if the program is being implemented as intended and when program revisions are needed
- Communicate the program purpose and the individual's progress
- Monitor IEP progress using the curriculum scope and sequence

Unit and Lesson Plans: Design units and lesson plans to maximize instruction

Plan to accommodate for learner characteristics and individual background

Understand that individuals with disabilities exhibit a unique array of characteristics such as limited attention span, distractibility, and hyperactivity (see Standard 6) 9.02.01.01

- Plan structured programs, class routines, and activities including instructional learning cues to maintain attention (see Standard 10)
- Select equipment that maintains attention such as considering color, size, and shape
- Plan a variety of presentations so that specific tasks can be altered if needed in order to maintain interest and attention
- Plan the use of a variety of teaching styles that will meet the needs of individuals with disabilities (see Standard 10)

Understand that the readiness level of individuals with disabilities may vary 9.02.01.02

- Plan programs to include appropriate modifications for individuals with disabilities who learn at slower or different rates
- Plan programs to include appropriate skills and activities based on individual's readiness level

Understand motivation levels of individuals with disabilities 9.02.01.03

- Plan programs with consideration of the teaching behaviors to promote and motivate the learner (see Standard 10)
- Plan programs with consideration to what the individual finds reinforcing to promote and motivate the learner

Understand the wide variety of individual differences among and within different types of individuals with disabilities 9.02.01.04

- Plan programs to account for individual differences among individuals with disabilities such as using various teaching styles
- Plan programs that include modified games and activities
- Plan programs for appropriate use of environment, equipment, rules, materials, and activities (see Standard 10)

Accommodate for the medical history of the individual within the instructional design

Understand the effect certain medical conditions may have when planning physical activity for an individual with a disability 9.02.02.01

- Check individual's medical records (file) and be aware of his/her current medical condition and medication being taken
- Consult with a physician and other medical staff regarding recommended and contraindicated activities as a result of the individual's medical condition/ medication
- Plan for recommended activities and exercises and avoid activities and exercises that are contraindicated such as butterfly swim stroke and diving activities for individuals with atlantoaxial instability
- Keep a schedule for medication and chart the effect certain medications (type, dosage) have on movement performance such as fatigue, errors in movement, and distractibility
- Organize the learning environment so that disabilities are not aggravated or exacerbated such as the removal of strobe lights, flickering fluorescent lighting, or sounds to prevent the inducement of seizures

Understand the effect medication (type and dosage) may have on the behavior and performance of an individual with a disability when planning activities 9.02.02.02

- Plan programs based on the effect the medication has on the individual's physical fitness and motor skill abilities and physical work capacity
- Plan programs based on the effect the medication has on the length of time the individual is able to remain on task

Plan for safety and risk management

Understand proper safety techniques and principles specific to individuals with disabilities 9.02.03.01

- Plan activities by taking into account the amount of risk involved by considering such factors as space available, floor surfaces, appropriate equipment, and types of activities offered
- Plan for such safety procedures as handling wheelchair transfers, securing and strapping techniques, negotiating stairs and inclines, bracing, reinsertion of tracheotomy tube, and guiding techniques
- Identify and post safety procedures for specific emergency procedures
- Use national, state, and/or community agencies that have health and safety information including voluntary health organizations and associations related to a specific condition and government office/agency

Plan for proper supervision following school policies

Understand potentially dangerous situations and activities specific to individuals with disabilities 9.02.04.01

- Identify and share information and procedures with general physical educators and others regarding individuals with disabilities and their special needs
- Develop and post emergency plans specific to individuals with a disability such as procedures to follow for an individual having a seizure
- Plan for directional, visual, auditory, and tactile signals for potentially dangerous activities and emergencies
- Develop specific supervision and spotting procedures

Understand LEA policies with regard to safety of individuals and staff 9.02.04.02

- Implement safety policies specific to individuals with disabilities
- Fill out appropriate accident forms as required by school policy

Consider student–teacher ratio

Understand that certain individuals with disabilities may need a small teacher–student ratio 9.02.05.01

- Plan for activities using paraprofessionals and peer tutors for individuals who require greater attention for such reasons as being disruptive to others, short attention span, or assistance with learning a skill
- Plan for activities varying the assistance of the teacher such as the use of stations or reciprocal style teaching (see Standard 10)
- Plan for training of paraprofessionals and volunteers to assist individuals with disabilities (see Standard 15)

Consider class size and composition

Understand the effect the arrangement of the class and various formations will have when planning activities specific to individuals with disabilities 9.02.06.01

- Design for smaller group formations such as shorter relay lines with individuals who are easily distracted and/or display difficulty staying on task
- Design a class formation for individuals who need to be near the teacher such as the deaf or hard of hearing
- Structure the class composition to be free of extraneous stimuli
- Design for the grouping of individuals with and without disabilities

Plan for physical education classroom management, organization, and routines

Understand the importance of developing class management rules, routines, transitions, and consequences specific to individuals with disabilities (see Standard 10) 9.02.07.01

- Develop signals for getting the class's attention and starting and stopping the class, taking into account various characteristics of learners
- Design consistent routines and transitional procedures that can be used with individuals with disabilities
- Use peer tutors to assist in class management

Plan for appropriate use of environment, equipment, rules, materials, and activities

Understand how to modify the environment, equipment, rules, materials, and activities specific to individuals with disabilities 9.02.08.01

- Use equipment that is developmentally appropriate and accommodates the needs of individuals with disabilities

- Plan for games such as beep baseball or goal ball to accommodate individuals who are visually impaired or blind

Plan for modifications of environment

Understand the concepts and strategies necessary to modify the environment, such as the play area, specific to individuals with disabilities 9.02.09.01

- Reduce the playing area for individuals who have limited mobility
- Use hard surfaces or play indoors for individuals such as those in wheelchairs
- Lower the basket or net to varying heights in such games as basketball or volleyball for individuals with low stamina or deficient skill levels
- Use sound devices, bright equipment, and hand signals or flags, and mark goals and boundaries for individuals with visual disabilities
- Increase the size of the goal for individuals with an eye–hand coordination problem
- Provide visual cues on wall to assist individuals with short-term memory or language barriers

Plan for modifications of equipment

Understand the concepts and strategies necessary to plan for the modifications of equipment specific to individuals with disabilities such as weight, size, color, and texture 9.02.10.01

- Use different size balls for individuals who are clumsy
- Use a contrasting background during activities such as when catching a ball outside (i.e., yellow ball against a blue sky)
- Use activities and equipment that are motivational such as brightly colored balls
- Use equipment that will attract attention such as beep baseball or bell ball for individuals who are blind
- Decrease the speed of a moving object by adding or reducing weight, deflating a ball, or putting a tail on the object
- Shorten the length of the handle on a striking implement such as a racket, bat, or golf club
- Use large visual targets for individuals with visual deficits
- Use soft and light equipment such as sponge Frisbee or ball for individuals who have difficulty handling objects
- Make objects stationary such as using a batting tee for individuals who have difficulty striking a moving object
- Use Velcro mitts and balls for individuals who have difficulty catching
- Change the texture of the object, such as using a foam ball, for individuals who are fearful of the object

Plan for modifications of rules

Understand the concepts and strategies necessary to modify rules specific to individuals with disabilities 9.02.11.01

- Use rules from various sport disability associations and organizations such as Challenger Little League Baseball, National Wheelchair Basketball Association (e.g., use two pushes in wheelchair basketball)
- Play with a different number of players on the floor than the rules permit to make the game more challenging or fair such as three players on a side for tennis or badminton
- Use modifications such as having individuals move closer to the net or over the serving line when serving in games like volleyball or badminton
- Reduce the number of rules to simplify game or activity
- Preserve purpose of the game when modifying rules

Plan for modification of activities and games

Understand the concepts and strategies necessary to modify activities and games specific to meet the needs of individuals with disabilities by incorporating such concepts as cooperative games or game interventions 9.02.12.01

- Avoid elimination games
- Keep collective score among teams by combining points of the teams
- Emphasize cooperation over winning among teammates as well as opponents
- Plan games and activities that stress participation for everyone

Plan for appropriate time spent in lesson

Understand the importance of planning to maximize learning time with individuals with disabilities 9.02.13.01

- Maximize learning time by matching the difficulty of the task with the unique ability levels of individuals with disabilities
- Plan for individuals with disabilities who require more time to complete tasks and need time for review
- Sequence lesson plan activities according to unique needs of individuals with disabilities
- Modify lesson plan format and activities according to unique needs of individuals with disabilities such as providing frequent rest periods for individuals with low physical vitality

Understand the importance of planning to optimize instruction time with individuals with disabilities 9.02.13.02

- Teach individuals using optimal communication modes
- Keep instructions to a minimum for individuals with cognitive disabilities
- Use key words or commands to elicit the desired response or behavior with individuals with disabilities

Understand the importance of planning to reduce transition time for individuals with disabilities 9.02.13.03

- Arrange environment to allow for smooth and quick transition when working with individuals who have limited attention spans or who need a longer period of time to move from one activity to another
- Allow for adequate time for individuals to change in and out of physical education clothes, and who require assistance in changing such as individuals with orthopedic disabilities and/or multiple disabilities

Determine individual progression through a formative evaluation plan (i.e., evaluate unit and lesson plans)

Understand the importance of evaluating the progress of individuals with disabilities (see Standards 4 and 8) 9.02.14.01

- Chart progress on the individual's IEP or IFSP
- Plan for the evaluation standards unique to individuals with disabilities that determine the mastery of a skill or activity such as using a task analysis
- Plan for the evaluation of individual program progression from dependent supervised training to independent completion of the activity

Understand the importance of selecting realistic lesson plan goals and objectives that can be successfully attained by individuals with disabilities 9.02.14.02

- Include individuals with disabilities as part of the planning process of goals and objectives selected

- When appropriate, include individuals with disabilities in recording progress using charts and tables
- Select functional skills for instruction and evaluation that match the needs of individuals with disabilities

Understand the importance of evaluating the functional aspects of performance for individuals with disabilities 9.02.14.03

- Evaluate performance in the environments in which individuals with disabilities will perform the skill
- Evaluate performance based on criteria determined as needed for successful participation in the community such as being able to bowl at a bowling center

Plan for paraprofessionals, volunteers, and peer tutors

Understand the importance of planning for paraprofessionals, volunteers, or peer tutors to assist with teaching individuals with disabilities 9.02.15.01

- Establish a system of recruiting, training, communicating, and providing feedback for paraprofessionals and volunteers/peer tutors such as providing training in techniques used in physical education like monitoring behaviors with a checklist or a rubric
- Provide individuals with disabilities with responsibilities that are compatible with their ability level

IEP and IFSP: Understand federal mandates involved in planning programs of physical education for individuals with disabilities

Know the IEP process

Understand present level of performance such as knowledge of the movement skill development in individuals 3 to 21 years old with disabilities that includes physical fitness, fundamental skills, games, sport, and leisure 9.03.01.01

- Write present level of performance statement based on assessment information such as using normative test scores, criterion-referenced test scores, and informal test methods (see Standard 4)
- Write present level of performance statement based on information from records, parents, and information from other professionals

Understand how to develop annual goals based on assessment data and the specific needs of individuals with disabilities 9.03.01.02

- Write annual physical and motor outcome statements based on present level of performance information
- Write observable and measurable goals

Understand that short-term motor instructional objectives in physical education lead toward performance mastery 9.03.01.03

- Write instructional objectives in behavioral terms based on present level of performance information
- Match objectives to previously established annual goals

Understand that a continuum of least restrictive environments in physical education exists 9.03.01.04

- Provide various physical education and adapted physical education delivery services to individuals with disabilities to meet specific learner needs

- Work with other physical education service delivery providers to meet the needs of individuals with disabilities

Understand that related services such as physical and occupational therapy are available based on the individual's needs 9.03.01.05

- Communicate and work with the related service providers in meeting an individual's established goals and objectives
- Monitor the effectiveness of the related service to the individual's overall physical education goals and objectives

Understand how to project dates for the initiation and duration of physical education services 9.03.01.06

- Coordinate the individual's physical education program with all service providers
- Implement a physical education program for the duration of needed services
- Monitor program progress for the duration of the established physical education program and until goals/objectives are met

Understand physical education transition from school to community 9.03.01.07

- Coordinate the transition skills needed within the existing physical education structure with community services
- Collaborate with the support services and service providers in implementing the transition plan
- Write age and ability transition goals and objectives according to the individual's ability and interest

Know the IFSP process

Understand child's present level of performance by identifying family's knowledge of their child's motor skills through various data collection methods including formal assessment, verbal communication, and observation 9.03.02.01

- Record the information collected from the family concerning child's motor skills
- Write present level of performance based on information gathered from assessment, verbal communication, and observations

Understand family's motor outcomes by developing a sequential instructional plan of motor skill activities that includes realistic goals and objectives for the family to implement with their child 9.03.02.02

- Write realistic annual goals for the child that include the needs of the family
- Write objectives that reflect the present level of performance
- Write a motor program that the family can implement that matches the stated goals and objectives

Understand how to determine family timelines to meet motor outcome progress 9.03.02.03

- Write timelines related to the mastery of a student's stated physical education or motor goals and objectives
- Write timelines that are monitored by the family and the instructor

Understand how to plan for services to meet family motor needs 9.03.02.04

- Monitor various services for the family to meet the established goals and objectives including community service, educational support, and other private and public services
- Coordinate various early intervention services that meet the motor development needs of the child so that cooperation occurs, and not duplication of services

- Monitor the various services the family has in order to assess their contribution to the child's progress in motor development

Understand how to establish dates for the implementation and evaluation of an IFSP 9.03.02.05

- Write dates for the implementation of the program, including gathering or purchasing of equipment, amount of time involved in teaching, and time to locate and schedule adequate space
- Coordinate the child's motor program with the family, early intervention service providers, and the child when appropriate
- Monitor motor development skill sequence and acquisition timeline
- Monitor program progress and service providers' ability to implement the child's established motor program for the duration of the needed service

Understand how to plan for motor transition from early intervention to school 9.03.02.06

- Determine the similarities and differences between the early intervention environment and that of the educational setting
- Determine the similarities and differences among available early intervention services
- Determine the similarities and differences between the individual's motor needs in the home in contrast to those same needs in school

Technology Applications: Demonstrate knowledge of communication systems sanctioned by the American Speech-Language-Hearing Association (ASHA)

Understand that verbal communication is a medium of oral communication that involves the use of linguistic code (language)

Understand the importance of using oral communication in physical education class with individuals with language disabilities 9.04.01.01

- Rephrase thoughts or ideas during communication
- Use appropriate vocabulary

Understand that nonverbal (alternative/augmentative) communication is any approach designed to support, enhance, or supplement the communication of individuals who are not independent verbal communicators

Understand how nontechnical aids augment communication for individuals with speech and language disorders such as the deaf and hard of hearing 9.04.02.01

- Collaborate with other professionals to determine the most appropriate nonverbal communication approach to use in a physical education environment
- Demonstrate a proficiency in communicating in physical education using sign language, Blissymbolics, rebus, communication boards, communication, typing, and/or writing

Understand how technical aids augment communication for individuals with speech and language impairments 9.04.02.02

- Collaborate with other professionals to determine the most appropriate technical aids to augment communication in a physical education environment
- Demonstrate a proficiency in communicating in physical education using a Touch Talker, Light Talker, Wolf, Canon Communicator, and/or notebook computer as a computer-based speaking and writing system

Assistive Devices: Knowledge of adaptation of assistive devices to enhance participation in physical education

Understand how physical positioning can facilitate movement in physical education

Identify types of equipment used to position individuals with disabilities 9.05.01.01

- Use bolsters for positioning to facilitate movement, wedges, and/or lying wedges
- Use strapping to maintain appropriate body alignment during physical education activities
- Use standing frame for positioning to facilitate movement

Understand how modified seating can enhance movement for individuals with disabilities 9.05.01.02

- Use adaptations to the wheelchair such as removal of armrests to facilitate movement
- Use alternative seating such as on a bench or on the floor to enhance movement in physical education

Understand how canes enhance mobility in physical education

Know types of canes used by individuals with lower limb disabilities 9.05.02.01

- Collaborate with other professionals to determine what type of cane would be the most appropriate to use in the physical education environment for an individual with lower limb disability
- Incorporate use of a quad cane and/or an ice gripper cane to enhance mobility

Understand how crutches enhance mobility in a physical education environment

Identify types of crutches that are most often used by individuals with disabilities such as amputees, long leg brace users, and individuals with a temporary disability 9.05.03.01

- Collaborate with other professionals to determine which type of crutches would be the most appropriate to use in a physical education environment for an individual with a lower limb disability
- Incorporate the use of the Lofstrand crutch or forearm support crutch, platform crutch, and/or underarm crutch

Understand how walkers can provide more stability than crutches during physical education activities

Know different types of walkers that are often used by individuals with lower extremity disabilities 9.05.04.01

- Collaborate with other professionals to determine which walker would be best to use during the physical education environment for an individual with a lower extremity disability
- Incorporate use of the pick-up walker, rolling walker, forearm support walker, and/or the Kaye posture control walker during physical education activities

Understand that an orthosis is a positioning device for support or immobilization, and is used to prevent or correct a deformity, or to assist or restore function

Know the types of orthotic devices for individuals with lower extremity disabilities 9.05.05.01

- Collaborate with other professionals to determine which type of orthotic devices would be appropriate to use in the physical education environment for an individual with a lower extremity disability

- Incorporate the use of ankle-foot orthoses, hip-knee-ankle-foot orthoses, knee-ankle-foot orthoses, and reciprocating gait orthoses during physical education activities

Know the types of orthotic devices for individuals with upper extremity disabilities 9.05.05.02

- Explain the use of different types of orthotic devices for individuals with upper extremity disabilities
- Incorporate the use of Hand Oppens Orthoses and/or serpentine splints during physical education activities

Understand that a prosthesis is a substitute for a missing extremity

Know prosthetic devices for lower extremity amputees 9.05.06.01

- Know prosthetic devices for use by individuals with a lower extremity amputation
- Incorporate the use of foot prostheses such as the Seattle Foot and lower limb prostheses during physical education activities

Know prosthetic devices for upper extremity amputees 9.05.06.02

- Know prosthetic devices for use by individuals with upper extremity amputation
- Incorporate the use of a myoelectric arm and/or upper extremity prostheses during physical education activities

Understand adaptations of equipment used for sport and recreational activities

Understand specific adaptations of equipment for individuals with visual impairments 9.05.07.01

- Collaborate with others to determine which specific equipment adaptations would be appropriate in the physical education environment for an individual with a visual impairment
- Use beepers to help locate a target
- Use handrails to adjust body posture
- Use beeper or bell balls in throwing, rolling, or catching activities

Understand specific adaptations of equipment for individuals with physical impairments 9.05.07.02

- Use strapping such as Velcro to attach striking implements to the arms of amputees or individuals who cannot grasp the implement
- Enlarge the handle for grasping striking implements
- Use Velcro gloves or mitts for individuals with upper extremity involvement to make catching easier
- Use modified skis such as sit skis to enable individuals with lower extremity involvement to ski
- Modify a walker by adding skis to enable individuals with lower extremity involvement to stand and ski

Mobility Devices: Knowledge of various mobility aids to enhance participation in physical education

Understand that wheelchairs either enhance mobility or provide total means of mobility for those who have lower extremity physical disabilities

Understand types of manual wheelchairs such as medical model, lightweight or sport, and racing or track wheelchairs 9.06.01.01

- Incorporate the use of stainless steel manual wheelchairs in physical education
- Incorporate safety travel/lift in space wheelchairs designed for individuals with severe physical disabilities in the physical education environment
- Incorporate lightweight or sport wheelchairs in physical education activities
- Incorporate track wheelchairs for racing

Understand components of manual wheelchairs 9.06.01.02

- Demonstrate ability to lock brakes and adjust armrests and footrests on a wheelchair to facilitate participation in physical activity
- Suggest modifications to casters, wheels, handrims, chair backs, and seats to facilitate participation in physical activity

Understand components of power or motorized wheelchairs used by individuals with disabilities 9.06.01.03

- Accommodate the use of standard upright powerchairs to facilitate participation in physical education activities
- Demonstrate use of control box mechanism to facilitate participation in physical education activities
- Explain procedure to engage/disengage motors

Understand that scooters are a means for increasing mobility and participation in physical education

Know a variety of scooter boards for individuals with disabilities such as lower extremity involvement 9.06.02.01

- Collaborate with others to determine the appropriate scooter board to use in the physical education environment for an individual with a lower extremity disability
- Incorporate use of regular and long scooter boards and/or modified scooters to facilitate participation in physical education activities

Understand that bicycles and tricycles increase mobility in physical education

Know various bicycles and tricycles used by individuals with physical or orthopedic impairments 9.06.03.01

- Collaborate with other professionals to determine the most appropriate bicycle or tricycle with possible modifications for an individual with a physical or orthopedic impairment
- Attach a unicycle to front of wheelchair to convert to a tricycle
- Incorporate the use of hand crank cycle and/or standard adult tricycle to facilitate participation in physical education activities

Know adaptations made to cycles to accommodate individuals with physical or orthopedic impairments 9.06.03.02

- Collaborate with other professionals to determine the appropriate adaptations for a cycle for an individual with a physical or orthopedic impairment
- Incorporate the use of foot sandals, hip and chest straps, and/or back and neck supports to facilitate participation in physical education activities

Understand how the use of mobility aids for individuals who are visually impaired enhances their participation in physical education activities

Know types of mobility aids for individuals with visual impairments 9.06.04.01

- Collaborate with other professionals to determine the appropriate mobility aids for an individual with a visual impairment participating in a physical education environment
- Incorporate cane walking, sighted guide techniques, partner assists, and/or guide wire or rope to enhance participation in physical education activities

Teaching

Teaching Styles: Demonstrate various teaching styles in order to promote learning in physical education

Understand the command style of teaching

Understand the effectiveness of using command-style teaching with individuals with disabilities in order to promote learning in physical education 10.01.01.01

- Provide clear, concise, and simple language when needed
- Use specific, clear, concise verbal cues to highlight points
- Use total communication as needed
- Use visual cues to demonstrate skill such as using a colored sock to show kicking foot

Understand the effectiveness of demonstrating an activity using a command-style approach for individuals with disabilities 10.01.01.02

- Secure students' attention through a command or other communication means before demonstrating
- Perform demonstrations in an environment that minimizes distractions for individuals who have short attention spans or who are easily distracted
- Perform demonstrations with verbal cues to maximize sensory information input
- Perform demonstration in a position that allows the individual to best receive information such as individuals who are deaf or hard of hearing

Understand the effectiveness of class organization and control using the command style of teaching 10.01.01.03

- Organize the class so that individuals with disabilities such as autism or mental retardation perform skills under structured class rules and conditions
- Structure the class so that individuals with disabilities complete assigned skills on command
- Establish a physical activity environment that remains the same in terms of format, procedures, and routines for individuals with disabilities, such as autism, mental retardation, and blindness
- Teach class so that individuals with a variety of disabilities practice the activity together under the direct supervision of the general physical educator

Understand the reciprocal style of teaching

Understand the effectiveness of using reciprocal-style teaching with individuals with disabilities in order to promote learning in physical education 10.01.02.01

- Guide students to be peer tutors or partners to teach individuals with disabilities
- Design activities that allow individuals to work together in pairs
- Design activities so peer tutors can see progress

Understand the importance of training peer tutors to effectively participate in reciprocal teaching environment with individuals with disabilities in order to promote learning 10.01.02.02

- Teach peer tutors to provide a continuum of prompts from minimum to maximum for individuals with disabilities
- Train peer tutors to communicate effectively with individuals with disabilities
- Train peer tutors to provide appropriate feedback to individuals with disabilities
- Train peer tutors to use their initiative and provide alternative progressions and skill techniques when their partner is not experiencing success with the activity being attempted

Understand what qualities to look for when selecting and assigning peer tutors to work with individuals with disabilities 10.01.02.03

- Identify peer tutors with a tolerant positive nature and mature disposition
- Identify peer tutors with good communication skills, preferably in more than one mode of communication, such as ability to use communication boards or an additional language such as sign language, Spanish, etc.
- Identify peer tutors with ability to model skills correctly

Understand the task teaching style

Understand the effectiveness of using task-style teaching with individuals with disabilities in order to promote learning in physical education 10.01.03.01

- Design activities and instructions to the ability level of the individuals with disabilities such as using picture activity cards to depict the desired skill to be performed
- Use a variety of equipment, modified if necessary, in each activity to ensure successful completion of each assigned task
- Select tasks that can be performed by the individual with a disability individually and safely
- Identify and create goal levels for each skill or activity that will allow all individuals with disabilities to achieve individual levels of success at the same task

Understand how to organize a class environment to promote a task-style teaching method for individuals with disabilities 10.01.03.02

- Design the class activities in a circuit type or station arrangement
- Arrange the class so that individuals with disabilities can move quickly and safely from one task to the next
- Arrange the class so that individuals with disabilities can perform tasks individually and safely
- Design tasks with multiple successful outcomes to allow individuals with disabilities to develop coping and adapting strategies

Understand how to effectively analyze progress and provide feedback to individuals with disabilities using a task-style teaching method 10.01.03.03

- Identify goals and objectives specific to the needs of the individual with disabilities
- Use self-recording to allow individuals with disabilities to monitor their own progress and assess their own gains

Understand individualized style of teaching

Understand the effectiveness of using individualized-style teaching with individuals with disabilities in order to promote learning in physical education 10.01.04.01

- Design physical activities based on the specific needs of the individual
- Create an individualized education program based on the specific needs of individuals with disabilities
- Use individualized charts and reports to determine the progress of individuals with disabilities
- Create activity opportunities with variable levels of success (e.g., using stations) to enable all individuals to achieve some measure of success in the same activity
- Provide instruction and feedback to the individual with disabilities in that individual's prime mode of communication

Understand how to assess individuals with disabilities to determine present level of performance and IEP 10.01.04.02

- Select appropriate assessment instruments specific to the individual with disabilities (see Standards 4 and 8)

- Develop instruments based on the task analysis
- Determine the level of independence for each individual based on assessment information

Understand how to provide effective feedback using an individualized style of teaching 10.01.04.03

- Provide personal recording methods such as self-recording progress cards and charts
- Design tasks and activities that provide individualized feedback of results and information on the successful completion of the task such as lights and buzzers that sound when the ball has gone through the hoop

Understand the guided discovery style of teaching

Understand the effectiveness of using guided discovery-style teaching with individuals with disabilities in order to promote learning in physical education 10.01.05.01

- Develop problem-solving techniques involving challenging questions and tasks to promote adaptation and coping strategies for individuals with disabilities
- Develop problem-solving techniques based on naturally occurring obstacles and challenges that occur in the everyday environment
- Guide the student, when appropriate, to efficient task completion
- Develop a hierarchy of problem solving from single to multiple tasks

Understand the divergent or exploratory style of teaching

Understand the effectiveness of using divergent- or exploratory-style teaching with individuals with disabilities in order to promote learning in physical education 10.01.06.01

- Select tasks for instruction that have multiple methods of successful completion for individuals with disabilities
- Choose activity areas that are appropriate for the future needs of the individuals with disabilities
- Use praise and feedback to foster alternative methods of completing the skill or task
- Use the concept of generalization to challenge the individual with disabilities to complete a specific task under different environmental conditions and circumstances
- Encourage and praise effort and creativity in addition to task completion

Understand how to present tasks using a divergent- or exploratory-style of teaching that is appropriate for the individual with disabilities 10.01.06.02

- Identify tasks and skills that are developmentally as well as age appropriate for individuals with disabilities
- Use group activities to promote cooperative learning and development

Understand how to effectively use feedback and praise when using a divergent or exploratory style of teaching for individuals with disabilities 10.01.06.03

- Use corrective feedback, which provides information that indicates the correct way to perform the task for individuals with disabilities
- Use comments that promote alternative variations to complete the task to foster independent coping and adapting strategies for the individual with disabilities

Understand the cooperative learning style of teaching

Understand the effectiveness of using the cooperative learning style of teaching with individuals with disabilities in order to promote learning in physical education 10.01.07.01

- Use group activities to foster incidental learning such as social values and interaction skills in individuals with disabilities
- Use noncompetitive tasks and environments to promote cooperation and interaction among individuals with disabilities and individuals without disabilities in a nonthreatening environment
- Use group activities that include individuals with disabilities to challenge current concepts on how some tasks should be performed and to promote variations that allow everyone to successfully complete the task
- Provide culminating activities that reinforce cooperation

Teaching Behaviors: Understand the various teaching behaviors needed to promote learning

Understand various instructional cues such as verbal directions, demonstrations, and physical guidance

Understand the importance of using various instructional cues to prompt certain individuals with disabilities to complete tasks 10.02.01.01

- Implement instructional and environmental cues based on the needs of individuals with disabilities from least to most intrusive
- Implement instructional and environmental cues based on the unique needs of the individual with a disability such as having an individual with mental retardation step in a hoop in order to cue him or her to step with opposition while throwing
- Avoid unknowingly eliciting abnormal reflexes when providing physical guidance
- Use other types of instructional cues if one is not effective in communicating to the individual's unique needs or disability such as Braille for an individual who is blind
- Use peers to demonstrate instructional cues such as demonstrating a skill to an individual with a disability
- Avoid overcueing or overdemonstrating in the selected modality for an individual with a disability such as an individual with attention-deficit/hyperactivity disorder
- Transition individual reliance on instructional cues to independent completion of the task

Understand the process of task analysis

Understand the use of task analysis procedures to promote skill learning in individuals with disabilities 10.02.02.01

- Break skills down along a hierarchy in order to meet the unique needs of individuals with disabilities
- Provide the prerequisite and ancillary skills needed to complete the skill targeted for instruction
- Develop an ecological task analysis that includes the unique needs of the learner and the environment such as teaching the skill in various settings (i.e., school and community)
- Assess skill development and progress using a skill- or student-specific task analysis testing tool (qualitative) that also accounts for level of independence/ dependence during evaluation and teaching (see Standard 8)

Understand the concept of time on task

Understand the importance of providing maximal time on task in each lesson to maximize learning for individuals with disabilities in physical education 10.02.03.01

- Plan lessons allowing the individual with disabilities to receive as many opportunities to perform the task as possible

- Organize the teaching environment so that transition time between task responses and activities is kept to a minimum
- Use behavior management techniques such as incentives/rewards for completing the task and teaching environment strategies such as removing other items or activities that may distract the student in order to sustain performance during time on task
- Keep instructional information concise such as focusing on key words and phrases

Understand qualitative skill teaching

Understand the importance of teaching qualitative aspects of skills and activities to individuals with disabilities 10.02.04.01

- Teach the correct form necessary to perform the skill
- Promote qualitative aspects of skills that facilitate normalization and are socially inconspicuous for individuals with disabilities such as pedaling an exercise bicycle
- Promote generalization such as how to correctly and safely use a stair climber exercise machine at the local gymnasium or health club
- Use modified equipment to enable the individual with disabilities to complete the task in as close to a normal manner as possible or on a functional skill level

Understand quantitative skill teaching

Understand the importance of using quantitative aspects of skills to teach individuals with disabilities in physical education 10.02.05.01

- Emphasize the product outcome of a skill such as scoring a basket in basketball
- Use group cooperation activities in integrated settings to promote task completion
- Emphasize outcome aspects of skill instruction that allow the individual with disabilities to successfully participate in socially normal environments such as hitting a tennis ball back over the net and into the court in a game of tennis
- Use adapted equipment such as using a bowling ramp to bowl that allows the individual with disabilities to participate successfully in socially normal environment (see Standard 9)

Understand teacher pacing of lesson

Understand the importance of pacing activities to meet the unique needs of the individual with a disability 10.02.06.01

- Time activities to maintain interest
- Plan activities of short duration in a lesson for individuals with a short attention span
- Plan frequent rest breaks in a lesson for individuals with disabilities such as those with low fitness levels or obesity
- Establish lesson activity sequence that alternates high- and low-intensity activities to foster fitness improvement

Understand how to communicate learner expectations and content

Understand the importance of using various means of communication to provide teacher expectations to individuals with disabilities such as the latest communication technology (see Standard 9) 10.02.07.01

- Communicate with individuals in their primary learning modality (e.g., total communication with individuals who are deaf)
- Keep communication simple for those students who are limited in cognition (e.g., posting pictures of class rules for those who cannot read)
- Allow individuals with disabilities to record their own results so they can monitor their progress toward the established goals

- Allow individuals with disabilities to be part of program planning and where applicable have them sign the program plan

Understand the type of social climate that promotes interaction

Understand how to use peer tutors to promote social interaction and normal social values with individuals with disabilities 10.02.08.01

- Select peer tutors with appropriate communication skills, social skills, and maturity level
- Select peer tutors from the community who demonstrate skills needed by individuals with disabilities
- Educate peer tutors to communicate and interact with individuals with disabilities
- Provide partner and group activities that foster appropriate interactions for individuals with and without disabilities
- Play cooperative games that foster social interaction and trust for individuals with and without disabilities (see Standard 9)

Understand knowledge of feedback, knowledge of performance, and knowledge of results

Understand the importance of providing positive, specific, immediate feedback to individuals with disabilities 10.02.09.01

- Provide feedback that individuals with disabilities can understand and comprehend such as using short action word statements for individuals with mental retardation
- Design activities for individuals with disabilities that provide knowledge of performance through auditory and visual feedback
- Provide immediate feedback for individuals with disabilities to establish a response–consequence relationship between the feedback and the performed behavior
- Provide the majority of feedback for individuals with disabilities in a positive way

Understand how to determine progress and make changes to fit individual needs

Understand the importance of monitoring progress specific to individuals with disabilities 10.02.10.01

- Use appropriate assessment that is relevant to the specific individual and his or her disability (see Standard 8)
- Conduct informal and formal assessment of the progress of individuals with disabilities on a regular basis
- Use multiple tests and assessment methods and criteria to determine the progress of individuals with disabilities

Understand how to make changes in teaching to meet the needs of individuals with disabilities based on assessment data 10.02.10.02

- Reevaluate goals and objectives (program, student, teacher) on a regular basis for individuals with disabilities
- Develop task analysis checklists with sequential steps that are appropriate to the needs and developmental level of individuals with disabilities
- Use task analysis breakdowns to determine intermediate steps for skills that have not been attained at the end of the teaching period for individuals with disabilities
- Use adapted equipment and/or alternative teaching techniques to make immediate changes during the lesson when an individual with disabilities continually fails to complete a task or activity with existing teaching methods

Applied Behavior Analysis Principles: Understand the principles of adapted behavior analysis to promote learning

Understand how to select and define specific behaviors to be changed or maintained

Understand that individuals with disabilities may exhibit more severe and unique behaviors (see Standard 6) 10.03.01.01

- Identify self-injurious behaviors that may be exhibited by individuals with autism, depression, serious emotional behaviors, and other disabilities
- Identify aggressive behaviors that may be harmful to others

Understand how to observe, chart, and analyze the behavior to be changed

Understand how to systematically observe, chart, and analyze the unique behaviors exhibited by individuals with disabilities 10.03.02.01

- Use members of multidisciplinary team to assist with observing, charting, and analyzing the behaviors exhibited by individuals with disabilities
- Analyze student information from a variety of formal and informal settings
- Use frequency, duration, and intensity recording procedures when needed (see Standard 4)
- Use continuous interval recording or time sampling procedures when needed (see Standard 4)

Understand a variety of strategies for changing behaviors

Understand that individuals with disabilities may require the application of a number of unique behavior change strategies and programs 10.03.03.01

- Implement a continuum of behavior change strategies depending on the needs of the individual with a disability from prevention to punishment
- Implement consistent behavior change strategies with other team members and when possible across various settings such as the classroom, physical education setting, and home
- Implement a variety of behavior change strategies as appropriate

Understand how to evaluate the behavior change plan

Understand the importance of evaluating the behavior intervention plan in individuals with disabilities in order to meet the unique needs necessary to change behavior 10.03.04.01

- Include behavior intervention plan information with the individual's IEP, teaching units, lesson plans, and other progress reports
- Communicate behavior change plan results with other team members who work with the individual

Preventive Strategies: Understand preventive management strategies in order to promote learning

Understand how to use signals for getting the class' attention and for starting and stopping the class

Understand the use of specific signals to get the attention of individuals with disabilities 10.04.01.01

- Use sound signals (i.e., tambourine, whistle) for individuals with disabilities such as those who are blind
- Use visual and tactile signals for individuals with disabilities such as those who are deaf

Understand how to use routines and transitional procedures from one activity to the next

Understand the routines and transitional procedures that can be used with individuals with disabilities 10.04.02.01

- Communicate class routines in a meaningful way such as posting schedules or using flip charts
- Communicate clear, concise transitional procedures such as rotating clockwise from one activity to the next

Understand how to organize the class into groups and formations based on the nature of the activity

Understand that certain individuals with disabilities may need a smaller student–teacher ratio (e.g., distribution of students) 10.04.03.01

- Use paraprofessionals and peer tutors for individuals who require more attention
- Use stations or a reciprocal teaching style
- Use small group formations (e.g., only one or two individuals at a station)

Understand how to deal with interruptions while teaching

Understand that certain individuals with disabilities such as those with attention span deficits may seek constant attention and interrupt the class 10.04.04.01

- Identify cause(s) of interruption(s) that may be specific to an individual with a disability
- Implement specific plans, strategies, and signals such as proximity control, extinction, or time-out procedures

Understand how to teach individual goal-setting strategies

Understand the importance of setting realistic goals based on the limitations, needs, and strengths of individuals with disabilities 10.04.05.01

- Use goal setting to motivate individuals with disabilities to participate in various adapted physical education environments
- Implement realistic sequential steps to achieve goals

Understand how to teach self-management

Understand the importance of self-management at a developmentally appropriate level for individuals with disabilities 10.04.06.01

- Identify the most appropriate self-management techniques for the developmental level of the individual
- Teach individuals with disabilities to use self-management techniques

Increasing Behaviors: Knowledge of positive teaching methods for maintaining and increasing student behavior in order to promote learning

Understand modeling as a teaching method

Understand the importance of the teacher and individuals without disabilities modeling appropriate behavior to individuals with disabilities 10.05.01.01

- Model appropriate behavior to individuals with disabilities
- Use peer tutor models to demonstrate appropriate behavior to individuals with disabilities

Understand prompting as a teaching method

Understand the use of prompts such as verbal, demonstration, and physical guidance and the hierarchy of prompts from less intrusive to more intrusive based on the individual's disability 10.05.02.01

- Select prompts based on individual needs (e.g., physical prompts for individuals who are blind)
- Use more intrusive prompts as needed
- Avoid physical guidance for individuals with tactile sensitivity
- Fade prompts while maintaining performance

Understand shaping as a teaching method

Understand how to use shaping strategies such as task analysis and successive approximation with individuals with disabilities 10.05.03.01

- Teach and reinforce only those parts of the skill that are necessary
- Use qualitative and quantitative aspects in developing a shaping plan for individuals with disabilities

Understand chaining as a teaching method

Understand when to use forward chaining, reverse chaining, and total task presentation depending on the individual's disability 10.05.04.01

- Use total task presentation prior to forward or backward chaining
- Implement different forms of progressive forward and reverse chaining of skills depending on the needs of the individual
- Use reverse chaining when needed

Understand social reinforcement as a teaching method

Understand how to use various nonverbal and verbal social reinforcement strategies based on the individual's disability 10.05.05.01

- Identify a variety of social reinforcers that may appeal to individuals with disabilities, such as age-appropriate social reinforcers (e.g., smile, high five, shaking hands)
- Use verbal reinforcement at a level the individual with a disability can comprehend such as using action words or simple two-word statements
- Use mercury switches to activate reinforcers

Understand tangible reinforcement as a teaching method

Understand the use of tangible reinforcers with individuals with disabilities 10.05.06.01

- Select reinforcers that are highly reinforcing for each individual
- Provide age-appropriate tangible reinforcers
- Continue social reinforcement and fade tangible reinforcers as appropriate
- Monitor progress when using tangible reinforcers
- Fade out tangible reinforcers

Understand physical activity reinforcement as a teaching method

Understand the use of physical activity reinforcers with individuals with disabilities 10.05.07.01

- Use physical activity reinforcers to assist individuals with disabilities to make progress toward IEP goals and objectives
- Use physical activity reinforcers to develop leisure and recreational choices for community involvement

Understand reinforcement menus, token economies, and point systems as teaching methods

Understand the use of reinforcement menus, token economies, and contingency point systems with individuals with disabilities 10.05.08.01

- Match system (e.g., token economy) to the individual's comprehension level
- Use age-appropriate items on reinforcement menu
- Identify individual reinforcers that are highly reinforcing
- Monitor progress when using these techniques
- Fade techniques while maintaining progress

Understand written contracts as a teaching method

Understand the value of written contracts when developing accountability in individuals with disabilities 10.05.09.01

- Use written contracts modified to the comprehension level of the individual
- Include essential components of a written contract such as the target behavior and consequences

Understand group and individual contingencies as teaching methods

Understand value of group and individual contingencies in changing behaviors in individuals with disabilities 10.05.10.01

- Use group contingencies when peer pressure is effective in changing behavior such as with individuals with a behavior disorder
- Provide contingencies that are achievable for the lowest functioning individual within a group
- Develop different individual contingencies for those individuals who cannot conform to the group contingency

Understand reinforcement schedules as a teaching method

Understand reinforcement schedules and their progression to use with individuals with disabilities 10.05.11.01

- Provide continuous reinforcement to those individuals learning a skill for the first time
- Provide reinforcement schedules such as ratio and interval reinforcement to assist individuals with disabilities who are learning to maintain or generalize a behavior over time
- Implement a ratio schedule of reinforcement by reinforcing the specified frequency of responses
- Implement an interval schedule of reinforcement by reinforcing the specified duration of the performance of behavior

Understand differential reinforcements (DR) as a teaching method

Understand that DR is a method of manipulating the reinforcement schedule and may be used to increase or decrease the rate at which an individual with a disability exhibits a behavior 10.05.12.01

- Identify DR as a viable strategy to increase appropriate behavior and decrease inappropriate behavior
- Use DR for omission of an inappropriate behavior for a specified period of time (0 times in 10 minutes)
- Use DR for maintaining a low rate of behavior for a specified period of time (less than 2 times in 15 minutes)
- Use DR to reinforce incompatible behaviors
- Use DR to reinforce alternative behaviors

Decreasing Behaviors: Use different methods, along a continuum from less to more intrusive, only after positive methods have been ineffective

Understand extinction as a teaching method

Understand the importance of using extinction for individuals with disabilities 10.06.01.01

- Ignore mild forms of inappropriate behavior with individuals who are constantly seeking attention while reinforcing alternative forms of appropriate behaviors
- Avoid using extinction with severe behaviors such as self-abuse
- Recognize that extinction is effective when attention is acting as the reinforcer

Understand response cost as a teaching method

Understand response cost as a technique that removes reinforcement and may be effectively used with individuals with disabilities 10.06.02.01

- Withdraw earned reinforcers contingent on the occurrence of the inappropriate behavior
- Use response cost as an alternative to physically or psychologically aversive strategies
- Use reinforcement of an appropriate behavior in conjunction with response cost to deter an inappropriate behavior
- Use response cost effectively with both individuals and groups

Understand overcorrection as a teaching method

Understand the value of overcorrection in teaching appropriate behavior while eliminating inappropriate behavior in individuals with disabilities 10.06.03.01

- Use restitutional overcorrection such as cleaning gymnasium walls by allowing the individual to experience the effort required by others to restore the damaged environment
- Use positive practice overcorrection by allowing the individual or group to practice the correct behavior numerous times

Understand time-out procedures as a teaching method

Understand that different time-out procedures are effective for individuals with disabilities such as observation, seclusion, and isolation 10.06.04.01

- Identify legal aspects involved with time-out procedures
- Administer the proper steps for using time-out procedures with individuals with disabilities

- Use observational time-out by having the individual placed in time-out and allowed to continue to observe the activity
- Use seclusion time-out by allowing the individual to remain in the geographical area but not observe the activity
- Use isolation time-out by requiring the individual to leave the physical activity environment under supervision

Understand paired stimuli (pairing primary and secondary reinforcers) as a teaching method

Understand that paired stimuli may be used for both increasing and decreasing behaviors in individuals with disabilities 10.06.05.01

- Use paired stimuli to reinforce incompatible behaviors
- Combine reinforcement and punishment techniques to increase the effectiveness of a form of punishment that is not effective in reducing a behavior
- Use pairing techniques with individuals with more severe disabilities

Understand strong punishers (corporal punishment) as a teaching method

Understand that the use of strong punishers with individuals with disabilities such as aversives, physical restraints, and corporal acts are very controversial and may not be allowed in many school districts or by a student's parents 10.06.06.01

- Modify management techniques based on the knowledge that the administration of strong punishers is usually not a behavior builder
- Modify management techniques based on knowledge that administration of strong punishers is usually considered beyond the expertise of the adapted physical educator and should only be used with proper training and documentation of the technique
- Explain the negative side effects of using corporal punishment
- Explain what the moral, ethical, and legal issues are for using corporal punishment

---

Other Management Methods: Use other management methods/models for increasing, maintaining, and decreasing student behavior in order to promote learning

---

Understand the value responsibility model as a teaching method

Understand that most individuals with disabilities can benefit from programs that promote self-control of behaviors 10.07.01.01

- Develop social skills by using the value responsibility model hierarchy of levels (e.g., irresponsibility, self-control, involvement, self-responsibility, and caring)
- Use appropriate strategies such as modeling, contracts, goal setting, reflection time, student sharing, and journal writing to implement the different levels of the value responsibility model

Understand teacher effectiveness training as a teaching method

Understand the value of effective communication between the teacher and individuals with disabilities 10.07.02.01

- Use effective communication methods with the individual such as active listening
- Use two-way communication to enhance learning and minimize behavioral problems in the physical education setting such as using a chalkboard to foster communication and questioning between an instructor and an individual who is deaf

Understand reality therapy as a teaching method

Understand that many individuals with disabilities can be taught to accept responsibility for their behavior 10.07.03.01

- Teach individuals with disabilities to acknowledge their behavioral deviations and be responsible for developing a plan to change
- Help individuals with disabilities focus on the here and now and develop a plan to achieve goals and stay on track
- Use questions and classroom meetings as potential methods for certain individuals with disabilities

Understand social discipline as a teaching method

Understand that communication between the teacher and individuals with disabilities involves social interaction 10.07.04.01

- Modify styles of interaction because misbehaviors may be the results of inappropriate needs such as attention, power, and getting revenge
- Use student reflection to identify antecedent behaviors
- Encourage and apply logical consequences as viable techniques for developing appropriate behavior in individuals with disabilities

Consultation and Staff Development

Motivation: Understand how motivation influences behavior

Understand Maslow's theory as the basis for planning consultation and staff development

Understand the motivation of general practitioners teaching individuals with disabilities 11.01.01.01

- Use a survey instrument to determine teachers' needs prior to inservice
- Use techniques to reduce intimidation and fear
- Provide successful experiences for teachers so they feel capable of teaching individuals with disabilities

Administrative Skills: Knowledge of program organization and administrative hierarchy

Understand administrative organizational structure of education agencies/services

Understand how decisions are made in education agencies/services 11.02.01.01

- Identify the key personnel in the decision-making process
- Implement strategies to change organizational behavior
- Encourage administrators' interaction with teachers during inservice presentation

Understand program organization

Understand how curriculum decisions are made for teaching individuals with disabilities 11.02.02.01

- Explain the ABC model which includes program planning, assessment, implementation planning, teaching, evaluation, and modification strategy
- Monitor implementation of individualized education program in general physical education class

Understand effects of the living environment and the parent/guardian intervention

Understand strategies for communication with living environments 11.02.03.01

- Instruct parents and guardians on how to teach physical fitness and motor skills at home
- Encourage parents and guardians to be proactive in providing sport and leisure opportunities on a segregated and integrated basis

Know how to describe legal rights and responsibilities of parents and guardians of individuals with disabilities 11.02.03.03

- Identify advocates to assist parents and guardians in ensuring appropriate physical education programming
- Inform parents and guardians of their right to due process

Understand the role of community-based activity programs

Know how to identify community resources for individuals with disabilities 11.02.04.01

- Facilitate transportation possibilities for individuals to participate in community programming
- Develop physical fitness and motor skills that facilitate transition to community recreation facilities

Understand identification of funding sources

Know how to describe how funds can be obtained at various levels 11.02.05.01

- Seek funding from community service organizations
- Contact grants officer for local education agency
- Contact grants officer for state education agency
- Contact foundations that fund programs and equipment for individuals with disabilities

Group Dynamics: Demonstrate knowledge of team approaches for providing educational programs for all individuals

Understand the team approach for providing educational programs

Understand the multidisciplinary team process related to individuals with disabilities (see Standard 15) 11.03.01.01

- Establish a working relationship with members of motor team such as physical therapists, occupational therapists, and speech therapists
- Use communication skills to enhance cooperation and mutual respect among team members

Understand the ecological approach related to individuals with disabilities 11.03.01.04

- Include families in the decision-making process (see Standard 15)
- Collaborate with the community professionals to provide physical education services to individuals with disabilities
- Use the available expertise when planning a physical education program for individuals with disabilities

Understand the nature of group cohesiveness

Understand the forces acting on members to remain in the group to improve physical education services provided to individuals with disabilities 11.03.02.01

- Create incentives for providing physical education services to individuals with disabilities
- Establish group goals so there is an expectancy of outcomes related to improving physical education services to individuals with disabilities
- Plan group activities that are valuable to the members and will improve physical education services to individuals with disabilities
- Evaluate success of group related to the expected outcomes of improving physical education services for individuals with disabilities

Understand situational leadership

Understand the importance of developing professional relationships related to working with others to provide physical education services to individuals with disabilities 11.03.03.01

- Develop positive interaction with teachers who have effective teaching behaviors
- Use teachers with effective teaching behaviors to mentor other teachers who are less effective

Understand task orientation related to working with others to provide physical education services to individuals with disabilities

- Use explicit communication related to expectations in terms of performance in teaching physical education to individuals with disabilities
- Provide physical educators with the information they need to acquire the technical competence to teach physical education to individuals with disabilities

Understand cultural issues related to group dynamics

Understand differences in the behavior and lifestyle of other cultures 11.03.04.01

- Appreciate and accommodate differences in the behavior and lifestyle of other cultures
- Determine what language is spoken in the home environment
- Refrain from stereotyping individuals who look similar
- Establish rapport with ethnically diverse individuals by being sensitive to their cultural belief systems related to sport and exercise

Interpersonal Communication Skills: Knowledge of the ability to interact with, discuss, and write about individuals

Understand active listening as a communication skill

Know how to identify components of active listening useful in communication as an adapted physical education consultant 11.04.01.01

- Establish a physical education environment that will allow for good communication between the teacher and the consultant
- Use active listening when communicating with others

Understand the dynamics of advocacy groups

Know how to identify strategies used by advocacy groups for individuals with disabilities 11.04.02.01

- Teach individuals with disabilities about the laws that govern their right to access quality physical education, recreation, and sport programs and services
- Promote and defend the rights of individuals with disabilities to have access to public recreational facilities

Psychological Dimensions: Knowledge of the cognitive processes that affect behavior

Understand attitude theories

Understand contact theory as related to individuals with disabilities 11.05.01.01

- Establish contact between individuals with and without disabilities that includes cooperative physical activities
- Establish contact between individuals with and without disabilities in a physical education setting that emphasizes the similarities between individuals with and without disabilities

Understand mediated generalization theory as related to individuals with disabilities
11.05.01.02

- Organize successful experiences in game and movement situations in which individuals with and without disabilities participate together
- Select game activities in which all individuals in an integrated physical activity program can perform and be successful

Understand assimilation-contrast theory as related to individuals with disabilities
11.05.01.03

- Use inservice training to promote positive attitudes toward individuals with disabilities
- Prepare the physical education class to receive a new student who has a disability

Understand stigma theory as related to individuals with disabilities 11.05.01.04

- Integrate individuals with disabilities into physical education activities with the support they need relative to type and degree of disability
- Integrate individuals with disabilities into activities that utilize abilities and strengths

Understand interpersonal relations theory as related to individuals with disabilities
11.05.01.05

- Design a peer tutoring program for physical education that is structured and long term (see Standard 10)
- Provide opportunities for individuals to observe highly competitive sporting events for individuals with disabilities, such as a track meet for individuals who are wheelchair users

Understand group dynamics theory as related to individuals with disabilities
11.05.01.06

- Provide input to teachers as to how their attitude toward individuals with disabilities affects others' attitudes
- Empower teachers to plan lessons that facilitate success and stress equity

Understand cognitive dissonance as related to individuals with disabilities
11.05.01.07

- Conduct activities that simulate disabling conditions during physical education
- Provide new experiences for students without disabilities, such as using a wheelchair for a day

Understand reasoned action theory as related to individuals with disabilities
11.05.01.08

- Provide a clear purpose and value for participation in adapted physical activities for all students before beginning the activity
- Motivate all students to participate together in an integrated physical activity setting

Consulting Models: Knowledge of how to utilize various consulting models

Understand prescription mode

Understand that adapted physical education consultants provide plans or aid in the selection of strategies for predetermined problems 11.06.01.01

- Conduct assessments and write the IEP for the direct service provider (see Standard 8)
- Provide one-to-one consulting sessions with the direct service provider

Understand provision mode

Understand that adapted physical education consultants provide direct services to individuals as needed 11.06.02.01

- Provide direct physical education services to individuals with disabilities when appropriate
- Model desired teaching behaviors

Understand collaboration mode

Understand that adapted physical education consultants respond to requests by engaging in mutual efforts to understand the problem, devise an action plan, and implement the plan 11.06.03.01

- Engage in a problem-solving relationship with the direct service provider
- Work with the direct service provider to select mutually agreeable strategies and ways to implement them

Understand mediation mode

Understand that adapted physical education consultants respond to requests from two or more consultees to help them accomplish an agreement or reconciliation by serving as a facilitator 11.06.04.01

- Facilitate solutions for quality physical education services for students with disabilities when teachers and administrators are in a disagreement
- Facilitate positive relationships between parents and guardians and direct service providers when disagreements occur, without dictating solutions

Program Evaluation

Student Outcomes: Understand the value to program evaluation of measuring student achievement

Monitor the effectiveness of the assessment plan and make appropriate revisions

Understand different methods for evaluating program effectiveness 12.01.01.01

- Use individual progress on goals and objectives as an indicator of program effectiveness
- Use unanticipated outcomes as an indication of program effectiveness

Understand the advantages and limitations of formal testing 12.01.01.02

- Describe how the attributes of learners influence formal testing procedures
- Explain the effect on formal testing procedures of the preferred learning style(s) of individuals with disabilities
- Select instruments that are valid for the age and suspected disability of the individual being tested
- Modify formal testing procedures to accommodate the preferred learning styles of individuals with disabilities

Understand the advantages and limitations of informal testing 12.01.01.03

- Use evaluation in the assessment process of determining motor performance needs of individuals with disabilities
- Use formative evaluation techniques and apply them to individuals with disabilities
- Use summative evaluation techniques and apply them to individuals with disabilities
- Modify evaluation instruments and explain the effect of these modifications on validity and reliability
- Write realistic and functional goals for individuals with disabilities utilizing appropriate standards of performance
- Explain the differences in validity and reliability between instruments that are used for making placement decisions and instruments used for determining individual progress

Understand how to use available resources to evaluate an individual's needs for modified equipment and/or learning materials 12.01.01.04

- Justify appropriate modification of equipment or materials
- Seek outside funding to supplement available resources as needed

Use existing criteria for quality physical education programs in terms of curriculum accessibility, appropriateness, and frequency and duration of program delivery

Understand how to compare curricula with existing criteria for quality physical education programs 12.01.02.01

- Use developmentally appropriate curricula for individuals with disabilities
- Use functionally appropriate curricula for individuals with disabilities

Understand how to justify program content based on evaluation standards 12.01.02.02

- Write goals and instructional objectives that are measurable and justifiable based on evaluation standards
- Discuss goals and instructional objectives with other professionals
- Use developmentally and functionally appropriate goals and instructional objectives for individuals with disabilities

Understand how to monitor the effectiveness of the program plan and make appropriate revisions in program content 12.01.02.03

- Select a timeline for implementing revised content for a smooth and easy transition for individuals with disabilities into general classes
- Document intended program outcomes

Understand how to match program content with program components of activities addressing physical and motor fitness; fundamental motor skills and patterns; skills in aquatics, dance, and individual and group games and sports; as well as functional living skills 12.01.02.04

- Compare duration of time spent on program components with needs of individuals with disabilities
- Compare the developmental and functional appropriateness of program components with needs of individuals with disabilities

Understand how to measure the effectiveness of program implementation based on the plan and make appropriate revisions 12.01.02.05

- Distinguish between effective and ineffective service delivery for each individual with a disability
- Modify the service delivery model to meet the individualized needs of the student

Understand how to evaluate the effectiveness of various service delivery models such as collaboration, consultation, inclusion, and integration 12.01.02.06

- Discuss the strengths and weaknesses of various service delivery models as they relate to meeting the unique needs of individuals with disabilities
- Discuss the degree to which different models are being implemented in the LEA

Program Operations: Understand the importance of monitoring the quality of program operations

Understand the legal requirements for accessibility of physical education facilities for individuals with disabilities (see Standard 5)

Understand how to recognize and use instruments for evaluating accessibility of physical education facilities 12.02.01.01

- Evaluate accessibility of physical education facilities using architectural standards to accommodate individuals with disabilities
- Recommend modifications or retrofitting where needed to aid facility accessibility for individuals with disabilities

Recognize the importance of properly functioning wheelchairs and orthopedic appliances

Understand how to evaluate the functional operations of wheelchairs and other orthopedic appliances (see Standard 9) 12.02.02.01

- Describe adjustments for wheelchairs enabling sport participation by individuals with disabilities
- Describe adjustments for braces and other appliances enabling sport participation by individuals with disabilities
- Recommend available resources for the repair of wheelchairs and other orthopedic appliances

Recognize the need for staff training, additional administrative support, and reallocation of resources for assessment

Understand how to contribute to staff training by submitting ideas for programs to meet the needs of personnel development 12.02.03.01

- Conduct sessions for staff training addressing needs of colleagues
- Participate in staff training to improve skills and competencies in adapted physical education (see Standard 13)

Understand how to contribute to training of parents and families by submitting ideas for presentations (see Standard 15) 12.02.03.02

- Develop videotapes for parent and family training on issues related to adapted physical education
- Conduct training sessions for parents and families on how to work with their children in physical activity

Understand various methods of describing and recording the results of measurement and evaluation

Understand systematic observational techniques for recording academic learning time (ALT) 12.02.04.01

- Use event recording techniques to observe behavior
- Use duration recording techniques to observe behavior
- Use interval recording techniques to observe behavior
- Use time sampling techniques to observe behavior
- Explain the uses and limitations of systematic observational techniques
- Use unobtrusive measures such as rating scales, case studies, and anecdotal records
- Graph baseline data that have been collected over a preset interval of time

Understand how to use student self-report and/or peer evaluation data 12.02.04.02

- Use student self-report data when appropriate in formulating individualized program plans and goals
- Use peer evaluation data when appropriate in formulating individualized program plans and goals

Use performance profiles in reporting student achievement

Understand how to interpret performance profiles in reporting student achievement 12.02.05.01

- Use age-appropriate award systems in rewarding and motivating achievers
- Use forms of recognition other than awards for student achievement

Use grades to report student progress

Understand how letter grades can be supplemented to report progress of individuals with disabilities 12.02.06.01

- Interpret letter grades with an accompanying narrative
- Use a performance profile to interpret letter grades

Recognize the need for staff training, additional administrative support, and reallocation of resources for reporting and recording

Know resources available to support staff training 12.02.07.01

- Locate and confirm presenters for staff training
- Obtain additional resources for staff training

Demonstrate the ability to evaluate the degree to which a program meets professional standards of quality

Know how to conduct a self-study of program strengths and weaknesses 12.02.08.01

- Study the quality of the school–community environment in terms of mission, philosophy, climate, recognition of accomplishments, parent involvement, communication, and public relations
- Study the quality of the physical education program in terms of goals and objectives, curriculum organization, IEPs, equity, program evaluation process, program implementation, and dissemination of evaluation results
- Study the quality of the instruction in physical education in terms of individual characteristics, teacher characteristics, teacher–student interactions, classroom management, discipline, and individual evaluation
- Study the quality of facilities, equipment and safety practices, safety considerations, school medical records, and procedures (see Standard 9)

Consumer Satisfaction: Monitor indications of consumer satisfaction

Demonstrate knowledge of the caregivers' role in gathering information regarding students' attitudes toward physical education

Understand how to communicate with parents and guardians regarding students' attitudes toward physical education 12.03.01.01

- Recommend community resources for parents and guardians
- Explain methods used to communicate with parents and guardians to other professionals
- Establish ongoing communication with parents and guardians to obtain their input

Understand strategies to survey parents and guardians on their satisfaction with the physical education program 12.03.01.02

- Conduct satisfaction survey of parents and guardians
- Explain how the results of a parent or guardian survey can be used
- Recommend physical activity resources for parents or guardians that they can use or make

Recognize the value of student feedback in program evaluation

Understand how to use different methods of soliciting feedback from individuals with disabilities regarding program merit and weaknesses 12.03.02.01

- Survey students regarding their attitudes toward physical education and suggestions on curriculum offering
- Survey individuals for suggestions on curriculum offerings in physical education

Understand how to survey students for suggestions on curriculum offerings in physical education 12.03.02.02

- Explain how the results of a student survey can be used
- Use individual survey results to influence curricular offerings

Monitor student's behavior relative to approaching or avoiding physical activity as an indication of their enjoyment or dissatisfaction with the movement medium

Understand how to use nonverbal indicators of student's satisfaction with curricular offerings 12.03.03.01

- Record how frequently individuals initiate physical activity given a choice to select from a variety of activities
- Provide recognition for individuals who engage in physical activity outside of school programs

Understand strategies for surveying individuals about the vigorousness of their leisure time activities 12.03.03.02

- Explain how survey results may be used
- Refer individuals to programs for leisure time participation
- Use survey results in program planning

Continuing Education

Professional Growth: Understand how to remain current on issues and trends that influence the field of physical education

Understand the impact of federal statutes and mandates on the provision of physical education service delivery

Understand how to locate the Federal Register in order to access information related to individuals with disabilities 13.01.01.01

- Apply information in the *Federal Register* to maintain compliance with current legislation related to individuals with disabilities such as in Individuals with Disabilities Education Improvement Act (IDEA, 2004) and Americans with Disabilities Act (ADA, 2002)
- Synthesize information with local practices pertaining to individuals such as making reasonable accommodations within physical education programs

Understand information provided in the U.S. Department of Education Annual Report to Congress related to individuals with disabilities 13.01.01.02

- Access a copy of the *Annual Report to Congress* related to individuals with disabilities
- Interpret statistics relative to the implementation of IDEA (2004) in state education agencies (SEAs) and local education agencies (LEAs)
- Compare an LEA's implementation of IDEA with that of other LEAs, as amended, within a region of the state
- Compare state statistics on implementation of IDEA (2004) with other states
- Assess LEA's program to determine compliance with IDEA

Understand the current federal nomenclature related to individuals with disabilities 13.01.01.03

- Interpret federal abbreviations and acronyms such as Office of Special Education and Rehabilitative Services (OSERS), free and appropriate public education (FAPE), and regular education initiative (REI)
- Use federal abbreviations and acronyms in communications pertaining to compliance with federal regulations in physical education for individuals with disabilities

Understand how to access information through local offices of congressional leaders who are influential on matters related to individuals with disabilities

Know how to obtain the names of local legislators who are instrumental in the passage of issues related to individuals with disabilities 13.01.02.01

- Contact legislators who are instrumental in the passage of issues related to individuals with disabilities
- Participate in advocacy groups that attempt to lobby legislators who are instrumental in the passage of legislation related to individuals with disabilities

Understand how to identify how legislators vote on critical issues related to individuals with disabilities 13.01.02.02

- Access information through newspapers or *Congressional Record*
- Use information from the voting records of decisions at the local, state, and federal levels regarding adapted physical education

Know current changes of public laws and how these changes affect adapted physical education 13.01.02.03

- Use information about current changes in public laws to influence LEA policies and procedures related to the provision of adapted physical education
- Use information about current changes in public laws to influence the best practices in adapted physical education

Access information through the state department of education

Know how to access SEA's state plan for the implementation of IDEA (2004) 13.01.03.01

- Evaluate whether state plan includes procedures for implementing physical education for individuals with disabilities
- Evaluate procedures for implementing physical education mandates for students with disabilities

Know how to access LEA plans for the implementation of IDEA (2004) 13.01.03.02

- Evaluate whether local districts have developed procedures for implementing physical education for individuals with disabilities
- Evaluate and compare procedures for implementing physical education mandates for individuals with disabilities

Understand current state and local nomenclature related to individuals with disabilities 13.01.03.03

- Interpret state and local terminology related to individuals with disabilities
- Use state and local terminology in communications pertaining to compliance with regulations that affect physical education for individuals with disabilities

Be aware of governance as it is conducted by LEA

Understand how school boards or their equivalent operate on issues related to individuals with disabilities including the provision for adapted physical education 13.01.04.01

- Assist LEA in monitoring compliance with legislation designed to ensure adapted physical education for individuals requiring such services
- Advocate for adapted physical education services when issues requiring public hearing are necessary

Be aware of the positions of various professional organizations and groups on issues related to individuals with disabilities

Understand how to access information through professional organizations related to individuals with disabilities 13.01.05.01

- Attend local and state meetings to acquire legislative updates on issues related to individuals with disabilities
- Discuss current issues related to individuals with disabilities with other professionals in adapted physical education

Understand how to access information from individuals with disabilities 13.01.05.02

- Discuss current issues with parents/guardians or other advocacy groups for individuals with disabilities
- Discuss current issues with friends or colleagues with disabilities

Understand the nature of parent–professional communication to assist in the development of parent understanding of adapted physical education (see Standard 15) 13.01.05.03

- Involve parents/guardians in adapted physical education by making presentations or otherwise keeping them informed about their child's rights under IDEA 2004
- Disseminate information to parents/guardians and community to assist them in determining if the provision for adapted physical education is appropriate
- Assist or organize parents/guardians to advocate for appropriate adapted physical education services in the community

Current Literature: Keep up to date with current literature in physical education

Subscribe to and read journals in physical education

Know how to review literature regarding physical education for individuals with disabilities 13.02.01.01

- Implement new teaching strategies and methods for use in adapted physical education
- Support and use innovative ideas
- Communicate with other professionals who work with individuals with disabilities relative to current literature related to adapted physical education
- Read journals from allied fields that address current issues related to the fields of adapted physical education

Understand the implications for adapted physical education as they pertain to the literature from allied fields 13.02.02.01

- Apply multidisciplinary teaching methods to improve quality physical education programming
- Use most recent information on medically restricted conditions to enhance the quality of adapted physical education programming

Professional Organizations: Interact with professional organizations that address issues involving physical education

Support the activities of state, regional, and national organizations that promote physical education

Know the importance of professional commitment through attendance at regional, state, and national meetings sponsored by AAHPERD and the National Consortium for Physical Education and Recreation for Individuals with Disabilities (NCPERID) 13.03.01.01

- Make presentations related to adapted physical education
- Serve on committees that support the efforts of the organization as they relate to adapted physical education

Know the importance of professional commitment through service to local, state, and national organizations involving adapted physical education 13.03.01.02

- Chair or serve on committees involved in influencing policies and procedures concerning issues and concerns about individuals with disabilities
- Chair or serve on committees involved in the planning and conduct of professional development activities

- Provide consultation services to community members regarding the area of adapted physical education
- Provide workshops to community leaders and professionals in the area of adapted physical education
- Support activities of other organizations that may address issues directly or indirectly related to physical education such as the Council for Exceptional Children

Know how to contact the state department of education to obtain necessary information regarding professional development activities related to individuals with disabilities 13.03.02.01

- Attend workshops/courses that address issues indirectly related to adapted physical education
- Present at workshops/courses that address issues related to adapted physical education

Know how to join associations or organizations related to research and practice in special and remedial education 13.03.02.02

- Provide professional development to school personnel and members of the community regarding adapted physical education
- Instruct other professionals about the benefits of adapted physical education

Technology: Understand how to use technology as a technique to disseminate information pertaining to physical education

Use Web pages, blogs, e-mail list serves, and Internet search engines as a means of posting and retrieving information pertaining to physical education

Understand how colleagues in LEAs, SEAs, and other professional organizations can access information related to individuals with disabilities 13.04.01.01

- Stay informed of current and new developments in special education and adapted physical education
- Share information with colleges and universities, special education centers, and schools
- Share information with local recreation centers, parks, and public facilities that provide community recreation programs for individuals with disabilities
- Access a variety of information retrieval systems such as ERIC

Know how to disperse information obtained from information retrieval systems to assist professionals and others to understand professional practice in adapted physical education 13.04.02.01

- Use information obtained from information retrieval systems to improve the quality of adapted physical education programming
- Use information obtained from information retrieval systems to assist professionals and others to remain updated with current theories, concepts, trends, and practices in adapted physical education

Know how computers can assist IEP management 13.04.03.01

- Use computers to facilitate record keeping and data storage
- Use computers to manage and analyze IEP assessment data
- Use computers to generate adapted physical education IEP goals and objectives
- Use computers to generate IEP progress reports to be given to students and parents
- Use computers to disseminate information to others regarding the effectiveness of their physical education program

Know how to use commercial word-processing programs to disseminate information related to adapted physical education 13.04.04.01

- Use word-processing programs to develop adapted physical education newsletters
- Use word-processing programs to produce personalized letters on issues related to adapted physical education

Know how to use commercial electronic spreadsheet programs as they relate to adapted physical education 13.04.04.02

- Use spreadsheet programs to manage and calculate students' grades in adapted physical education
- Use spreadsheet programs to manage the adapted physical education budget

Know how to use commercial database programs as they relate to adapted physical education 13.04.04.03

- Use a database program to manage student performance data such as physical fitness and motor skill data in adapted physical education
- Use a database program to develop and maintain mailing lists of adapted physical education professionals

Teaching Certification: Understand the need to maintain current teaching certifications

Understand what mechanisms are available to maintain current teaching certifications

Know how to access professional development activities related to physical education for individuals with disabilities 13.05.01.01

- Enroll in adapted physical education coursework at local college/universities
- Participate in adapted physical education workshops offered by non-degree-granting agencies
- Use alternative means for acquiring or maintaining certifications such as online coursework

Ethics

Understand the need for professional standards

Understand and respect the roles and responsibilities of educators and other school-related professionals (see Standard 15)

Understand the need for standards for professionals who work closely with adapted physical educators, including special educators and related personnel such as occupational and physical therapists 14.01.01.01

- Apply the professional and ethical standards associated with preparation and certification as adapted physical educators
- Uphold the standards associated with certification as a teacher and an adapted physical educator
- Respect the need to monitor and enforce professional standards for adapted physical educators

Understand and value appropriate professional conduct

Accept the need for standards for a professional engaged in the education of children, youth, and adolescents

Understand the responsibility for developing and providing appropriate adapted physical education experiences 14.02.01.01

- Develop and implement programs that are based on research findings and acknowledged best practices as related to the education of individuals with disabilities
- Respect confidentiality and right to privacy in all matters related to the education of individuals with disabilities, including evaluation, assessment outcomes, and report writing

Understand the need to be respectful of all individuals, parents, advocates, and other professionals 14.02.01.02

- Interact with individuals with disabilities, parents, surrogates, advocates, and others in professional and courteous manner
- Use appropriate terminology such as person-first language
- Create an environment of respect and equality

Understand the need for continuous professional development

Understand the opportunities to participate in meetings, seminars, and conferences related to the education of individuals with disabilities (see Standard 13) 14.02.02.01

- Attend courses, conferences, seminars, and other continuing education experiences on a regular basis
- Provide and share professional information with others, including parents, guardians, and related personnel, that is accurate, current, and free of personal bias (see Standard 15)

Understand the responsibility to advocate for the educational needs of individuals with disabilities

Understand issues confronting individuals with disabilities and the relationship of these to programs designed to provide opportunities for physical activity 14.02.03.01

- Articulate the challenges individuals with disabilities experience in accessing health-related facilities and programs
- Support and promote individuals and organizations that provide physical activity programs for individuals with disabilities
- Cooperate with parent or guardian organizations and professional societies in promoting the health and fitness of individuals with disabilities (see Standard 15)

Understand the need to maintain credentials and professional standards

Understand the responsibility to earn credentials as an adapted physical educator as required by the state and/or a professional society 14.02.04.01

- Advocate for the requirement of professional standards
- Adhere to the requirements of professional standards and credentials in the practice of providing adapted physical education services
- Suggest changes or modifications to professional standards or procedures for assessing standards to state, district, and/or professional society

Understand the need to advance the professional knowledge base

Understand the need to conduct and support various forms of research (e.g., action, field, laboratory, qualitative) designed to expand the knowledge base

Understand the need to support research endeavors that advance programs and services for individuals with disabilities 14.03.01.01

- Engage and support research with special populations if it adheres to appropriate standards (i.e., approved by human subjects' board)
- Use an informed consent process and respect the rights of individuals with and without disabilities who choose to participate in research studies
- Synthesize and report findings of studies that involve special populations to others
- Accept responsibility to conduct research that is relevant to the needs of individuals with disabilities (e.g., field based, socially valid)
- Acknowledge the contributions of others, including research participants, to the research endeavor

Understand the responsibility to incorporate research findings into practice

Know journals that provide current information about latest research regarding programs and activities for individuals with disabilities 14.03.02.01

- Use research findings and incorporate promising practices into adapted physical education programs and activities
- Evaluate new program ideas incorporated from research to assess their effectiveness on individual outcomes

Advance the profession

Serve on professional committees

Know adapted education professional organizations and their committee structures 14.04.01.01

- Volunteer to serve on committees and actively contribute
- Respond to requests for assistance from professional organizations such as completion of a survey data form
- Retain the rights to agree and disagree over professional matters, recognizing the need to do so in a courteous and professional manner
- Accept leadership opportunities consistent with talent, available time, and other responsibilities

Communication

Parents and Families: Communication with parents and families

Understand the importance of parent and family intervention

Understand the importance of family support during the individualized education program (IEP), the individualized family service plan (IFSP), and other parent/teacher conferences/meetings 15.01.01.01

- Explain the motor components of the IFSP to family members
- Assist family members with the transition of the physical fitness and motor component from the IFSP to the IEP
- Explain physical education IFSP to family members

Understand the management skills needed to encourage families to participate in play, sport, and physical activity with individuals with disabilities 15.01.01.02

- Develop a management plan specific to family's needs
- Provide families with the specific management skills needed to implement a play, sport, or physical activity program
- Provide families with strategies and teaching techniques to increase their effectiveness as instructors

Be a family advocate and counselor of physical activity

Understand the importance of family advocacy meetings where parents can meet and learn about physical activity programs for individuals with disabilities 15.01.02.01

- Be an advocate for programs by working closely with the press and media such as writing newsletters
- Volunteer to be a speaker at parent advocacy meetings

Understand about already developed home-based physical activity programs 15.01.02.02

- Design family home-based physical activity programs
- Teach parents to implement a plan that includes long-range goals, behavioral objectives, lesson plans, teaching cues, and strategies for charting child progress
- Provide homework assignments for home-based activity programs

Acquire knowledge of national agencies, organizations, and community programs that assist families in play, sport, and physical activity such as Special Olympics and the United States Association of Blind Athletes 15.01.02.03

- Assist families in contacting and getting involved in such national agencies, organizations, and community programs
- Assist families in appropriate assessment procedures for placement in play, sport, and physical activity
- Assist families in utilizing and adapting equipment in order to participate in physical activities

Public Relations: Communicating the role of physical education (see Standards 5 and 13)

Acquire knowledge of physical education and ability to communicate the importance of physical activity

Understand and communicate the importance of physical activity for individuals with disabilities in the schools and community 15.02.01.01

- Integrate the adapted physical education program with other subject areas including general physical education
- Plan and implement programs that promote adapted physical education for parents and other groups
- Take community-based educational trips and provide feedback relative to body and space management for individuals with disabilities
- Take integrated groups to such community-based activities as ice skating, bowling, and fitness centers
- Be an advocate in a consulting role for adapted physical education person on transition teams
- Collaborate with local physicians regarding the importance of adapted physical education programs
- Involve oneself in assessment, placement, and programming
- Advocate for inclusion of individuals with disabilities in intramural and athletic programs
- Communicate with local business and municipal recreation leaders about the need to market recreational activities for all individuals, including those with disabilities; offer to help/consult
- Speak to civic organizations about the rights to recreate for individuals with disabilities such as addressing specific community needs to offer inclusive recreation/leisure opportunities

Roles of Other Professionals: Understand other professionals who work with adapted physical educators and serve individuals with disabilities

Acquire knowledge of the roles and responsibilities of occupational therapists

Understand how occupational therapist can assist in programs of physical activity for individuals with disabilities 15.03.01.01

- Confer with the occupational therapist on activities of daily living (ADL)
- Meet regularly about progress of individuals with disabilities relative to self-care, work skills, and daily activities to ensure that work toward goals is congruent
- Observe an occupational therapist working with individuals with disabilities and invite occupational therapist to observe physical education/adapted physical education classes where an individual receiving occupational therapy is present
- Assist individuals with disabilities in identifying special interests in recreation/ physical education that may require occupational therapist services

Acquire knowledge of the roles and responsibilities of physical therapists

Understand how the physical therapist can assist in programs of physical activity for individuals with disabilities 15.03.02.01

- Confer with physical therapist on such activities as use and safety of wheelchairs and orthotics, wheelchair transfers, and positioning of individuals with reflexive movements

- Communicate with physical therapist regarding assistive devices such as sport wheelchair for active and least restrictive involvement of individuals with disabilities
- Collaborate with physical therapist for most appropriate stretching exercises for individuals with specific physical disabilities

Acquire knowledge of the roles and responsibilities of therapeutic recreators

Understand how the therapeutic recreator can assist in community-based leisure activities for individuals with disabilities 15.03.03.01

- Confer with therapeutic recreator to identify leisure needs
- Confer with therapeutic recreator to identify what community recreation/leisure opportunities exist
- Confer with therapeutic recreator regarding ecological inventory and task analysis of community/recreation/leisure activities
- Accompany individuals with disabilities on recreation/leisure trips to assess adapted physical education needs
- Contact agencies such as Easter Seals with the intent to cooperatively expand recreation activities such as horseback riding
- Confer with therapeutic recreator regarding camping, climbing, and canoe paddling activity options for individuals with disabilities

Acquire knowledge of the roles and responsibilities of vocational specialists

Understand the importance of physical fitness to enhance job skills and productivity 15.03.04.01

- Design physical fitness and physical activity programs for vocational work sites
- Accompany the vocation specialist to study work site to assess physical abilities needed
- Collaborate with vocational specialist to teach proper posture and body mechanics during manual labor
- Explore how physical fitness activities can be combined with work experiences such as walking or biking to work, stretching during work breaks, and performing low back exercises during breaks

Acquire knowledge of the roles and responsibilities of general physical educators

Understand how the general physical education teacher can assist in curricular and scheduling decisions for individuals with disabilities 15.03.05.01

- Consult with general physical educator to make appropriate adaptations to activities
- Observe individuals with disabilities in inclusive settings
- Collaborate with the general physical educator during assessment, writing of goals and objectives, and recommending placement
- Confer with general physical educator to identify and access appropriate community recreation opportunities
- Work with general physical educator to include individuals with disabilities in intramural programs
- Write grants cooperatively to improve programs such as acquiring sport wheelchairs to be used in physical education classes by individuals who ambulate with crutches when appropriate

Acquire knowledge of the roles and responsibilities of special education classroom teachers

Understand how the special education classroom teacher can assist in the appropriate placement of individuals with disabilities in such least restrictive environments as general or special education 15.03.06.01

- Collaborate with special education classroom teacher regarding written work required
- Collaborate with special education classroom teacher regarding behavior management in order to keep management techniques consistent across settings
- Inform special education classroom teacher when routines or activities of individuals with disabilities will be changed in physical education classes
- Assist in establishing community recreation/leisure involvement
- Assist with prerequisite physical skills needed for transitioning to community workforce
- Assist in developing activities for special education classroom teacher and general education classroom teacher for individuals with disabilities to practice in the classroom, during recess, at home, or in the community

Acquire knowledge of the roles and responsibilities of paraprofessionals and other volunteers

Understand how paraprofessionals and other volunteers can assist in the adapted physical education program 15.03.07.01

- Demonstrate for paraprofessionals and volunteers how to physically assist individuals with disabilities
- Model for paraprofessionals and volunteers how to sufficiently challenge individuals with disabilities during programming
- Teach paraprofessionals and volunteers how to encourage peer partners
- Ask paraprofessionals and volunteers to assist during assessments
- Train paraprofessionals and volunteers to take a lead role in teaching when adapted physical educator is absent due to involvement in assessments or IEP meetings (depending on LEA policy)
- Teach paraprofessionals and volunteers how to use specialized equipment
- Evaluate the effectiveness of paraprofessionals and volunteers

Acquire knowledge of the roles and responsibilities of other school-based professionals who work with adapted physical educators and serve individuals with disabilities

Understand how to collaborate with these professionals to provide the appropriate educational services for individuals with disabilities 15.03.08.01

- Understand the roles and responsibilities of professionals such as principals, psychologists, physical educators, special educators, occupational therapists, physical therapists and therapeutic recreators
- Collaborate with other professionals regarding assessment and programming for individuals with disabilities
- Collaborate with other professionals regarding legal issues
- Collaborate with other individuals about issues related to school, state, and federal policies

Team Approach: Communicate effectively using a team approach

Acquire knowledge of differences among various team approaches

Understand which collaborative team approach should be used (see Standard 11)
15.04.01.01

- Collaborate and work effectively in a team by using such methods as consensus forming with the various members of the team
- Collaborate with other professionals regarding individual goals and objectives
- Explain how adapted physical education contributes toward the total growth of individuals with disabilities

National Consortium for Physical Education and Recreation for Individuals with Disabilities

The purpose of the National Consortium for Physical Education and Recreation for Individuals with Disabilities (NCPERID) is to promote, stimulate, and encourage the conduct of service delivery, professional preparation, and research in physical education and recreation for individuals with disabilities. NCPERID provides public information and education, promotes the development of programs and services, and disseminates professional and technical information. The organization succeeded the National Committee on Physical Education and Recreation for Handicapped Children and Youth, formed in 1973. Members of the organization are primarily professionals in adapted physical education and therapeutic recreation employed in colleges and universities throughout the United States. Other members include individuals and organizations that advocate for people with disabilities.

Related to the areas in the purpose of the organization, the membership works diligently to stimulate and/or conduct research efforts directed toward improving the lifestyle and well-being of individuals with disabilities through physical education and recreation. In part, the membership works to monitor available research funding from governmental agencies by articulating current needs and collectively advocating for funding related to our mission. In addition, the membership works to serve as a liaison to legislative organizations at the national, state, and local levels. An essential function of NCPERID is to develop and/or foster the adoption of standards related to staff qualifications, services facilities, and recommended levels of support for recreation and physical education programs for persons with disabilities at national, state, and local levels.

An added goal of NCPERID is to serve as a professional voice and collective force in support of physical education and recreation for all people. This may be articulated through the development of national policy and position statements reflecting the contribution of physical education and recreation to the lives of people with disabilities. Efforts are made to communicate effectively within the membership of NCPERID and with other professional organizations that advocate for the rights of people with disabilities.

How the Adapted Physical Education Standards and National Certification Examination Were Developed

The purpose of this five-year special project from the U.S. Department of Education, Office of Special Education and Rehabilitation Services to NCPERID was to ensure that physical education instruction for students with disabilities was provided by qualified physical education instructors. This purpose was designed to be achieved by meeting the following goals:

1. Develop national standards for the field of adapted physical education
2. Develop a national certification examination to measure knowledge of the standards

The first two years of the project were devoted to developing the national standards. These standards would serve as the foundation for creating a national certification examination in years 3 and 4, which would be administered nationally during the fifth year of the project. It is important to note that what was proposed and funded was a dynamic process for achieving these goals. This process served as the initial framework and was continually shaped and refined by input from a variety of constituencies and the ongoing evaluation process.

Committees

The workforce for the standards project was composed of four committees and the project staff. Each of the major committees is described briefly in this section in terms of its membership and responsibilities.

Executive Committee (6 Members)

This committee was responsible for ensuring that the project was implemented as intended, for making all policy decisions, and for approving all materials and products produced by the various committees.

- Luke Kelly (University of Virginia), chair, project director, and past president of NCPERID
- Jeff McCubbin (Oregon State University), former president of NCPERID
- Patrick DiRocco (University of Wisconsin at La Crosse), official liaison between the project and the American Alliance for Health, Physical Education, Recreation and Dance (AAHPERD) (member from the NCPERID board of directors)
- Hester L. Henderson (University of Utah), official liaison between the project and the Council for Exceptional Children (CEC) (member from the NCPERID board of directors)

- Smokey Davis, representing National Association of State Directors of Special Education
- Martha Bokee, member representing the U.S. Department of Education, Office of Special Education and Rehabilitation Services, Department of Personnel Preparation

Steering Committee (7 Members)

The members of this committee applied for these positions and were reviewed and selected by the executive committee. The responsibilities of the steering committee were to develop credentialing procedures and criteria for selecting the members of the six standards committees and the evaluation/review committee; draft, implement, and monitor the development of the standards and the exam; chair one of the standards committees; and report progress on a regular schedule to the executive committee.

- Luke E. Kelly, chair and project director, University of Virginia
- John M. Dunn, Oregon State University
- G. William Gayle, Wright State University
- Barry Lavay, California State University at Long Beach
- Monica Lepore, West Chester University
- Michael Loovis, Cleveland State University
- Janet A. Seaman, California State University at Los Angeles

Standards Committees (72 Members)

Each of the six standards committees was chaired by a member of the steering committee. The members on these committees applied for the positions and were selected by the steering committee and assigned to a standard committee based on their area(s) of expertise and experience. The responsibilities of the standards committees were to delineate the scope and sequence of the content in the standards they were assigned; revise the content based on the evaluation/review committee's feedback; develop test items to measure the standards; and revise the test items based on the evaluation/review committee's feedback. The members of the standards committees are listed in Figure B.1. Fifty-four percent of the committee members were female, and 46% were male. The committee members were from 26 states and from both K-12 schools (45%) and colleges and universities (55%).

Evaluation/Review Committee (300+ Members)

Members volunteered for the evaluation/review committee (ERC) and were appointed by the steering committee based on credentials. For evaluation tasks, multiple subevaluation groups composed of 30 members each were randomly formed from the pool of ERC members. The project director was responsible for instructing and monitoring the work of this committee. The ERC's responsibilities included validating the draft content of the standards and test items developed by the various standards committees. A total of 977 professionals expressed interest in working on the ERC. From this pool, 300 were selected to evaluate the draft standards based on their willingness to perform this task and evidence that they were in fact practicing adapted physical educators with one or more years of teaching experience. See Appendix D for the names of these ERC members. Descriptive data on the ERC are shown in Table B.1. A review of the data in Table B.1 reveals that 90% of the committee members were K-12 adapted physical educators. They had a mean age of 40.36 years and an average of 11.28 years of teaching experience, and they represented 40 of the 50 states.

APE National Standards: Standards Committee Members

Judy Alexander	Bernadette Ascareggi	James Ascareggi	Ted Baumgartner
David Bermann	Nick Breit	Sandy Brungardt	Ellen Campbell
Alana Campbell	Judy Chandler	Charlie Daniel	John Downing
Gail Dummer	Charles Duncan	Peter Ellery	Steven Errante
M. Rhonda Folio	Sherry Folsom-Meek	Taralyn Garner	Georgia Frey
Michael Berick	Wanda Gilbert	Mike Haeuser	Constance Hayes
John Herring	Ric Hogerheide	Mike Horvat	Cathy Houston-Wilson
Joseph Huber	Charlotte Humphries	Daniel Joseph	Monica Kleeman
Ellen Kowalski	Karen Leightshoe	Lauren Lieberman	Dwayne Liles
Patrice Manning	Nancy Markos	Deborah Maronic	Elaine McHugh
Robert Merrifield	William Merriman	Sue Ellen Miller	Duane Millslagle
Thomas Murphy	Kathy Omoto	Michael Paciorek	Gloria Palma
Jan Patterson	Vicki Vance	Thomas Pennewell	Virginia Politino
Lynda Reeves	Jim Rimmer	Catherine Schroeder	Cindy Slagle
Stephen Butterfield	Christine Stopka	Perky Stromer	Christine Summerford
Paul Surburg	Ric Tennant	Kathleen Tomlin	April Tripp
Terri Troll	Garth Tymeson	Dale Ulrich	Paul Vogel
Bill Vogler	Tim Wallstrom	Robert Weber	Andrea Williams

Figure B.1   Standards committee members.

TABLE B.1   Evaluation/Review Committee Demographic Data

Variables	n	%		
Gender				
Male	90	30		
Female	10	70		
Training				
Bachelor's	279	93		
Master's	210	70		
Doctorate	45	15		
Teaching level				
K-12 schools	269	90		
University	31	10		
State represented	40	80		
Variables	n	Minimum	Maximum	Mean
Age	300	22.0	66.0	40.36
Years teaching	300	1.0	30.0	11.28
% time teaching APE	300	10.0	100.0	80.54

Project Staff

The project staff was composed of the project director, a research consultant, a project assistant, and a clerical assistant. The project director was Luke E. Kelly, who was a past president of NCPERID and director of the graduate adapted physical education programs at the University of Virginia. The research consultant was Bruce Gansneder from the Bureau of Educational Research, Curry School of Education, University of Virginia. The project assistant responsibilities were distributed across four doctoral students at the University of Virginia during the first two years of the project: Katie Stanton, Jim Martindale, Morris Pickens, and David Striegel. The clerical assistant responsibilities were distributed across a number of graduate students during the first two years of the project, most notably Karen Etz, Alyssa Watkins, and Jennifer Williams.

Standards Development Process

The first year of the project was devoted to achieving three objectives. The first of these objectives was to review and compare our proposed procedures with those of other professional organizations that had already gone through the process of developing standards and national exams. The second objective was to identify the roles and responsibilities adapted physical educators were being asked to perform in our nation's schools as well as the perceived needs of these educators. The final objective for year 1 was to interpret the job analysis data to determine the content that adapted physical educators need to know to perform their roles and responsibilities and to create a means of organizing this content.

Because a number of other professional organizations had already developed national standards and certification exams, it seemed prudent to contact these organizations to see what could be learned from their experiences. To this end, the executive committee identified six professional organizations that were viewed as having elements of similarity to adapted physical education. Some of these elements were size, focus, need, and purposes for creating their standards and exams. These six organizations were the American College of Sports Medicine, the American Occupational Therapy Certification Board, the American Physical Therapy Association, the National Athletic Trainers' Association, the National Council for Therapeutic Recreation Certification, and the National Organization for Competency Assurance. Extensive telephone interviews were conducted with key members of these associations who had been involved in the standards and/or exam development processes of their respective organizations. The results of these interviews were compiled and reviewed by the members of the executive committee.

Based on the review of the telephone interviews, the executive committee decided to invite three representatives to a two-day work session to discuss the proposed procedures for our project. These representatives were Ms. Patricia Tice, representing the American Physical Therapy Association; Ms. Maureen Plombon, representing the American College of Sports Medicine; and Mr. Paul Grace, representing the National Athletic Trainers' Association and the National Organization for Competency Assurance. Prior to the work session, each representative was sent a complete copy of the proposed project and the five-year project management plan. At the work session, the proposed procedures for developing the adapted physical education national standards and certification examination were confirmed by the representatives. They also provided a number of helpful suggestions, particularly related to developing and administering the exam, that have subsequently been added to the project management plan.

Determining the current roles, responsibilities, and perceived needs of practicing adapted physical educators required the following:

1. The development of an appropriate tool to collect this information
2. The identification of a representative sample of practitioners to supply the needed information

The first step in this process was to review previous needs assessment instruments that had been used in the profession and to solicit input from the executive and steering committees. With this information, the project staff developed a draft survey using the total design method (Dillman, 1978). The draft survey was reviewed by the executive and steering committees and revised accordingly by the project staff. The revised draft was field tested using small groups (total $n = 36$) of adapted physical educators identified by members of the steering committee. The field test results were compiled and reviewed by the steering committee, and final revisions were made to the instrument.

The second task related to the job analysis was to identify a representative sample of practitioners to receive the survey. The initial plan was to use the AAHPERD Adapted Physical Activity Council (APAC) membership list as the pool and to sample from this by region for the job analysis survey. However, a survey administered by the project director (Kelly, 1991a, 1991b) using this method revealed a number of limitations with this sampling plan. For example, the APAC membership list did not distinguish between K-12 and college/university adapted physical educators, nor did it distinguish between members interested in adapted physical education and those who were actually practitioners. Kelly (1991c) drew a random sample of 600 from the membership list of 1,500+ members. Based on a return rate of 81% ($n = 491$), only 22% of the respondents were full-time adapted physical educators at the K-12 level. Because it was essential that the job analysis be completed by teachers who were actually practicing adapted physical educators, a more appropriate sampling plan was needed.

Based on the recommendation of the steering committee, it was ultimately decided to identify K-12 adapted physical educators in each state and then to use this group as the sample. A stratified sampling plan was developed. Each member of the steering committee was assigned several states. The steering committee members then contacted key leaders in adapted physical education in each of their assigned states. Depending on the size of the state, the initial contact in a given state may have been asked to identify other leaders within the state to ensure that the entire state would be represented. The contacts in each state were asked to collectively provide a specific number (based on state size) of names of adapted physical education practitioners in the state. The sample size obtained by state is illustrated in Table B.2. This process resulted in a total sample size of 585, with each state contributing a weighted number of subjects based on the population of the state. Two states were unable to produce the requested number, resulting in the final sample size of 575.

The results of the job analysis are contained in a separate report (Kelly & Gansneder, 1998). The final return rate was 55% (316/575). These results were reviewed by the steering committee, who then divided the content needed by practicing adapted physical educators into the 15 broad standard areas shown in Table B.3 (see page 168). The members of the steering committee were then assigned two or three of these standard areas for which they were responsible for delineating the content with their standards committee.

One of the key decisions the steering committee had to make early on was the degree to which the content should be delineated. For example, should the standards be limited to just the unique content that adapted physical educators should know, or should they include the prerequisite content that general physical educa-

TABLE B.2 Job Analysis Sample Distribution by State

State	Sample	State	Sample
Alabama	10	Montana	5
Alaska	5	Nebraska	5
Arizona	10	Nevada	5
Arkansas	10	New Hampshire	5
California	40	New Jersey	20
Colorado	10	New Mexico	5
Connecticut	10	New York	30
Delaware	5	North Carolina	15
Florida	25	North Dakota	5
Georgia	15	Ohio	25
Hawaii	5	Oklahoma	10
Idaho	5	Oregon	10
Illinois	25	Pennsylvania	25
Indiana	15	Rhode Island	5
Iowa	10	South Carolina	10
Kansas	10	South Dakota	5
Kentucky	10	Tennessee	10
Louisiana	10	Texas	20
Maine	5	Utah	5
Maryland	10	Vermont	5
Massachusetts	15	Virginia	15
Michigan	20	Washington	10
Minnesota	10	West Virginia	5
Mississippi	10	Wisconsin	10
Missouri	15	Wyoming	5

tors would be expected to know? In making this decision, the steering committee considered the following factors:

1. A delineation of what regular physical educators should know relative to the proposed 15 standards does not exist.
2. The standards developed would be used by parents, state department officials, and others who probably would not have the training to deduce the prerequisite content.

TABLE B.3 Adapted Physical Education National Standards

Standard	Title	Chair
1	Human Development	John M. Dunn
2	Motor Behavior	Michael Loovis
3	Exercise Science	Willie Gayle
4	Measurement and Evaluation	Janet A. Seaman
5	History and Philosophy	Monica Lepore
6	Unique Attributes of Learners	Monica Lepore
7	Curriculum Theory and Development	Michael Loovis
8	Assessment	Janet A. Seaman
9	Instructional Design and Planning	Barry Lavay and Willie Gayle
10	Teaching	Barry Lavay
11	Consultation and Staff Development	Willie Gayle
12	Student and Program Evaluation	Janet A. Seaman
13	Continuing Education	Michael Loovis
14	Ethics	John M. Dunn
15	Communication	Barry Lavay

3. What is defined as the minimum standards to be qualified may be interpreted by others as the absolute criteria.

Based on these considerations, the steering committee decided that the delineation should include both the prerequisite content a general physical educator should know and the content an adapted physical education specialist should know. As a result, the content in each standard area was divided into five levels.

The first three levels of each standard represent content that should be known by all physical educators. These levels were developed by the steering committee and reviewed and validated by the standards committees. The Level 4 content represents the additional content adapted physical educators need to know to meet the roles and responsibilities of their positions. Level 5 contains example applications of the Level 4 content that adapted physical educators would be expected to be able to demonstrate.

The majority of the work during year 2 of the project was devoted to delineating and validating the Level 4 and Level 5 content for each standard. The following process was used to create and validate the content:

1. The steering committee members developed an example for each of their standards illustrating the five levels of content. The steering committee members then provided their standards committee members with the first three levels of the standard and an example of how to delineate the specific content they were being assigned to develop.

2. The standards committee members delineated the content they were assigned and returned this information to their chair. Each chair then edited

and compiled the results into a draft document that was submitted to the project director.

3. The project staff entered the draft standard content into a database and produced an ERC evaluation instrument. The typical ERC instrument was 8 to 10 pages in length and contained 50 to 60 content items to be evaluated. For some of the larger standards, the content was divided into two or more ERC instruments to keep the amount of content reviewed in any given evaluation reasonable.

4. This project staff randomly drew a sample of 30 ERC members from the database of 300+ and sent them the ERC instrument. The ERC members were asked to complete and return the instruments as soon as possible. When the ERC instruments were returned, the project staff entered the ERC ratings into an SPSS data file. Summary statistics were computed and entered into the database for each content item.

5. The steering committee members reviewed the summary statistics for their standards and decided what revisions were warranted. This information was sent to the standards committee members with the request to revise and/or expand the content as indicated by the evaluation data.

The previous process was repeated for the Level 4 and 5 content of each standard until the steering committee, as a group, agreed it was acceptable. At this time, the steering committee identified and defined any terms they felt should be included in the glossary and added cross-references within the standards.

Dissemination

Given the goal of this project, to ensure that all students with disabilities receive appropriate physical education services delivered by a qualified physical educator by developing national standards, a plan was included in the original proposal to disseminate the products of this project. Complimentary copies were sent to the following recipients:

1. All state directors of special education
2. All state directors of physical education
3. All members of the National Consortium for Physical Education and Recreation for Individuals with Disabilities
4. All identified directors of college/university adapted physical education programs
5. Members of the executive, steering, and standards committees
6. The executive directors of select professional and advocacy groups associated with physical education and/or serving the needs of individuals with disabilities

Disclaimers

Although significant progress has been made in defining the scope and sequence of the content that adapted physical educators should know, the current standards are viewed as only the initial steps of what will be an ongoing evolutionary process.

It was accepted as a limitation at the start of this project that measuring an individual's knowledge through the use of a paper-and-pencil test was no guarantee that the knowledgeable individual would correctly apply this information when delivering services to individuals with disabilities. However, it was also clear that if teachers did not know what should be done or why, there was little likelihood that they would do it correctly. Therefore, it appeared reasonable, given the financial and time constraints of this project, to delimit this project to developing the initial version of the standards and a written test to measure knowledge of this content. It is anticipated that in the coming years the standards will be expanded and the examination revised to include measures of knowledge, application, and demonstration.

The standards described in this document were developed in response to the roles, responsibilities, and perceived needs of practicing adapted physical educators. Although many faculty from institutions of higher education (IHE) were involved, there was no attempt to limit the standards to either what was currently being offered by IHEs or to what higher education faculty felt could be easily accommodated. As a result, it is possible that many IHEs may need to revise their personnel preparation programs to adequately meet these standards. Any implications for change emerging from this project are intended to be positive and proactive and not threats or criticisms of current training programs.

It may also be the case that the standards presented in this document vary from the standards in the 14 states that have established state certifications or endorsements for teachers of adapted physical education. The current standards were not developed with the intent of challenging or interfering with state requirements. In fact, states that have credentials should be acknowledged for their initiative and proactive compliance with the mandates of IDEA (2004). Hopefully, these states can take advantage of the up-to-date and national representation involved in the current standards and use these standards as a basis for evaluating—and, if needed, updating—their state standards.

Finally, the standards were developed and reviewed independently by many professionals using all available resources. Any specific mention in the standards to any specific products, projects, programs, terms, resources, or references should not be interpreted as endorsements. Rather, these references should be viewed solely as illustrative examples.

Frequently Asked Questions

Over a decade, numerous professionals in numerous professions have had questions related to the Adapted Physical Education National Standards (APENS). The most commonly asked questions are related to the background, development, and history of the APENS and the APENS exam, eligibility to take the exam, and how to earn the CAPE (certified adapted physical educator) status. To clarify some of these issues, we will respond to those questions. If you require further information, contact the APENS national office at 1-888-APENS-EXAM or visit the APENS Web site at www.cortland.edu/APENS.

Adapted Physical Education National Standards

Why national standards for adapted physical education (APE)?

The Individuals with Disabilities Education Act (IDEA, 2004), mandates free and appropriate public education services for all children and youth with disabilities be provided by "highly qualified professionals." The definition of special education within this law included the discipline of physical education. Interestingly, physical education for children with disabilities was the only specific curricular area identified. Although physical education was specifically addressed in the federal legislation, the state educational agencies were given the responsibility to interpret the term "qualified professionals" within their respective states in order to develop or amend existing certification and/or licensing qualifications. Unlike other special education areas (teaching individuals with mental retardation, learning disabilities, etc.), adapted physical education did not have defined certifications in most states. Although 14 states did have an endorsement or certification in adapted physical education at the time of this writing, 36 states and eight territories had not yet defined the qualifications teachers need to provide adapted physical education services to their students with disabilities (Kelly & Gansneder, 1998). Subsequently, a baseline or standard was needed that defined what an adapted physical educator should know in order to provide services to children with disabilities.

When were the APENS first developed?

In the spring of 1991, the National Consortium for Physical Education and Recreation for Individuals with Disabilities (NCPERID), in conjunction with the National Association of State Directors of Special Education (NASDSE) and Special Olympics International, conducted an "Action Seminar" on adapted physical education for state directors of special education and leaders of advocacy groups for individuals with disabilities. This conference had two goals: (a) to identify the barriers that were preventing full provision of appropriate physical education services to individuals with disabilities and (b) to establish an action agenda for resolving these problems. Although numerous barriers were identified by the group, the most significant for state education leaders were that they did not know what adapted physical education was, how individuals with disabilities could benefit from appropriate physical education programming, or what competencies teachers needed to deliver appropriate physical education services to students with disabilities. In response to this need, it was recommended that NCPERID develop professional standards and a means for evaluating these standards.

Adapted physical education is a field that draws on more than 100 years of history, having its roots in the 19th-century efforts at medically directed remediation of disabilities. Since then, a body of scientific research has expanded our understanding of the field to the point where it now constitutes a knowledge base appropriate for a specialist. The field continues to grow exponentially, and keeping up with it is essential if students who require adapted physical education are to receive the full benefit of the instruction to which they are entitled. The only realistic means available to school districts and parents for ensuring that those students are receiving that benefit is to rely on a national certifying authority to maintain an updated standard and to regularly certify that its members are current in their understanding and practice of those skills and knowledge.

How were the APENS developed?

One of the many outcomes established during the 1991 Action Seminar was a recommendation that national standards be developed to guide the future of adapted physical education. Based on this recommendation, the NCPERID board voted unanimously to assume responsibility for developing national standards for adapted physical education. A grant proposal was submitted to the U.S. Department of Education, Office of Special Education and Rehabilitation Services, Division of Personnel Preparation (#H029K20092), which funded a five-year project to develop national standards and a national certification examination for adapted physical education.

The first year, 1992, was devoted to conducting a national job analysis to determine what roles and responsibilities adapted physical educators were being asked to perform in their jobs. The second year focused on developing and validating content standards based on these roles and responsibilities. The third year involved developing and evaluating a database of over 2,000 test questions from which to develop a set of certification exams. The fourth year was devoted to conducting a national validation study on the test items. Finally, the fifth year focused on creating and administering the first national certification exam, which was conducted at 46 sites across the country on May 10, 1997.

How do I know whether the APENS are valid?

As part of a doctoral dissertation (Davis, 2001), the APENS policies and procedures for development were reviewed and sources of validity evidence established under the guidelines of the 1999 *Standards for Educational and Psychological Testing*. Specifically, five sources of validity evidence were used to investigate the validity of the APENS and the national certification exam. The five sources were (a) evidence based on test content, (b) response processes, (c) internal structure, (d) relationships to other variables, and (e) consequences of testing. Results of the data analyses indicated there was sufficient evidence to support the validity for four of the five validity sources. Evidence based on test content indicated that the APENS exam measures what it purports to measure and that a test specification framework was used to guide the test item development. Expert judges were used throughout the entire APENS and national certification exam development process. Finally, issues surrounding the under- or overrepresentation of the construct, including bias, were controlled through a strong internal validity design.

Evidence based on response consequences supported the validity argument in that responses from a test validation study conducted during the test item development phase of the project were used to inform the item writing and selection process. Responses from exam candidates were analyzed using multiple regression. The findings support the eligibility criteria established to take the exam as well as the certified adapted physical education (CAPE) specialist profile. Predictors were in agreement with both the eligibility and CAPE criteria. Evidence based on internal structure suggested that the process and procedure used to develop the APENS and the national certification exam were sound and controlled to construct irrelevant bias. An exploratory factor analysis was conducted on the results from the 219 candidates who took the 1997 APENS national certification exam. It was hypothesized that no factors would emerge because of the unique design and nature of the test items written for the exam.

What major organizations have endorsed the APENS?

- American Alliance for Health, Physical Education, Recreation and Dance (AAHPERD)
- American Association for Active Lifestyles and Fitness (AAALF)
- Adapted Physical Activity Council (APAC)
- National Association for Sport and Physical Education (NASPE)
- American Association of School Administrators (AASA)
- National Association of State Directors of Special Education (NASDSE)
- National Association of Secondary School Principals (NASSP)

APENS Exam

When is the APENS exam offered?

The APENS national certification exam is offered every year on the first Saturday in June. In addition to the national testing date, exams are available through state AHPERD associations, conferences, and at the national AAHPERD convention held in a different location each spring. Finally, test dates can be individually contracted by contacting the APENS national office.

Where can I take the APENS exam?

Applicants who submit materials to take the exam on the national exam date (first Saturday in June) will be asked to indicate the three colleges/universities they could travel to for the exam from a list supplied in the application. After the applications are received, the site data will be analyzed to determine which sites will be used. Applicants will then receive notification in the mail as to which site they have been assigned to take the examination. Teachers also have the option to take the exam in conjunction with the AAHPERD national convention. For more information on these options, contact the APENS office at 1-888-APENS-EXAM.

How much does it cost?

The application and exam fee is $100.

How is the APENS exam formatted?

The exam is composed of 100 multiple-choice questions designed to measure knowledge of adapted physical education. Teachers are given three hours to complete the exam. The questions will be derived from the Level 4 content from each of the 15 standard areas in the APENS manual. Within compliance of Section 504 of the Rehabilitation Act of 1973 and the Americans with Disabilities Act, persons with documented disabilities (according to the legal definition) who require specific testing accommodations are granted a reasonable accommodation.

Who is eligible to take the APENS exam?

To be eligible to sit for the exam, teachers must have the following:

- A bachelor's degree in physical education (teaching) or equivalent
- Twelve credits of course work in adapted physical education
- Two hundred hours of supervised teaching experience with students with disabilities in physical education
- A current valid teaching license in physical education (or related field) for the state where you work

What do you receive for passing the APENS exam?

Individuals that pass the exam will be certified by NCPERID for a period of seven years. These individuals will be listed in NCPERID's national registry of certified adapted physical educators based in the APENS national office. They will also be given a one-year membership in NCPERID. In addition, successful candidates will be awarded a certificate documenting that they are nationally certified adapted physical educators and will be able to list the initials CAPE after their names. It is important to note that the APENS have earned endorsements from a variety of national organizations (see page 173). This growing recognition forms the backbone of a unified voice to gain professional recognition and commensurate compensation from school districts across the nation.

How was the APENS exam developed?

The APENS exam is the product of five years of development and evaluation work performed by over 500 members of the profession. During Year 3 of the project, a database of over 2,000 potential test questions was developed based on the Level 4 content in the APENS manual. Each of these test questions was sent to 30 adapted physical educators, chosen from the larger group, who were asked to evaluate the item according to eight criteria. Their responses were compiled and analyzed, and the questions were revised accordingly.

During the fourth year of the project, the test items were administered to a national sample of 3,000 preservice and inservice teachers including adapted physical educators, special educators, general physical educators, and nonteaching physical education majors. The responses of these groups were used to calculate the psychometric measures to test each item (item difficulty, discrimination index, etc.). Test items were reviewed by standard, and appropriate items were selected to be included in the national test item database. Test items were then randomly selected by standard to produce the 100-item exam. The results from several pilot tests and from the first administration of the national exam were analyzed against existing standards of validity. Evidence of validity is used to determine whether an exam actually measures what it is intended to measure, in this case, and whether the performance of an applicant on the exam is an indicator of job performance. Findings indicate that comprehensive evidence exists to support the question of validity.

Earning the CAPE Status

How do I become a CAPE?

The method to become a CAPE is to take the APENS national certification exam. The exams are held several times each year and can be taken at a campus near you. You must apply for this by means of an application form. To make things easier, the form has been divided into two sections, one for sitting for the exam and one for obtaining certification when you pass the exam.

Why should I become a CAPE?

The roots of adapted physical education extend back into the mid-1800s, when physicians prescribed "remedial exercises" in an attempt to correct or ameliorate "handicaps." Adapted physical education has gone through a variety of transformations over the intervening century and a half. A great deal of thorough research has been conducted that brings to light effective methods for adapting physical education to meet the needs of people with disabilities. The preparation of those who provide adapted physical education has evolved to exacting levels. Finally, society has come to realize that people with disabilities are actually a minority who possess different abilities from the mainstream and, as such, have the same rights to a free and appropriate education as the rest of society.

The time has come for those prepared and charged with providing this specialized education to be recognized as being specialists who bring unique skills and insight to the teaching of physical education. The APENS define the foundation of those skills and knowledge and provide a proven method for certifying those who possess them.

NCPERID has launched a coordinated program to bring about appropriate professional recognition. APENS and NCPERID will be undertaking the following:

- Obtaining federal government endorsement of the APENS
- Getting individual states to adopt APENS certification
- Providing assistance to individual CAPEs wishing to gain recognition from their school boards
- Establishing a means whereby CAPEs can exchange "best practices" that will keep them abreast of the latest developments in the field
- Establishing an annual conference of CAPEs that would be a forum where those in the profession can meet and exchange ideas and experiences
- Conducting ongoing review and revision of the 15 standards and the exam to ensure that they are up-to-date with current practice

By becoming a CAPE, you will have an opportunity to personally help give the field of adapted physical education a unified voice and, with that, the recognition it deserves.

Web Site Information

Where can I obtain more information about the APENS (e.g., applications, standards updates, newsletters, and resources)?

The APENS Web site can be viewed by visiting www.cortland.edu/APENS. Other physical education Web sites, including AAHPERD and PE Central, are linked to our

Web site. Additional information can be obtained by contacting our office directly as follows:

APENS
E224 Park Center
Department of Physical Education
SUNY Cortland
Cortland, NY 13045
1-888-APENS-EXAM
APENS@cortland.edu
www.cortland.edu/APENS

Evaluation/Review Committee Members

Pamela Abeling	John Adair	Beverly Adam	Jeff Adams
Hezi Aharoni	Constance Alchus	Elizabeth Anderson	Kim Anderson
Lisa Ash	Peter Aufsesser	Brad Bacaro	Cindia Badger
Mary Kay Baker	Karen Barnhart	Joe Barry	Greg Bayley
Elizabeth Bayuk	Kristi Beach	Christine Belanger	Kathy Bell
Eileen Bender	Jim Bennink	Walt Bergman	Alice Berkner
Cynthia Berrol	Maria Bertolucci	Heidi Bickel	William Bishop
John Boeltar	Aaron Bond	Donald Bornell	Wayne Boudreau
Peanuts Boyer	Gail Brevig	Dawn Bridges	Kathy Brinker
Sally Bruce	Juan Bruno	Cathy Bryan	Joy Bryceson
Louise Burbank	Teresa Burgess	Lee Burkett	Allen Burton
Sharon Burton	Howard Cadenhead	Kittie Callaway	Sal Caminada
Ellen Campbell	Stacey Carniglia	Marcia Carrillo	Sam Cerceres
Denise Chang	Jo Chew	Rose Chew	Christine Chiodo
Penny Christensen	Kara Christian	Gail Clark	Doug Collier
Jan Collings	Sue Combs	Gail Conrad	Judy Conroy
Erin Coolman	Kathleen Cooney	Jill Corti	Judy Cox
Connie Custer	John Dagger	Denise Darvel-Citana	Tim Davis
Ron Davis	Jennifer Davis	Cindy Dawley	Michelle De Lorm
Debby Dearden	Jim Decker	Frank Degnan	Brenda Dessauer
John Dlabal	Victor Dominocieo	Ann Dorrance	Anne Duncan
Carl Eichstaedt	Janice Elix	Cindy Elrod	Mame Engleking
Lorri Engstrom	Catherine Erhard	Julie Erickson-Hines	Glendora Estacion
Elizabeth Evans	Jean Evans-Kent	Gretta Fahey	Anita Farnholtz
Manny Felix	Beverly Fillingin	Janet Fisher	Ann Fleury
Susan Floethe	Mary Frampton	Rikki Gans	Tom Gentry
Pat Giebink	Kris Gilmore	Pamela Glueck	Elly Goldman
Joanne Gonzalez	Mary Goodwin	Craig Gordon	Glen Graham
Hollis Green	Ann Griffin	Dale Grupe	Nancy Guggenheim
Linda Gunning	Christine Guzzo	Carlton Hansen	Karen Happke
Jerry Harris	Lois Harris	Virginia Harris	Aleita Hass-Holcombe
John Hassenzahl	Ruth Haynes	Marsha Heath	Paul Heine
Betty Heising	Nancy Henderson	Tina Herring	Todd Herrington

Michele Herzing	Kathy Hixon	Chris Hopper	Jane Horner
Denise Horpedahl	Charles Howe	Carol Huettig	Linda Huntimer
Diane Hursky	Patsy Jackson	Paul Jansma	Melanie Jernigan
Leon Johnson	Edwin Johnson	Steve Johnston	Jean Jones
Phyllis Jorgensen	Jennifer Kahaian	Lyn Kalinowski	Susan Kasser
Billy Keel	Chuck Keller	Brian Kelly	Diane Kime
Pamela Kissler	Kirk Klucznik	Barbara Knipe	Karl Knopf
Deborah Konar	Sharon Kounas	Claire Kzeski	Luigi Lettieri
Kim Lewolt	Ingrid Loen	Carol Lynch	Rose Lyon
Kay Mabry	Julienne Maeda	Raye Maero	Doug Malay
Shelley Mallue	Susan Mangel	Brent Mangus	Jean Margolis
Michael Marsallo	Larry Martin	Janet McCauley	Deann McCormick
Skip McCrory	Jana McKinley	Linda McMorran	Nancy McNamee
Gail Meacham	Nancy Megginson	Howard Menton	Corine Meyer
Mike Miley	Glenn Mills	Jerri Miner	Linda Mitchell
Ron Moon	Kathleen Morland	Dennis Morrow	Kimble Morton
Paul Motley	Ginny Mott	Sue Moucha	Eugene Mulcahy
Peggy Munten	Nathan Murata	Terry Murray	Diana Nelson
Sue Nestor	Gerry O'Brien	Rita O'Loughlin	Carolyn Oborny
Robin Olberding	Stephanie Ontiveros	John Oppliger	Brad Osato
Linda Osborn	Patricia Osborne	Patty Osborne	Carol Outhier
Stephen Overby	Shelia Owen	Patricia Owens	George Pacheco
Ann Page	Chris Pappas	Jocelyn Paré	Lee Parks
Bill Payret	Steve Peak	Peter Pedroza	Randi Perkins
Karlene Peterson	Jeannie Phillips	Lisa Picini-Asman	David Poretta
David Potter	Richard Powell	Kathy Powell	Joan Pylman
Doreen Ramsey	Linda Raphael	Terrie Rauzon	Tim Ray
Belinda Rector	Patricia Reed	Helen Rehm	Barbara Rethans
Peter Richter	Jim Rimmer	Terry Rizzo	Ted Robertson
Pat Robinson	Robert Roesch	Jessica Rogers	Trish Rogers-McIntyre
Monica Rogerson	Barbara Rohleder	Robynn Rome	Jody Rose-Dressler
Susan Rosenthal	Debe Rougeau	Mary Ann Rounds	Mark Runac
Ronda Runyon	Kathryn Russell	Carol Ryan	Jack Sage
Susan Schakel	Leigh Schmidt	Roger Schoonover	Lisa Schreeder
Steven Seymour	Bill Shannahan	Carolyn Sharp	Vicky Sheesley
Carol Shenosky	Marge Shively	Susie Shurmur	Lisa Silliman
Bob Sinibaldi	Linda Skinner	Janet Sklenar	Marie Slusser
Carolyn Snyder-Sain	Chet Spencer	David Stabelfeldt	Allan Stanbridge
Alex Streltzov	Diane Swanson	Jayne Swercinski	James Sylvis
Diane Symons	Sue Tarr	Terri Taylor	Noel Teichman
Mary Thompson	Margery Thompson	Debbie Tillett	Joan Tomaszewski
Michelle Trujillo	Deb Turner	Louise Van Zee	Elinor Vandegrift
Joanie Verderber	Paul Vogel	Patty VonOhlen	Julie Wally

Debbie Watson

Nancie Whiteside

Debbie Williams

Gwen Wilson

Lynde Woolace

Julia Young

Diane Wetherill

Bettie Wickersham

Beverly Williamson

Pam Witzmann

Joan Worley

John Zerkle

Sue Wheeler-Ayres

Ann Wilber

Susan Williford

Pamela Wolosky

Jennifer Wright

Hedy Zikratch-Marches

Nancy Whitehurst

Kathy Wildermuth

Penny Wills

Joanne Woodruff

Marnie Young

GLOSSARY

academic learning time (ATL)—A unit of time in which an individual is engaged in activities related to class objectives.

achievement-based curriculum (ABC)—A model for integrating program planning, assessing, prescribing, teaching, and evaluating so that the physical education needs of all individuals can be addressed.

activities of daily living (ADL)—Skills that are necessary to perform everyday functions such as walking and dressing.

adapted physical education (APE)—Programs designed to develop physical and motor fitness; fundamental motor skills and patterns; and skills in aquatics, dance, and individual and group games and sports so that the individual with a disability can ultimately participate in community-based physical activity programs to enjoy an enhanced quality of life. Diversified programs generally have the same goals and objectives as general physical education, but are modified when necessary to meet the unique needs of each individual.

administrative feasibility—A number of factors such as cost, time, training, and specialized equipment required to use an assessment instrument accurately and reliably (Kelly & Melagano, 2004).

afterload—Additional load placed on the muscle during contraction (McArdle, Katch, & Katch, 2001).

agonist—A muscle acting to cause a movement (Hall, 2003).

allied educators—Professionals who provide instruction to individuals with disabilities.

alternative/augmentative communication—Supplemental communication techniques that are used in addition to whatever naturally acquired speech and vocalization exists, to include such things as sign language and gestures. Also called alternative/augmentative modes.

American Sign Language—The primary language of the deaf, using hand signs and finger spelling. Signs are concept based and are grammatically and symbolically different from English.

amplitude—The distance between two target centers in an aiming task.

annual goals—General statements of student outcomes, projected over the school year.

antagonist—A muscle that in contracting tends to produce movement opposite to that of the agonist.

antecedent stimuli—Stimuli that occur prior to a response.

anticipation—The ability to predict what is going to occur in the environment and when it will occur, and then to perform various information-processing activities in advance of the event.

APE with collaboration—Physical education services implemented and provided together to accomplish a common goal.

APE with consultation—Ideas and suggestions communicated between the APE specialist and other service providers for individualizing physical education instructional strategies, equipment, and curriculum.

applied behavior analysis—Techniques derived from the principles of behavior that are systematically applied to meaningfully enhance socially significant behavior and demonstrate experimentally that the technique used caused the improved behavior.

appropriate education—Education that is specifically designed to meet the unique needs of an individual with a disability.

arousal—An internal state of alertness or excitement.

assessment—The interpretation of measurements for the purpose of making decisions about placement, program planning, and performance objectives by qualified professionals.

assessment plan—Predetermined procedures and instruments for gathering, interpreting, and reporting data gathered in the assessment process.

ataxia—A type of cerebral palsy that is characterized by hypotonia, poor coordination, and poor balance.

atlantoaxial instability—The misalignment of the first and second cervical vertebrae, which can cause permanent damage to the spinal cord during hyperflexion or hyperextension of the head or neck.

attention—The ability to direct senses and thought processes to particular objects, thoughts, and feelings.

augmented feedback—Information in addition to sensory feedback that is provided by a source external to the person making the movement.

automatic processing—A mode of information processing that is fast, not attention demanding, parallel, and often involuntary.

automaticity—A process to deal with information that is (a) fast; (b) not attention demanding, in that such processes do not generate significant interference with other tasks; (c) parallel, occurring together with other processing tasks; and (d) involuntary, often unavoidable (Schmidt & Lee, 2005).

axis—An imaginary line or point about which a body or a segment rotates (Kreighbaum & Barthels, 1996).

backward chaining—Process of selecting a desired behavior by beginning with the last behavioral link in the chain of behaviors.

balance—A process where the body's state of equilibrium is controlled for a specific purpose (i.e., stork stand, jackknife dive) (Krieghbaum & Barthels, 1981).

baseline behaviors—Behaviors or scores used to set goals and establish criteria for measuring change.

behavior disorders—A condition exhibiting one or more of the following characteristics over a long period of time and to a marked degree, which adversely affects educational performance: (a) an inability to learn that cannot be explained by intellectual, sensory, or health factors; (b) an inability to build or maintain satisfactory interpersonal relationships with peers and teachers; (c) inappropriate types of behavior or feelings under normal circumstances; (d) a general pervasive mood of unhappiness or depression; or (e) a tendency to develop physical symptoms or fears associated with personal or school problems.

behavior management—Strategies that educators use to develop, increase, maintain, or decrease the behavior of students. See *applied behavior analysis*.

biomechanics—An area of study in which knowledge and methods of mechanics are applied to the structure and function of living humans.

bleed—The characteristic of individuals with hemophilia in which bleeding occurs into joints or muscles, leading to joint damage; most commonly in the knee, ankle, and elbow.

blind—Visual impairment so severe that, even with correction, educational performance is adversely affected. Legal definition is 20/200 or greater in the better eye, after maximum correction, or field of vision of 20 degrees or less.

Blissymbolics—A graphic, meaning-based communication system capable of conveying aspects of human experience; basic symbol elements, pictographs, and ideographs can be used to construct compound symbols, giving the system the potential to provide a large vocabulary.

blood pressure—Resistance in the arterial system that the heart must pump against. The two components of blood pressure are systolic pressure, which is the higher pressure that is created when the heart ejects the blood into the arterial system, and diastolic pressure, which is the lower number or resting pressure between heartbeats (McArdle, Katch, & Katch, 2001).

body composition—Component parts of the body that are mainly fat and fat-free weight.

brittle diabetes—Insulin-dependent diabetes that is not well controlled and has increased potential for symptoms to occur at any time such as dizziness, nausea, and loss of consciousness.

calorimetry—The measurement of heat expressed in calories.

Canon Communicator—Portable tape typewriter with a control display that contains the letters of the alphabet. The interface consists of multiple switches or keys that the user depresses as selections are made.

carbohydrate—Chemical compound containing carbon, hydrogen, and oxygen. Some important forms of carbohydrate are the starches, celluloses, and sugars. Carbohydrate is one of the basic foodstuffs (McArdle, Katch, & Katch, 2001).

caregiver—The guardian of an individual with a disability who provides care. This includes parents, guardians, supervisors, and full-time home staff.

chain—Sequencing of a series of learned behaviors presented in a fixed order to achieve a more complex terminal response (Lavay, French, & Henderson, 2006).

child kinship—Relationships between a child and significant people in his/her life, including natural and adopted parents and other adults who assume responsibility for the child.

choice reaction time—The time involved in choosing one response from a selection of possible movements selected in advance.

circuit or station type of teaching—The creation of discrete learning areas within the general teaching area where individuals work on activities independently and at their own rates; very helpful with groups displaying a wide range of abilities.

closed loop control—A system control mode involving feedback and error detection and correction; applicable to motor behavior.

closed skill—A movement skill undertaken in an environment that is stable and predictable, allowing for advanced organization of movement (Schmidt & Wrisberg, 2004).

collaboration—Working jointly with others to accomplish a common goal such as making decisions or implementing assessment plans and programs.

command style of teaching—A teaching style in which the teacher makes all of the decisions regarding the organization of the lesson (starting, stopping, activities to be performed, how they are performed, etc.), and the student is only required to respond to the teacher's command signals (Mosston & Ashworth, 2001).

communication—A means by which an individual relates experiences, ideas, knowledge, and feelings to another (includes speech, sign language, gestures, writing).

communication board—An apparatus on which the alphabet, numbers, and commonly used words are represented; used when oral expression is difficult or cannot be obtained.

community resources—Personnel, materials, services, and facilities available in the community for use by educators to enrich IEPs, facilitate IFSPs, and actualize transition plans for individuals with disabilities.

community-based programming—Programming in which the individual is involved in real-life experiences inside and outside the school environment.

consistent mapping—The process of having the same stimulus always leading to the same response.

consultation—Providing (a) support services to parents, teachers, and other professionals; (b) adult education, which may include various forms of inservice education, parent training, and collaborative teamwork; and (c) expert advice and contract services, such as assessment or evaluation for a school district (Sherrill, 2004).

contained choices—A limited amount of choices given to an individual.

content-referenced standards—Established expectations in terms of the content of components of the task to be mastered.

contingency—The relationship between the target behavior to be changed and the events or consequences that follow that particular behavior (Lavay, French, & Henderson, 2006).

contingent observation time-out—A combination of modeling and time-out procedures in which the individual is removed from the group but is left near enough to observe peers demonstrating appropriate behavior.

continuous reinforcement—A schedule of reinforcement based on the individual being rewarded immediately and each time the target behavior is successfully met.

continuous skill—A skill in which the input or action repeats a pattern without a recognizable beginning or end.

continuum of placement—The offering of appropriate placements in educational programs along a continuum from least to most restrictive educational settings.

contractibility—The ability of the muscle to contract or shorten.

contraindicated—A term used to describe conditions, activities, or tasks that may aggravate or exacerbate a condition of a disability.

controlled processing—A mode of information processing that is slow, serial, attention demanding, and voluntary (Schmidt & Lee, 2005).

cooperative learning —A situation in which an individual learns from others in the class by working in teams that allow those with abilities in specific areas to help others in the group. Individual accountability is fostered. The group, not the individual, reaches the goal, giving all members of the group a feeling of success. The intent is social outcomes along with content mastery.

coping and avoiding strategies—Techniques used by individuals with disabilities to avoid practicing learning the tasks being taught.

corrective physical education—A historic term used to describe physical education activities of a prescriptive nature that involve a body part(s), posture, and/or remediation, or correction of specific weaknesses.

criterion-referenced instrument—A standardized or non-standardized instrument designed primarily to collect process measures, which are then compared to established reference standards (Kelly & Melograno, 2004).

criterion-referenced standards—The description of an explicitly defined task or behavior to be mastered.

cues—Stimuli that are used by the individual to make a discrimination. See *prompt*.

curriculum-embedded—The ongoing and continuous process of gathering data during the instructional phase of teaching. See also *content-referenced standards*.

Data-Based Gymnasium—A systematic approach used to assess and teach physical education to individuals with severe disabilities developed by Dunn, Morehouse, and Fredericks (1986). The curriculum requires the use of cues, consequences, and data analyses.

demonstrations—The exhibition of the task/behavior so that the individuals may have a visual representation of the task in order to model the task appropriately. The demonstration is often accompanied by verbal cues.

developmental coordination disorder —A condition in which a child has difficulty with motor coordination. Other terms for this disorder are *clumsy, physical awkwardness,* and *developmental dysphasia* (Clark, Betchell, Smiley-Ogen, & Whitall, 2005).

developmental delay —The discrepancy between an individual's chronological age and functional age in the cognitive, motor, or affective domains.

developmentally appropriate activities—Activities designed to meet the developmental needs, capabilities, and limitations of students in physical education.

differential reinforcement—The process of reinforcing an appropriate response in the presence of one stimulus while extinguishing an inappropriate response in the presence of another stimulus.

direct measures—Data-gathering techniques used to measure movement parameters directly through the use of instrumentation that often does not require the performance of a skill or pattern.

direct service (physical education)—Delivery of physical education services by an adapted physical educator including screening, evaluation, assessment, and implementing individualized education programs.

discrete skill—A skill in which the action is usually brief and with a recognizable beginning and end.

discrimination reaction time—The time required to respond to a specified stimulus given multiple stimuli.

distributed practice—A practice schedule in which the amount of rest between practice trials is long relative to the trial length.

divergent or exploratory teaching styles—Teaching styles in which the learner is encouraged to develop multiple responses to a single question or problem (Mosston & Ashworth, 2001).

domain-referenced—Tests that measure a general ability from which inferences are made about a student's general capability. See also *performance sampling.*

due process—A legally defined set of procedures available to individuals with disabilities to ensure that their rights are not violated. These procedures include mediation hearings and court actions.

duration recording—A process of recording the number of minutes (duration) the behavior occurs during a predetermined period of time—for example, the number of minutes a student is exhibiting on-task behavior.

dwarfism—A form of short-stature syndrome in which either the trunk is average sized with short arms and legs, or all body parts are proportionate but abnormally short.

dynamic lung volume—Lung volume measured during exercise.

dynamic systems theory—The belief that a movement pattern can be created as a result of a near infinite combination of interactions of component parts, and that the development of these patterns is discontinuous or constantly changing (Payne & Isaacs, 2005).

dynamics—A branch of mechanics associated with systems in motion (Hall, 2003).

ecological task analysis —An analysis of the subskills and progressions needed to complete tasks and skills that are appropriate to the individual with a disability within the specific environment in which these skills will be performed (Block, 2006); also referred to as ecological inventories.

ecological theory—Interactions between the individual and everything in the individual's environment. In teaching and learning, this suggests that environmental factors, as well as personal factors, must be considered.

economy (of measurement instruments)—Desirable test characteristics having minimal cost in terms of time, personnel, and equipment needed to administer. See also *administrative feasibility.*

encephalitis—An infection resulting in inflammation of the brain.

endocrine control—Controlled by hormones.

endurance—The ability to continue a movement activity for an extended period of time (McArdle, Katch, & Katch, 2001).

equilibrium—The state of a system whose motion is not being changed, accelerated, or decelerated (Kreighbaum & Barthels, 1996).

equilibrium reactions—Automatic reactions that the body uses for maintaining or controlling its center of gravity.

ergometry—Technique to measure work output usually by means of a collaborated apparatus such as an arm crank ergometer.

ERIC—The Educational Resources Information Center.

error detection capability —The learned capability to detect one's own error through analyzing response-produced feedback (Schmidt & Lee, 2005).

evaluation—The process of comparing initial assessment data with reassessment data to make informed decisions (Kelly & Melograno, 2004).

event recording—Recording the number of times the behavior (event) occurs during a predetermined period of time.

Everyone CAN—A model elementary physical education program based on the ABC model composed of assessment items and extensive instructional materials.

extinction—The process of eliminating or reducing the occurrence of a conditioned response by not administering any form of reinforcement.

extrinsic feedback—Feedback provided artificially over and above that received naturally from a behavior.

extrinsic reinforcers—Reinforcers provided artificially over and above those naturally occurring in the environment in which the behavior is being performed.

facilitated communication—A method of enabling individuals with disabilities to communicate using an alphabet board, a handheld typewriter, or a computer.

fading—The gradual removal of a cue, prompt, or reinforcer.

feedback—Performance-related information about the cause and outcome of a movement.

flexibility—The range of motion of a joint (static flexibility); opposition or resistance of a joint to motion (dynamic flexibility) (McArdle, Katch, & Katch, 2001).

fluid mechanics—The effects that a fluid environment (i.e., air, water) have on the motion of a body (Kreighbaum & Barthels, 1996).

force—The product of mass and acceleration (Hall, 2003).

formative evaluation—The measurement and evaluation of an individual's performance using a predetermined standard; parallels ongoing assessment and focuses on the process and interpreting why certain results occur; used to make short-term instructional decisions (Kelly & Melograno, 2004).

functional skills—Skills with everyday relevance for an individual. See also *activities of daily living (ADL)*.

functionally appropriate—Describes motor activities or tests that have everyday relevance for an individual.

game intervention or cooperative games—Games designed with alternative approaches in order to effectively accommodate and include all participants.

general physical education—A physical education program that includes goals in one of the following areas: physical and motor fitness; fundamental motor skills; and aquatics, dance, and individual and group games.

generalization—The process of applying what is learned in a class to other, unpracticed tasks of the same class or in another environment.

generalization activities—Activities that allow an individual to apply a learned behavior in another environment in which the behavior was not learned.

gestational disorders—Various anomalies that occur when the developing human organism is in the uterus.

group contingency—The presentation of a highly desired reinforcer to a group of individuals based on the behavior of one person or the group.

guidance—A procedure used to reduce errors in practice in which the learner is physically or verbally directed through the performance to reduce errors.

guided discovery teaching style—A teaching style in which the learning environment is arranged by the teacher to lead the individual to the learning outcome (Mosston & Ashworth, 2001).

heart rate—The number of times the heart beats per minute.

hemiplegia—Paralysis of the arm and leg on the same side of the body.

heredegenerative—A condition in which a congenital disorder becomes evident later in life.

home-based physical activity—Activities provided by caregivers and/or siblings providing physical activity for individuals with disabilities outside the school physical education setting.

hydrocephalus—An abnormally large head caused by an accumulation of cerebrospinal fluid (Berkow, 1987).

I-CAN—An extensive set of preprimary, primary, and secondary teaching resources based on the ABC model composed of performance objectives, assessment items, instructional activities, and games.

ideographs—Symbols representing ideas.

impulsivity—The tendency to react without carefully considering the alternatives (American Psychiatric Association, 2000).

incidental learning—Learning that is not a result of formal instruction (Schmidt & Wrisberg, 2004).

inclusion—The placement of an individual with a disability (even a severe disability) into general classes with peers in a neighborhood school. The individual is not an occasional visitor, but a viable member of the class with appropriate support services provided in the general classes.

individual family services plan (IFSP)—A written document that provides information about the free appropriate educational services needed and the process by which the services are provided for children with disabilities under the age of three years.

individualized education program (IEP)—A written statement of instruction and services to be provided based on a multidisciplinary assessment of the needs of each child with a disability; includes goals and objectives, evaluation methods, personnel responsible, and dates for initiation and completion of services (Dunn & Leitschuh, 2006).

individualized teaching style—Focuses on the concept of student-centered learning through an individualized and personalized curriculum (Pangrazi, 2004).

integrated settings—Physical education class settings that include individuals with disabilities learning together with nondisabled individuals. See *inclusion*.

interaction skills—Personal skills such as communication and social behavior required by individuals to enable them to successfully work with and relate to others around them.

interdisciplinary—A philosophical approach that facilitates a sharing of information among professionals for the purpose of increased service to individuals with disabilities.

intertrial interval—The time separating two trials of a task.

interval reinforcement—A schedule of reinforcement based on the individual being rewarded over a certain period of time for performance of a specific behavior.

intoxicants—Chemical toxins such as alcohol and cocaine that, when ingested by a woman during pregnancy, place the developing fetus at high risk for brain-related disorders.

intrinsic feedback—Feedback naturally received from performing a movement. See also *extrinsic feedback*.

involuntary—A muscle that is not under voluntary control.

Karvonen formula—A method for determining heart rate reserve; used to establish target heart rate for exercise programs.

kinematics—An area of study related to time and space factors in the motion of a system.

kinesiology—The study of human movement related to form, pattern, or sequencing of movement related to time (Hall, 2003).

kinesthesis—A sense derived from muscular contractions during purposeful movements; related to proprioception.

kinetics—An area of study related to the forces of the movement pattern produced.

knowledge of performance—Augmented feedback that describes a feature of the movement pattern produced.

knowledge of results—Information about success in meeting a movement goal; refers to the outcome or product (i.e., goals scored, distance covered) (Kelly & Melograno, 2004).

lactate threshold—The point at which lactate accumulates at rates faster than expected.

least intrusive level of prompts—The lowest level on the continuum of prompts ranging from physical assistance (most intrusive) to natural cues in the environment (least intrusive) (Block, 2006).

least restrictive environment (LRE)—An educational setting in which the individuals can safely and successfully function and meet the goals and objectives prescribed based on assessment results.

leisure counseling—Counseling involving a knowledge and understanding of leisure, the importance of leisure lifestyles, personal concepts of leisure choices, and the exploration of personal resources including skills, finances, experiences, and home/community resources.

lifespan—The continuous and cumulative process of development originating at birth and ending at death.

Light Talker—An augmentative device, similar to the Touch Talker, that uses a scanning device activated by a switch for individuals who cannot directly select symbols.

local education agency (LEA)—An educational agency such as a school, school district, or county that is responsible for the education of students.

long-term goals—Broad general statements of student outcomes.

long-term memory—Information that has been collected over a period of time; it may be essentially limitless in capacity. See *short-term memory*.

massed practice—A practice schedule in which the amount of rest between trials is short relative to the trial length.

mechanical—The ability of the human body to produce efficient mechanical work such as walking, running, and cycling.

medical gymnastics—A system popularized by Dudley Sargent in the early 1900s in which exercise was prescribed for various physical disabilities.

meningitis—An infection resulting in an inflammation of the covering of the brain (meninges).

mental practice—A practice procedure in which the learner imagines successful action without overt physical practice.

mercury switch—A device that uses a mercury switch attached by Velcro to the individual's body or clothes. When the individual performs the desired movement, the mercury switch completes the electrical circuit, allowing a reinforcer such as a light or music to be activated.

metabolic equivalent (MET)—Resting energy requirement, estimated to be 3.5 milliliters of oxygen per kilogram of body weight per minute.

metabolic rate—Energy expended by the body per unit of time (Spence & Mason, 1992).

metabolism—The total of all chemical reactions that occur in the body during the production of energy for work.

microcephalus—An abnormally small head.

mineralization—Mineral deposits in the tissues.

modeling—A procedure in which another person demonstrates the correct performance of the task/behavior to be learned.

modified physical education—General physical education class or program that involves appropriate modifications or adjustments suited to the needs, capabilities, and limitations of individuals with disabilities.

moral development—A process whereby humans progress from behaving in a way that receives rewards and avoids punishment to the desired stage of unselfish concern for human rights. Cognitive thought process and moral reasoning are believed to be parallel.

motor fitness—Components of physical performance such as agility, coordination, speed, and power that contribute to success in various physical activities.

motor program—A centrally located symbolic representation of movement that defines the essential details of skilled action.

multidisciplinary—A broad term indicating that many disciplines are involved in the service delivery process; involves separate evaluations and prescriptions from different specialists (various team members).

multidisciplinary model—Involves separate evaluations and prescriptions from different specialists assigned to identify the individual's specific problem.

muscular endurance—The ability of a muscle or a muscle group to perform repeated contractions against a light load for an extended period of time (McArdle, Katch, & Katch, 2001).

muscular strength—The amount of force exerted or resistance overcome by a muscle for a single repetition (McArdle, Katch, & Katch, 2001).

myoelectric arm—A type of prosthesis for individuals who have a portion of their arms amputated. The arm, which operates by means of a small battery-driven motor, obeys signals received from electric energy produced by movement of the remaining muscle groups. This allows control of elbow or hand strength of motion.

negative reinforcement—The removal of an aversive event as a consequence of a behavior in order to increase the frequency of the behavior (Lavay, French, & Henderson, 2006).

negative transfer—Occurs when the experience with a previous skill hinders or interferes with the learning of a new skill.

neurodevelopmental theory—A theory that suggests that (a) delayed or abnormal motor development is the result of interference with normal brain maturation, (b) interference is manifested as an impairment of the postural reflex mechanism, (c) abnormal reflex activity produces an abnormal degree and distribution of postural and muscle tone, and (d) righting and equilibrium reactions should be used to inhibit abnormal movements while simultaneously stimulating and facilitating normal postural responses.

nonverbal communication—Any approach designed to support, enhance, or supplement the communication of individuals who are not independent verbal communicators in all situations.

normalization—The principle of instructing persons with disabilities in community settings so that the activity can be generalized to the setting in which it will typically be performed. In this principle, socially acceptable ("normal") behavior is emphasized to reduce the obviousness of a disability and allow more natural blending in with others.

objective taxonomy —An approach to specifying curriculum content that focuses on how the learner acquires knowledge, skills, attitudes, normative social behaviors, and values.

occupational therapy—A form of therapy primarily concerned with the components of performance to maintain the individual's self-care, work, and leisure activities. Major components include motor functioning, sensory integrative functioning, and cognitive functioning.

open loop control—A mode in which instructions for the effector system are determined in advance and run off without feedback (Schmidt & Wrisberg, 2004).

open skill—A skill performed in an environment that is unpredictable or unstable, preventing advanced organization of movement.

operant conditioning—The use of a consequence to increase the probability that a behavior will be strengthened, maintained, or weakened (Lavay, French, & Henderson, 2006).

opportunity to respond—The number of appropriate learning trials (opportunities) a student has during a lesson.

order effect—The influence of other test items on the performance of a test item as a result of the order in which the performances were sampled.

organizing centers—Focal points for the curriculum and learning; they are the frame of reference, emphasis, or theme around which the subject matter is designed (Kelly & Melograno, 2004).

orientation and mobility training—Training provided to individuals who are visually impaired or blind in order to assist in independent travel.

orthoptic vision—Refers to the activity of the six external muscles of the eye that move the eyes up, down, in, out, and in diagonal directions.

orthosis—Straightening or correcting a deformity or disability.

outcome-based goals and objectives —Goals and objectives that focus on the result or outcome of the completed task and not the way the task is completed.

overcorrection—A technique to reduce inappropriate behavior while also providing training for appropriate alternative behaviors (Lavay, French, & Henderson, 2006).

overfat—Having a proportion of body fat that exceeds recommended limits, usually over 15% for men and 24% for women (McArdle, Katch, & Katch, 2001).

overlearning—Additional practice beyond the amount needed to achieve a performance criterion.

overload—Resistance greater than that which a muscle or muscle group normally encounters. The resistance (load) can be maximal or near-maximal (McArdle, Katch, & Katch, 2001).

overweight—A condition in which the body weighs more than normal based on height–weight charts.

oxygen consumption —The volume of oxygen used for energy expenditure. It is usually expressed in liters per minute or, in a relative term, milliliters per kilogram per minute (ml/kg/min) (McArdle, Katch, & Katch, 2001).

oxygen transport—The function of the cardiorespiratory system, which is composed of the stroke volume (SV), the heart rate (HR), and the arterial mixed venous oxygen difference (McArdle, Katch, & Katch, 2001).

pairing techniques—Matching or associating of a primary reinforcer with a secondary reinforcer (that is perhaps more socially normal and acceptable), which gradually replaces the primary reinforcer.

paraplegia—Paralysis or involvement of the lower extremities and trunk resulting from a spinal lesion or neurological dysfunction.

paraprofessionals—Individuals who do not have the formal education to teach physical education but who can assist the physical educator in tasks such as securing materials and equipment and working in one-on-one situations with students who need more personalized attention.

pathobiomechanics—The study of the nature and cause of disease that involves changes in the structure and function of the mechanics of the human system (Kreighbaum & Barthels, 1996).

pathokinesiology—The study of the nature and cause of disease, which involves structural and functional changes in the ability of a human body to move (Kreighbaum & Barthels, 1996).

peer tutor—A student with or without a disability serving as an aide in order to assist individuals with a disability.

perception—The process by which information is interpreted within the cortical areas of the brain, or the process of obtaining meaning from sensation and thus having knowledge of the environment (Sherrill, 2004).

performance generalization—The process in which a skill learned in one context is applied in another.

performance sampling—The practice of measuring representative factors of motor performance as a means of obtaining an overview of an individual's true ability.

perseveration—Persistence or fixation on a single feature or source of stimuli; manifests in repetitive behavior such as vocalizations, hand gestures, and fixation on a task.

personality disorders—A broad category of disorders that characterizes individuals whose personality traits are inflexible and maladaptive and significantly impair social, leisure, or vocational functioning (American Psychiatric Association, 2000).

phenylketonuria—A recessive genetic disorder accompanied by an enzyme dysfunction interfering with food metabolism. If untreated, brain damage and mental retardation may result.

physical activity reinforcement—A systematic procedure in which a structured time to choose among various preferred physical activities is contingent on the individual's meeting of a predetermined criterion of behavior (Lavay, French, & Henderson, 2006).

physical guidance—The most intrusive level of cueing or prompting. Physical guidance can range from the touch of a body part, to the physical manipulation of the individual's limbs and body so that the individual can complete a movement sequence (Block, 2006).

physical or psychological aversive strategies—The application of a stimulus that the individual does not like that reduces the likelihood that the inappropriate behavior will not be performed again.

physical restraints—Equipment or personnel used to control or reduce freedom of movement to prevent individuals from causing injury to themselves and others.

physical therapy—The identification, prevention, remediation, and rehabilitation of acute to prolonged movement dysfunction. Treatment occurs by physical means and treating through physical therapeutic measures as opposed to medicines or surgery.

Piaget's theory of cognition—A theory that describes the process by which infants and children acquire knowledge; the interaction between the individual and the environment is viewed as critical to learning.

pictographs—Symbols that look like the things they represent.

positive practice—A process by which an individual is required to practice an appropriate behavior for an extended period. For example, if an individual becomes angry and refuses to shake hands with another person after a contest, the individual might be required to shake hands with several individuals (Lavay, French, & Henderson, 2006). See *overcorrection*.

positive reinforcement—The process by which the increase in the frequency of a response (behavior) will occur when it is followed by a favorable consequence (Lavay, French, & Henderson, 2006).

positive specific immediate feedback—Feedback given to the individual immediately upon completion of the behavior that reinforces a specific aspect of the behavior and increases the likelihood that it will be done again (Schmidt & Wrisberg, 2004).

positive transfer—Occurs when experience with a previous skill aids or facilitates the learning of a new skill.

post delay knowledge of results—The interval of time between the presentation of knowledge or results and the next response (Schmidt & Lee, 2005).

postural reflexes—Automatic reactions that the body uses for maintaining or controlling its center of gravity.

power—The application of force and speed in relation to the quantity of work done per unit of time (Hall, 2003).

Prader-Willi syndrome—A congenital disorder characterized by excessive eating and mental retardation.

preload—Load on the muscle at rest (McArdle, Katch, & Katch, 2001).

Premack principle—A more preferred behavior by the individual is provided contingent upon the successful completion of a less preferred behavior (Lavay, French, & Henderson, 2006).

present level of performance—A written summary of a comprehensive assessment of the student's current baseline.

primary mode of communication—A method of communication with which an individual with a disability is most comfortable and competent.

primary reinforcers—Stimuli or events that by their biological importance (food, water, warmth, etc.) can act as rewards to behaviors that precede them (Lavay, French, & Henderson, 2006).

primitive reflexes—Reflexes that appear during gestation or at birth and typically become suppressed by approximately six months of age.

problem-solving techniques—Techniques used with guided discovery, divergent, or exploratory teaching styles to allow divergent responses and variations for the completion of any task or activity (Siedentop & Tannehill, 2000).

professional development—See *staff development*.

program evaluation—A process by which program merit can be determined by measuring student outcomes, consumer satisfaction, and the quality of program operations for the purpose of improvement, accountability, and enlightenment.

prompt—A cue that increases the probability of the behavioral response, usually in the form of physical guidance to initiate a proper movement (Block, 2006).

proprioception—Sensory information arising from within the body, resulting in the sense of position and movement; similar to kinesthesis.

proprioceptive neuromuscular facilitation (PNF)—A series of therapeutic techniques designed to enhance the neural muscular response (relaxation or contraction) of a body part; based on neuropsychological principles (Anshel, 1991).

prosthesis—An artificial substitute for a missing body part, such as an artificial extremity.

protein—Basic foodstuff that contains amino acids.

public accommodation—Equal access and equal services in the public domain. Making programs accessible and facilities architecturally accessible in the public domain as described in the Americans with Disabilities Act.

pulmonary system—A system of blood vessels that carries the blood between the heart and lungs.

punishment—Any aversive event or consequence that decreases the occurrence of a particular behavior.

quadriplegia—Paralysis or involvement of all four extremities in the trunk, resulting from a cervical spinal lesion or neurological dysfunction.

qualitative aspects of skills—Elements of the skill that relate to how the skill is performed rather than the outcome (quantitative) of the skill. Evaluation of the qualitative aspects of a skill is conducted using criterion-referenced tests and assessments (Auxter, Pyfer, & Huettig, 2005).

quantitative skill teaching—Skill instruction in which the emphasis lies in the final product (outcome or result) of the skill and not the way the skill was performed. Evaluation of this kind of instruction is done using normative assessment tools and objective assessment measures (Siedentop & Tannehill, 2000).

random practice—A practice sequence in which tasks from several classes are experienced in random order over consecutive trials.

ratio reinforcement—A schedule of reinforcement based on the individual being rewarded for a certain number of occurrences of the specific behavior.

reaction time—An interval of time from a suddenly presented, unanticipated stimulus until the beginning of the response.

reality therapy—The making of accommodations for individuals with disabilities that is an approach to managing behavior in schools based on the need to give and receive love and the need for self-worth; developed by Glasser.

reasonable accommodation—Modifications that may include (a) making existing facilities used by employees readily accessible to and usable by individuals with disabilities and (b) job restructuring, part-time or modified work schedules, reassignment to a vacant position, acquisition or modification of equipment or devices, appropriate adjustment or modifications of examinations, training materials or policies, the provision of qualified readers or interpreters, and other similar accommodations.

rebus—A puzzle representing a word, phrase, or sentence by letters, numerals, pictures, and so on, often with pictures of objects whose names have the same sound as the words represented; used as an alternative method of teaching reading.

reciprocal style of teaching—A style of teaching in which the teacher has the learner work with a partner. Partners offer and receive feedback based on criteria prepared by the teacher (Mosston & Ashworth, 2001).

reflexes—Automatic reactions to stimuli.

refractive error—Refers to problems of visual acuity associated with inappropriate bending of light rays before reaching the retina (e.g., myopia and hyperopia) (Sherrill, 2004).

regular education initiative (REI)—A term used to describe the goal of keeping as many students as possible in the regular education setting.

reinforcement event menu—A list of highly desirable reinforcers displayed for individuals to observe. These items can be earned as a result of exhibiting appropriate behavior.

reinforcement schedule—A set of rules or a plan that outlines the number of times or length of time a behavior must be performed before reinforcement is given to the individual performing the behavior; used to strengthen the occurrence of a behavior.

related services—Supportive services required to assist an individual with a disability to benefit from special education. These include physical therapy, occupational therapy, speech therapy, and so on.

response cost—The withdrawal of a positive reinforcer as a consequence of the occurrence of an undesirable behavior in order to decrease the frequency of occurrence of that behavior. Examples would be fines or loss of privileges.

response programming—Involves organizing the motor system for the desired movement.

response selection—Involves deciding what movement to make given the nature of the environment.

restitutional method—A method in which individuals are required to remediate disruptions they have caused. For example, an individual who fails to put equipment back in its proper location would be required to put the piece of equipment away and then straighten or replace additional equipment.

RPE—Ratings of perceived exertion.

satiation—The elimination of the effectiveness of a reinforcer on a behavior caused by excessive application.

secondary reinforcers—Stimuli or events that have acquired reinforcing capabilities (e.g., money or tokens).

self-actualization—As proposed by Maslow, refers to making actual, or realizing, one's potential. Emphasis is on internal rather than external motivation and personal responsibility.

self-efficacy—A situation-specific form of self-confidence based on the conceptual framework proposed by Bandura.

self-monitoring—A process by which people keep track of their own behavior such as using self-recording and monitoring heart rate.

self-recording—Recording personal scores on a log, journal, and so on.

self-stimulatory—Refers to behaviors that are self-induced, repetitive, and non-goal-oriented and that provide stimulation.

sensory integration—A theory that the inability to organize sensory information for use accounts for some aspects of learning disorders. It is theorized that enhancing sensory integration will make academic learning easier.

sensory receptors—Devices sensitive to light, heat, radiation, sound, or mechanical or other physical stimuli.

seriously emotionally disturbed—A condition in which an individual exhibits one or more of the following characteristics over a long period of time and to a marked degree, which adversely affects educational performance: (a) an inability to learn that cannot be explained by intellectual, sensory, or health factors; (b) an inability to build or maintain satisfactory interpersonal relationships with peers and teachers; (c) inappropriate types of behavior or feelings under normal circumstances; (d) a general pervasive mood of unhappiness or depression; or (e) a tendency to develop physical symptoms or fears associated with personal or school problems.

shaping—Reinforcing small steps or approximations of the desired target behavior.

short-term memory—A workspace (also referred to as "working memory") where controlled information-processing activities can be applied to relevant information.

short-term objectives—Statements written in measurable, behavioral terms, consisting of the following components: (a) performance/behavior, (b) condition, and (c) evaluation criteria (Short, 2000).

short-term sensory memory—The most peripheral aspect of memory; involves processing in the stimulus-identification stage, resulting in memory of the environmental sensory events that are stored for a maximum duration of about one-fourth of a second.

shunt—A device implanted in the body to remove or drain excess cerebrospinal fluid.

social imperception—The inability to gather information from the environment to utilize in determining the appropriateness of one's actions.

social reinforcers—Actions provided by the instructor of a social nature (physical contact, standing close to the student, verbal praise, etc.) that reinforce the desired behavior.

social values—Rules, morals, and ethical standards that, when exercised, reflect socially appropriate behavior.

special education—Specifically designed instruction at no cost to the parents to meet the unique needs of a child with a disability including classroom instruction, instruction in physical education, home instruction, and instruction in hospitals and institutions.

specially designed physical education—A physical education program designed to address the unique physical education needs of a student with a disability.

specificity hypothesis—A view that many motor abilities within a person are unrelated to each other.

speed–accuracy trade-off—The tendency for accuracy to decrease as the movement speed or velocity of a movement increases.

staff development—Any systematic attempt to educate school personnel.

standardized instruments—Tests that specifically describe procedures for administration including set of conditions, equipment, and instructions (standardized administration) to which data collection must conform in order for the data to be considered valid.

static lung volume—Lung volume measured during rest.

statics—A study of nonmoving systems (Hall, 2003).

stimulus identification—Primarily a sensory stage that requires analyzing environmental information from a variety of sources, such as vision, audition, touch, and kinesthesis, to decide whether a stimulus has been presented and, if so, what it is.

stimulus overselectivity—An abnormally limited attentional scope; an inability to select relevant cues and to see the whole.

stroke volume—The amount of blood pumped by the left ventricle of the heart in one contraction or beat (McArdle, Katch, & Katch, 2001).

structure-of-content—An approach to specifying curriculum content that uses a logical analysis of the subject matter and builds from a base of specific elementary content to complex, comprehensive content.

Sturge-Weber syndrome—A congenial syndrome characterized by port-wine stains on the body; associated with mental retardation, epileptic seizures, and glaucoma.

summative evaluations—The measurement and evaluation of an individual's performance using a predetermined standard that focuses more on the overall outcomes of instruction over time; done periodically and designed to address larger programmatic decisions such as whether students are mastering objectives on schedule (Kelly & Melograno, 2004).

tactile defensive—An individual who is hypersensitive to touch and/or pressure.

tangible reinforcement—An object or activity that, when given after the performance of a behavior, increases the likelihood that the behavior will be performed again.

task analysis—The breaking down of a skill into its component parts (Kelly & Melograno, 2004); sequenced subskills and/or intermediate progressions that a student must generally learn in order to complete the next or more complex subskill.

task description—An approach to specifying curriculum content that describes in a step-by-step progression the elements of a task; the outcome generated by this task analysis process is a series of descriptions that follow the progress of a given task through its various component operations.

task style of teaching—A teaching style in which the teacher determines the basic framework to the lesson (e.g., what tasks will be learned, in what order they will be learned, etc.) and students are permitted to make decisions on the pace at which they work and how the skill is to be executed (Mosston & Ashworth, 2001).

task variation—A practice sequence in which tasks from several classes are experienced in random order over consecutive trials.

Tay-Sachs disease—A metabolic disorder involving lipid storage that results in mental retardation.

technical aids—Computer-based speaking and writing systems, such as laptop computers, using standard hardware and customized software.

therapeutic recreation (TR)—A profession that promotes wellness and improves the quality of life through leisure activities for individuals with disabilities. Professionals in this field are called therapeutic recreation specialists.

thermoregulation—The ability of the body to regulate its temperature according to environmental conditions (e.g., sweating).

time on task—Time spent in the lesson or task in which the student is actively involved in the assigned activity.

time-out—The removal of an individual for a period of time from a reinforcing environment. This is contingent upon the emittance of inappropriate behavior in an attempt to decrease that particular behavior (Lavay, French, & Henderson, 2006).

token economy reinforcement—A system in which tokens, check marks, points, or chips are earned for meeting a predetermined criterion of behavior in order to increase the future occurrence of that behavior. The tokens are later exchanged for items that are reinforcing and of value to the individual.

top-down model—A process for developing a curriculum based on creating goal statements that define specifically what students will be able to do when they complete the program. These goal statements are then broken down into developmental lists of objectives that are sequenced across the various grade levels in the program (Kelly & Melograno, 2004).

total communication—A combination of communication modes (e.g., verbal, gestural, pictorial) that offers the individual with a hearing impairment an extended range of communication options.

total inclusion—A philosophical model that places and instructs all students, including those with disabilities, in a general education environment regardless of the type or severity of the disability. Multidisciplinary teams of professionals bring their collective skills and knowledge together to provide personal programs for each student (Kelly & Melograno, 2004).

Touch Talker—An augmentative device that allows nonverbal students to directly select (point to) symbols (ranging from 8 to 128) to communicate their wants and needs.

transdisciplinary model—A model of communication that encourages a sharing of information and cooperation among team members throughout the implementation of services to the individual.

transfer of learning—The gain or loss in proficiency on one task as a result of the practice or experience of another task.

transition time—Time spent during a lesson in organizational and nonacademic activities.

traumatic brain injury—A disability to the brain caused by concussion, contusion, or hemorrhage that results in permanent damage.

tuberous sclerosis—A syndrome manifested by convulsive seizures, progressive mental disorder, adenoma sebaceum, and tumors of the kidneys and brain with projections into the cerebral ventricles.

underweight—A condition in which body weight is lower than normal weight calculated from skeletal measurements, body weight is lower than the 20th percentile by height-for-age, and percent body fat is lower than 17% (McArdle, Katch, & Katch, 2001).

utility of measurement instruments—A desirable test characteristic referring to the usability of the data as well as the usability of the instrument. See also *administrative feasibility.*

variable practice—A practice sequence in which individuals rehearse a task in a number of different ways during a session.

ventilation—Movement of air into and out of the lungs (McArdle, Katch, & Katch, 2001).

verbal communication—A medium of oral communication that employs a linguistic code (language); through this medium one can express thoughts and feelings and understand those of others who employ the same code.

verbal directions—The least intrusive level of cueing or prompting that consists of the instructor verbally explaining to students what they should do in order for them to respond and complete the task (Block, 2006).

vestibular—A sensory system in the inner ear that provides signals to the brain related to movement of the body in space.

vocational specialist—A vocational educator who provides services to individuals with disabilities who cannot succeed in a general vocational setting. These professionals provide various services such as modified instruction, guidance counseling and testing services, employability skill training, and communication skill training.

von Recklinghausens disease—A disorder caused by multiple neurofibromata of nerve sheaths occurring along peripheral, spinal, and cranial nerves. The individual may experience pressure and pain on the spinal cord or on the brain.

BIBLIOGRAPHY

Abbott, M., Franciscus, M., & Weeks, Z.R. (1998). *Opportunities in occupational therapy careers.* Lincolnwood, IL: National Textbook Company.

American Education Research Association, American Psychological Association, and The National Council on Measurement in Education (1999). *Standards for educational and psychological testing.* Washington, DC: American Psychological Association.

American Physical Therapy Association. (1980). *Definition and guidelines.* Rockville, MD: Author.

American Psychiatric Association. (2000). *Diagnostic and statistical manual of mental disorders—revision* (4th ed.). Washington, DC: Author.

Anshel, M.H. (Ed.). (1991). *Dictionary of sport and exercise science.* Champaign, IL: Human Kinetics.

Auxter, D., Pyfer, J., & Huettig, C. (2005). *Principles and methods of adapted physical education and recreation* (10th ed.). St. Louis, MO: McGraw-Hill.

Ayres, A.J. (1981). *Sensory integration and learning disorders.* Los Angeles: Western Psychological Services.

Barnes, M.R., Crutchfield, C.A., & Heriza, C.B. (1979). *The neuropsychological basis of patient treatment, Vol. 2: Reflexes in motor development.* Atlanta, GA: Stokesville.

Baumgartner, T.A., & Jackson, A.S. (1991). *Measurement for evaluation in physical education and exercise science* (4th ed.). Dubuque, IA: Brown.

Berkow, R. (Ed.). (1987). *Merck manual of diagnosis and theory* (15th ed.). Rahway, NJ: Merck Sharp & Dohme Research Laboratories.

Bigge, J.L. (1991). *Teaching individuals with physical and multiple disabilities.* New York: Macmillan.

Block, M.E. (2006). *A teacher's guide to including students with disabilities in general physical education* (3rd ed.). Baltimore: Paul H. Brooks.

Carlson, N.R. (1991). *Physiology of behavior.* Boston: Allyn & Bacon.

Cartwright, G.P., Cartwright, C.A., & Ward, M.F. (1989). *Educating special educators* (3rd ed.). Belmont, CA: Wadsworth.

Clark, J.E., Betchell, N., Smiley-Ogen, A.L., & Whitall, J. (2005). Developmental coordination disorder: Issues, identification, and intervention. *Journal of Physical Education, Recreation and Dance, 76* (4), 48-53.

Cooper, J.M., Adrian, M., & Glassow, R.B. (1982). *Kinesiology.* St. Louis, MO: C.V. Mosby.

Cooper, J.O., Heron, T.E., & Heward, W.L. (1987). *Applied behavior analysis.* Columbus, OH: Merrill.

Cowden, J., & Tymeson, G. (1984). *Certification in adapted/special education: National status-update.* Dekalb, IL: Northern Illinois University.

Craft, D. (1994). Inclusion: Physical education for all. *Journal of Physical Education, Recreation and Dance, 65* (1), 22-23.

Davis, T. (2001). *A validation study of the 1997 Adapted Physical Education National Standards (APENS) certification exam.* Dissertation, University of Virginia, Charlottesville.

Dillman, D. (1978). *Mail and telephone surveys: The total design method.* New York: John Wiley & Sons.

Dreikurs, R., & Cassel, P. (1991). *Discipline without tears* (2nd ed.). New York: Penguin.

Dummer, G.M., Reuschlein, P.L., Haubenstricker, J.L., Vogel, P.G., & Cavanaugh, P.L. (1993). *Evaluation of K-12 physical education programs: A self-study approach.* Dubuque, IA: Brown.

Dunn, J.M., & Leitschuh, C.A. (2006). *Special physical education* (8th ed.). Dubuque, IA: Kendall/Hunt.

Dunn, J.M., Morehouse, J.W., & Fredericks, H.D.B. (1986). *Physical education for the severely handicapped.* Austin, TX: Pro-Ed.

Education of All Handicapped Children Act of 1975 (PL 94-142, Nov. 29, 1975), *United States Statutes at Large, 89,* 773-796.

Education of the Handicapped Act Amendments of 1990, Pub. L. No. 101-476, 104 Stat. 1103, codified as amended at 20 U.S.C.A. SS 1400-1487 (West 2000 & Supp. 2006).

Eichstaedt, C.B., & Lavay, B.W. (1992). *Physical activity for individuals with mental retardation: Infancy through adulthood.* Champaign, IL: Human Kinetics.

Fiorentino, M. (1981). *A basis for sensorimotor development: Normal and abnormal.* Springfield, IL: Charles C. Thomas.

Fisher, A., Murray, E., & Bundy, A. (1991). *Sensory integration: Theory and practice.* Philadelphia: F.A. Davis.

Fox, E.L., Kirby, T.E., & Fox, A.R. (1987). *Bases of fitness.* New York: Macmillan.

French, R., Lavay, B., & Henderson, H. (1985). Take a lap. *Physical Educator, 42,* 180-185.

Gabbard, C. (1992). *Lifelong motor development.* Dubuque, IA: Brown.

Gagne, R.M., & Briggs, L.J. (1979). *Principles of instructional design.* New York: Holt, Rinehart, and Winston.

Gallahue, D.L. (1989). *Understanding motor development in children* (2nd ed.). Indianapolis, IN: Benchmark.

Graham, G., Holt-Hale, S., & Parker, M. (1993). *Children moving* (3rd ed.). Mountain View, CA: Mayfield.

Hall, S.J. (2003). *Basic biomechanics* (4th ed.). Boston: McGraw-Hill.

Harrison, J.M., & Blakemore, C.L. (1992). *Instructional strategies for secondary physical education.* Dubuque, IA: Brown.

Hay, J.G. (1993). *The biomechanics of sport techniques* (4th ed.). Englewood Cliffs, NJ: Prentice Hall.

Hellison, D. (1985). *Goals and strategies for teaching physical education.* Champaign, IL: Human Kinetics.

Hole, J.W., Jr. (1992). *Essentials of human anatomy and physiology* (4th ed.). Dubuque, IA: Brown.

Individuals with Disabilties Education Act (IDEA) Amendments of 1990, 20 U.S.C. 1400 et seq.

Individuals with Disabilities Education Act (IDEA) Amendments of 1997, Pub. L. No. 105-17, 111 Stat. 37, codified as amended at 20 U.S.C.A. SS 1400-1487 (West 2000 & Supp. 2006).

Individuals with Disabilities Education Improvement Act (IDEIA) of 2004, Pub. L. No. 108-446, 118 Stat. 2647, codified at 20 U.S.C.A. SS 1400-1487 (West Supp. 2006).

Jansma, P., & French, R. (1994). *Special physical education* (2nd ed.). Englewood Cliffs, NJ: Prentice Hall.

Kelly, L.E. (1991a). National standards for adapted physical education. *Advocate, 20* (1), 2-3.

Kelly, L.E. (1991b). Is there really a national need for more adapted physical educators? *Advocate, 2* (1), 7-8.

Kelly, L.E. (1991c). Developing outcome standards for adapted physical education. Unpublished raw data.

Kelly, L.E. (1992). *National standards for adapted physical education* (Grant No. H029K20092). Washington, DC: United States Department of Education, Office of Special Education and Rehabilitation Services.

Kelly, L.E. (Ed.). (2006). *APENS study guide* (2nd ed.). Charlotteville, VA: NCPERID-APENS.

Kelly, L.E., & Gansneder, B.M. (1998). Preparation and job demographics of adapted physical educators in the United States. *Adapted Physical Activity Quarterly, 15*, 141-154.

Kelly, L.E., & Melograno, V.J. (2004). *Developing the physical education curriculum: An achievement-based approach.* Champaign, IL: Human Kinetics.

Kreighbaum, E., & Barthels, K.M. (1996). *Biomechanics: A qualitative approach for studying human movement* (4th ed.). San Francisco: Benjamin Cummings.

Lavay, B., French, R., & Henderson, H. (2006). *Positive behavior management in physical activity settings* (2nd ed.). Champaign, IL: Human Kinetics.

Lieberman, L.J., & Houston-Wilson, C. (2002). *Strategies for inclusion.* Champaign, IL: Human Kinetics.

Magill, R.A. (1993). *Motor learning: Concepts and applications* (4th ed.). Dubuque, IA: Brown.

McArdle, W.D., Katch, V.I., & Katch, V.L. (2001). *Exercise physiology: Energy, nutrition, and human performance* (5th ed.). Philadelphia: Lippincott, Williams & Wilkins.

Mohram, D.E., & Heller, L.J. (1986). *Cardiovascular physiology* (2nd ed.). New York: McGraw-Hill.

Moon, M.S., & Bunker, L. (1987). Recreation and motor skills programming. In M.E. Snell (Ed.), *Systematic instruction of persons with severe handicaps.* Columbus, OH: Merrill.

Morris, G.S.D., & Stiehl, J. (1989). *Changing kids' games.* Champaign, IL: Human Kinetics.

Mosston, M., & Ashworth, S. (2001). *Teaching physical education* (5th ed.). San Francisco: Benjamin.

National Association for Sport and Physical Education. (2001). *Standards for advanced programs in physical education.* Reston, VA: Author.

National Association of State Directors of Special Education. (1991). Physical education and sports: The unfulfilled promise for students with disabilities. *Liaison Bulletin, 17* (6), 1-10.

National Consortium on Physical Education and Recreation for the Handicapped. (1991). Summary of the NCPERID board meeting, Arlington, VA, July 20, 1991. *Advocate, 20* (1), 4-5.

National Resource Center for Paraprofessionals in Special Education. (1988). *A training program for paraprofessionals working in special education and related services.* New York: New Centers Training Laboratory.

Nicolosi, L., Haryman, E., & Kresheck, J. (1989). *Terminology of communication disorders.* Baltimore: Williams & Wilkins.

No Child Left Behind Act of 2001, Pub. L. No. 107-110, 115 Stat. 1425, codified as amended at 20 U.S.C.A. SS 6301-7941 (West 2003 & Supp. 2006).

Orlick, T. (1982). *The second cooperative sports and games book.* New York: Pantheon.

Pangrazi, R.P., (2007). *Dynamic physical education for elementary school children* (15th ed.). San Francisco: Pearson.

Payne, V.G., & Isaacs, L.D. (2005). *Human motor development: A lifespan approach* (6th ed.). Boston: McGraw-Hill.

Randall, L.E. (1992). *The student teacher's handbook for physical education.* Champaign, IL: Human Kinetics.

Rimmer, J.H. (1994). *Fitness and rehabilitation programs for special populations.* Dubuque, IA: Brown.

Rink, J. (1993). *Teaching physical education for learning.* St. Louis, MO: Mosby.

Sage, G. (1984). *Motor learning and control: A neuropsychological approach.* Dubuque, IA: Brown.

Schmidt, R.A. (1988). *Motor control and learning: A behavioral emphasis.* Champaign, IL: Human Kinetics.

Schmidt, R.A. (1991). *Motor learning and performance: From principles to practice.* Champaign, IL: Human Kinetics.

Schmidt, R.A., & Lee, T.D. (2005). *Motor control and learning* (4th ed.). Champaign, IL: Human Kinetics.

Schmidt, R.A., & Wrisberg, C.A. (2004). *Motor learning and performance* (3rd ed.). Champaign, IL: Human Kinetics.

Seaman, J., DePauw, K., Morton, K.E., & Omota, K. (2003). *From theory to practice in adapted physical education.* Scottsdale, AZ: Holcomb Hathaway.

Sears, C.J. (1982). The transdisciplinary approach: A process for the compliance with Public Law 94-142. *Journal of the Association for the Severely Handicapped, 6*, 22-29.

Sherrill, C. (1988). *Leadership training in adapted physical education.* Champaign, IL: Human Kinetics.

Sherrill, C. (2004). *Adapted physical activity, recreation, and sport: Crossdisciplinary and lifespan* (6th ed.). Dubuque, IA: McGraw-Hill.

Short, F.X. (2000). Individualized education programs. In J.P. Winnick (Ed.), *Adapted physical education and sport* (pp. 47-60). Champaign, IL: Human Kinetics.

Siedentop, D. & Tannehill, D. (2000). *Developing teaching skills in physical education* (3rd ed.). Mountain View, CA: Mayfield.

Siedentop, D.J., Herowitz, J., & Rink, J. (1984). *Elementary physical education methods.* Englewood Cliffs, NJ: Prentice Hall.

Snell, M.E., & Grigg, N.C. (1987). Instructional assessment and curriculum development. In M.E. Snell (Ed.), *Systematic instruction of persons with severe handicaps.* Columbus, OH: Merrill.

Spence, A.P., & Mason, E.B. (1992). *Human anatomy and physiology* (4th ed.). St Paul, MN: West.

Thomas, C.L. (Ed.). (1989). *Taber's cyclopedia medical dictionary* (16th ed.). Philadelphia: Davis.

U.S. Department of Education, Office of Elementary and Secondary Education. (2002). *No child left behind: A desktop reference.* Washington, D.C.: GPO.

Van Houten, R. (1980). *Learning through feedback: A systematic approach for improving academic performance.* Blaine, WA: Kluwer.

Walker, J.E., & Shea, T.M. (1991). *Behavior management: A practical approach for educators* (6th ed.). New York: Macmillan.

Williams, H. (1983). *Perceptual and motor development.* Englewood Cliffs, NJ: Prentice Hall.

Winslow, R.M. (1989). Therapeutic recreation: Promoting wellness through leisure. *California Association for Health, Physical Education, Recreation & Dance Journal, 51* (6), 11-12.

Wolfgang, C., & Glickman, C.D. (1986). *Solving discipline problems.* Boston: Allyn & Bacon.

ABOUT THE EDITOR

Luke E. Kelly, PhD, is a certified adapted physical educator, professor of kinesiology, holder of the Virgil S. Ward endowed professorship, director of the graduate programs in adapted physical education, and chief technology officer for the Curry School of Education at the University of Virginia. He has 30 years of experience working with public schools in evaluating and revising their physical education curricula to meet the needs of students with disabilities. Dr. Kelly has written extensively about the achievement-based curriculum model, assessment, and the use of technology in physical education. Dr. Kelly has served as the president of the National Consortium for Physical Education and Recreation for Individuals with Disabilities (NCPERID) and directed the NCPERID adapted physical education national standards project from 1992 to 1999. Dr. Kelly is a fellow in the American Academy of Kinesiology and Physical Education. He has also received the G. Lawrence Rarick Research Award and the William H. Hillman Distinguished Service Award from NCPERID. His hobbies and interests include fly-fishing, reforestation, and carpentry.

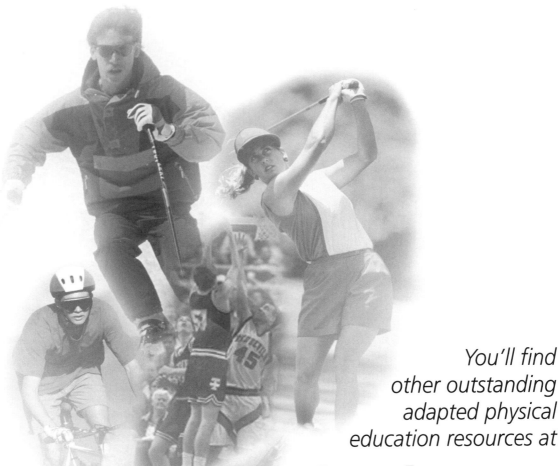

*You'll find
other outstanding
adapted physical
education resources at*

www.HumanKinetics.com

In the U.S. call

1-800-747-4457

Australia..08 8277 1555
Canada 1-800-465-7301
Europe...+44 (0) 113 255 5665
New Zealand.......................................0064 9 448 1207

HUMAN KINETICS
The Information Leader in Physical Activity
P.O. Box 5076 • Champaign, IL 61825-5076 USA